JOHN HAGEE

DAILY TRUTH

Published by Worthy Books, an imprint of Worthy Publishing Group, a division of
Worthy Media, Inc., One Franklin Park, 6100 Tower Circle, Suite 210, Franklin, TN
37067.

WORTHY is a registered trademark of Worthy Media, Inc.

HELPING PEOPLE EXPERIENCE THE HEART OF GOD

eBook available wherever digital books are sold.

Library of Congress Cataloging-in-Publication Data

Names: Hagee, John, author.
Title: Daily truth : a 365-day devotional / John Hagee.
Description: Franklin, TN : Worthy Pub., 2016.
Identifiers: LCCN 2016011305 | ISBN 9781617957550 (hardcover)
Subjects: LCSH: Devotional calendars.
Classification: LCC BV4811 .H235 2016 | DDC 242/.2--dc23
LC record available at http://lccn.loc.gov/2016011305

For foreign and subsidiary rights, contact rights@worthypublishing.com

ISBN: 978-1-61795-755-0

Cover Design: James Hall
Cover Photos: iStock

Printed in China

16 17 18 19 20 RRD 8 7 6 5 4 3 2

JOHN HAGEE

DAILY TRUTH

✠

A 365-DAY DEVOTIONAL

Deuteronomy 28:7
"The LORD will cause your enemies who rise against you
to be defeated before your face; they shall come out
against you one way and flee before you seven ways."

———— ·•·—•——·•· ————

*H*appy New Year! Today I want you to see the walls of resistance crumbling before you. I want you to see God taking on your enemies and handcuffing them—they are powerless when you hand them over to the Lord. I want you to see the mountains of impossibility that you are facing being cast into the sea.

Start telling God the desires of your heart and watch as He begins to make your paths straight. Watch as He begins to bring things to pass in your life that you never thought possible.

Focus your faith on the outcome. Right now the circumstances may look grim, but these are just mere stepping-stones in the overall story of your life. Keep marching forward. God sees your end from the beginning! Stay focused on Him!

I have read the book of Revelation, and we win! Great things are in store for you when you turn your life over to the King of kings.

Habakkuk 2:3
"The vision is yet for an appointed time; but at the end
it will speak, and it will not lie. Though it tarries, wait for it;
because it will surely come, it will not tarry."

If you pray for something and it doesn't happen right away, keep praying. For some of you, 30 minutes after the prayer has left your lips you are wondering why God hasn't heard you. Guess what? He heard you. Right this second might not be the timing He has in mind for your big finish. Hang on!

The God of the mountaintop is the God of the valley. Anyone can sing when the sun is shining, but you also need a song in your heart at night. It's not what you're going through; it's what you're going to that matters. Keep your eye on the prize!

Write down your proclamation of faith and begin watching for every sign that God is on the horizon, diligently working on your behalf. Anyone can look at the bitter facts of life and abandon their faith. Anyone can rush to disbelief. It takes a person of faith, courage, and purpose to focus on the finish line.

Focus on the joy of victory! Focus on the impact of living life without limit! Focus on the fact that the God we serve cannot fail!

1 Thessalonians 5:17
"Pray without ceasing."

———◆◆◆———

This is the year of your breakthrough! This is the year of great harvest in your life. Start declaring the good things of the Lord in your life today and watch as things begin to fall in line as the Holy Spirit moves.

This is the year that God answers the prayer you've been praying for years! This is the year that you and God are going to climb to the top of the mountain together, and the possibility you never thought would happen in your life becomes a reality.

Every miracle has two parts: your part and God's part. Take the initiative today and start walking in faith toward the answer you are seeking. The Bible says to ask and then you will receive. Call upon the Lord and He will answer. Start asking, and get ready for the floodgates to be opened to you in Jesus' name!

Psalm 103:2-3
"Bless the LORD, O my soul,
And forget not all His benefits:
Who forgives all your iniquities,
Who heals all your diseases."

The God that we serve is a God of might and miracles, hope and healing, life and liberty.

When Sarah cried out to God, He gave her a miracle baby at 90 years of age. By the Lord's infinite mercy Isaac, the son of laughter, was born. As you read through the pages of God's Holy Word, you will discover one miracle after the other. The Red Sea was parted for Moses, and the Israelites walked across on dry ground. Pharaoh and his army were defeated.

God is the all-mighty, all-powerful One who reigns over heaven and earth. He is the Living Water. He held the sun still for Joshua while he defeated Israel's enemies. And He can do the same for you today.

Are you looking for a healing in your life? It doesn't have to be a physical healing. You might need healing in your home, in your marriage, in your business, in your finances. Know that all things are possible to him who believes. Ask for God to move the mountain of impossibility in your life! The Healer is in the house!

Psalm 27:1–3
"The LORD is my light and my salvation; Whom shall I fear?
The LORD is the strength of my life; Of whom shall I be afraid?
When the wicked came against me To eat up my flesh,
My enemies and foes, They stumbled and fell.
Though an army may encamp against me..."

———— ✦ ————

"*M*y heart shall not fear; though war may rise against me, in this I will be confident."

David had it right. When God is on your side, your victory is inevitable! Failure is not an option; not even on the menu. You almost have to feel sorry for the other guys. Almost.

We serve a miracle-working God who says we have nothing to fear. So what are we so worried about all the time? Why are we taking anti-anxiety medications? We should be living a full life through the power of Almighty God!

You are never beyond the help or the hope of Jesus Christ. No matter what your doctor tells you, what your attorney tells you, what your spouse tells you . . . He is still a miracle-working God, and He is waiting to touch that part of your life that needs Him most. All you have to do is ask.

Fear not! Christ has overcome the world! If He has won the victory over death, hell, and the grave, certainly He can help you overcome this dark hour of your life. His light shines brightest in the dark recesses of our lives.

Psalm 17:7–8
"Show Your marvelous lovingkindness by Your right hand,
O You who save those who trust in You
From those who rise up against them.
Keep me as the apple of Your eye;
Hide me under the shadow of Your wings"

---

*H*ave you ever had an enemy? Someone who was trying to tear you down, even though you didn't deserve it? Invite Jesus into your situation and realize that He can make the difference. He is all-powerful and all-knowing, and He can protect you in the middle of your storm.

The Bible records that Jesus prayed for people in person and long distance, because prayer has no distance. And how powerful is He? Even those who were in His shadow were healed.

Brothers and sisters, that is power! And the best part is that He wants us to share in this very same power. Jesus said, "Greater things than these shall you do." Miracles are not a thing of the past. They are for the church today. They are for YOU!

What He did on the shores of Galilee so many years ago, He can still do today. In the precious name of Jesus—the name that is above all other names—you can have the total victory. Get ready to watch as the Master completes His good work in you!

John 3:16
"For God so loved the world that He gave
His only begotten Son, that whoever believes in Him
should not perish but have everlasting life."

———— ⊰•⊱ ————

This year I am praying that God brings you to a new destiny, a new spiritual high—a new destination with your Lord and Savior Jesus Christ—like never before. As He saturates your life, may you begin to experience the rich fullness that only comes with being in His presence, in sheer obedience to His Word.

You were created by a sovereign act of God, and you are so deeply loved by Him that He gave His only begotten Son to die in your place and redeem you from your sins. If you were the only one on planet earth, Jesus Christ still would have died to redeem YOU! That is how loved you are.

If you live captive to habits, emotions, addictions, or harmful relationships and you desire to be set free, I'm telling you that by the precious blood of Jesus Christ, TODAY you can have total freedom!

Lay your past at the foot of the Cross and begin to live a victorious life in Jesus' mighty name!

The Pastor's Blessing

And now may the Lord bless you and keep you. May the Lord make His face to shine upon you and be gracious unto you, giving you His peace. May you walk every day of this new year in the divine assurance that God is taking you to your promised land that is flowing with milk and honey; that your enemies will be defeated and your foot will be on the neck of your adversary. May the grapes of your harvest be abundant and the vats of new wine overflow. The wheat will be as golden grain because the Lord is the Lord of abundance and He is the God who is looking after you. Rejoice and be exceedingly glad! Our hope is in the Lord!

Psalm 27:5
"In the time of trouble He shall hide me in His pavilion;
In the secret place of His tabernacle He shall hide me;
He shall set me high upon a rock."

When you want what you've never had, you need to do what you've never done. This is "Thinking Outside the Box 101." Seek first the Kingdom and find out where God is leading you, what His desire is for your life. Have faith in God!

Faith starts out before you know how things are going to turn out. By faith Noah built the ark. Think about what would have happened if Noah had decided his idea was better than God's? Maybe he didn't like his neighbors ridiculing him so he decided not to build the ark? Noah had never seen one drop of rain, and yet he had total faith in God. And the faith of this one man saved his entire family (not to mention the entire human race).

We walk by faith, not by sight. Faith is what you do in the spiritual; sight is what you do in the physical. Virtually nothing happens by sight. Those things that are not seen are far greater than the tangible things right in front of us.

Everything from heaven's pantry comes out of faith. If you are facing the impossible, seek God's face and He will save you and your family. He is the God who never fails.

Joel 2:27
"I am the LORD your God And there is no other.
My people shall never be put to shame."

———— ◆◆◆ ————

*B*reak the shame barrier from your past tragedy. If you feel like there is a flaw you can't scrub out, know that Jesus Christ went to the Cross and took on your shame and sin so that you might be made clean. You do not have to carry the guilt of your past any longer. The past is OVER!

Recognize that because of the Cross, your shame is buried in the deepest sea, no longer to be remembered against you. Live, love, laugh, and be happy! This is a great day to be a child of God!

You are as pure as the blood of Jesus Christ can make you: whiter than snow. Your past is forgiven; God says He has forgotten it. You are princes and princesses—sons and daughters of the Most High God. You are loved and precious, blessed beyond measure. You are justified by faith. What does justified mean? Just as if you had never sinned. Stand up and shout! Today is going to be a great day in Jesus' name!

Isaiah 53:5
"He was wounded for our transgressions,
He was bruised for our iniquities."

"The chastisement for our peace was upon Him, and by His stripes we are healed."

We serve a healing Jesus. At one time Jesus healed a man by putting dirt in His hand and then spitting in it, mixing them together. Why? The Jewish people believed there was healing power in the spittle of the firstborn son of every family.

By this simple act, Jesus was saying He was the firstborn of God the Father and the Great Physician with the power to heal.

Jesus didn't just have sympathy for us as sinful beings; He didn't just feel badly for us when we became sick or when our lives were scarred by the effects of sin. He carried all of this away. At Golgotha's Cross, He was our scapegoat. He didn't just talk about healing us; He did something about it. On that sacred hill, death died. In John 6:47 Jesus affirmed, "Most assuredly, I say to you, he who believes in Me has everlasting life." At that moment sickness and disease died. The grave lost its sting.

We no longer have to worry about what tomorrow holds because we know WHO holds tomorrow. Everything is going to be alright.

Psalm 103:19
"The LORD has established His throne in heaven,
And His kingdom rules over all."

The God of the natural is the God of the supernatural. The God who enforces the law of gravity enforces the law of God.

What corrupts God's law? Sin. Exposure to disease causes physical corruption in your body. Exposure to sin causes spiritual corruption in your soul.

The Bible says to bless the Lord at all times and to let His praise be continually in your mouth. Don't wait for sin to harden your heart like a disease. First, treat the spiritual body (sin), and then treat the physical body (sickness and disease). Once the sin is forgiven, all diseases are healed in Jesus' name. This is God's promise to us.

When the Israelites were delivered from Egypt, they were given a promise. Exodus says they were told to diligently heed the voice of the Lord and do what was right... and God would put none of Egypt's diseases on them. And for 40 years as they wandered the desert, not one among them was sick as long as they obeyed. I would say that's a pretty good health plan!

If you need a healing touch in your life, the Bible says to call upon the Lord and He will "show you great and mighty things which you know not." Stand firm and He will rebuke the devourer for your sake.

Hebrews 12:14
"Pursue peace with all people, and holiness,
without which no one will see the Lord."

In ancient Israel there were seven feasts. Yom Kippur was the feast of repentance among the Israelites. During this celebration two goats were brought to the high priest. The first goat was slaughtered to forgive the sins of the priest because God demands holiness from His children, starting with the leaders of His people.

The priest who was presenting the offering had to be made pure before he could even ask God for forgiveness on behalf of his congregants. Then the high priest put the blood of the first goat in a bowl and dipped his fingers in it, placing some of the blood on the head of the second goat. The second goat became the scapegoat, the one that symbolized God's forgiveness of Israel's sins.

Jesus was our scapegoat, dying on the Cross in our place. He also took the place of the first goat as He redeemed us from our sin. God placed the blood on Jesus' brow, and with the Son's words "It is finished," our sin was buried in the deepest sea, never to be remembered again. Jesus paid it all.

Hebrews 13:8
"Jesus Christ is the same yesterday, today, and forever."

———————

$\mathcal{F}$aith is contagious. Faith is transferable.

What do I mean by that? You can pray over someone who is sick and they will recover through the power of Jesus Christ. When Jesus walked on the earth He performed great miracles that irrevocably changed the lives of the people He touched. Even as spectacular and truly awesome as these events were, He said that we would have the power (through Him) to do even greater things.

Are you sick in your body? Pray! Do you need a financial miracle? Pray! Is your marriage falling apart? Pray! God's power can invade your life today and restore that which the enemy has taken from you.

If you are looking for a touch from God, you must follow the rules outlined in the Bible. Anytime you are asking God to do something, you must follow His commands. You can't eat one tiny spiritual snack each week on Sunday morning and then expect to have a Miracle Ministry. You must devour God's Word. You must pray and fast, seeking His face, asking what His will is for your life... not giving Him your recommendations.

God is waiting to see miraculous things done in you and through you. Are you ready for what God can do when He unleashes His power upon your life? Get ready, because it could happen this very day!

3 John 1:2
*"Beloved, I pray that you may prosper in all things
and be in health, just as your soul prospers."*

———————

Are you having a bad day? I mean, a really bad day? Are you ready for the rain to stop pouring down on your parade? Look up! Your help comes from your Redeemer, the Light of the World! If you can't think of anything else to do, or the exact words to pray, just begin to PRAISE: Bless the LORD, O my soul; and all that is within me, bless His holy name!

Read through the Psalms and listen to the words of David, which repeat over and over that we are to praise the Lord, in good times and bad. As you praise Him, you will feel His anointing wash over you like a tidal wave of blessing. Joy unspeakable will flood your soul. You will feel overwhelming peace in your spirit. The exhaustion in your heart, soul, mind, and body will disappear as you invite Jesus to be the Lord and Master of your situation. Just the mention of His name will defeat any enemy you are facing.

Today you can prosper in all things; you can have peace of mind and health in your body. Begin by praising Him, and know that He is right beside you every step of the way!

The Pastor's Blessing

And now may the Lord bless you and keep you. May the Lord make His face to shine upon you and be gracious unto you, giving you His peace. May you live under the spiritual authority of God. May Jesus Christ be the Lord and Savior of your life. May the Kingdom of God on earth begin to manifest itself because of your obedience to the will of God. May His favor, His power, and His blessing be poured upon you because you have submitted to the ultimate power, the spiritual authority of God Himself. In Jesus' name, Amen!

Isaiah 61:1-2
"[The LORD] has sent Me to heal the brokenhearted,
To proclaim liberty to the captives,
And the opening of the prison to those who are bound;
to proclaim the acceptable year of the LORD."

———⋯———

*A*re parts of your life completely broken? Has the enemy destroyed prominent relationships? The Word promises that God sent Jesus to restore all things! No matter how shattered the pieces of our life, God can completely heal it and restore its beauty.

Proclaim a year of restoration where your broken relationships are made whole in Jesus' name. This can be your marriage, a relationship between yourself and a family member, or any person you have been separated from over petty issues. Receive the goodness of God and start loving one another in the unity of the faith.

Based on the Word of God, declare a year of deliverance and not disaster. Be set free immediately from the pain and guilt of your past. Don't focus on what has gone wrong, but realize what can go right. For whom the Son sets free is free indeed!

Psalm 86:8-9
"Among the gods there is none like You, O Lord;
Nor are there any works like Your works.
All nations whom You have made
Shall come and worship before You, O LORD."

"And shall glorify Your name. For You are great, and do wondrous things; You alone are God."

God's greatness is measured by what He can't do. Yes, it's an oxymoron. God cannot be given a problem He cannot solve. With men this is impossible, but with God ALL things are possible.

There is no god like our God.

Are you facing a Red Sea, an impossible trial? Is the path before you full of danger? Are you confronted by powerful enemies? You serve a majestic God with no limit, a strong tower you can run into in times of trouble. Call upon Him; He has promised to answer and show you great and mighty things which you know not. This means you don't have to try and come up with an answer on your own... you have the ultimate Resource immediately at your disposal.

The blast of His nostrils can rip the cedars of Lebanon. No good thing will He withhold from those who diligently seek Him. No matter how tumultuous your circumstance, He will always be just a prayer away.

Psalm 50:15
"Call upon Me in the day of trouble;
I will deliver you, and you shall glorify Me."

———————

God can't deliver anyone who isn't in trouble... or who won't admit it. How can you know God is your Physician without being sick? How can you know that He is your Provider unless you have a need? How can you know that God is a Friend who sticks closer than a brother without being lonely and rejected? How can you know He heals broken hearts without sobbing in some personal Gethsemane?

When God seems so silent and the night is so long and so black... how can you know God is a Deliverer unless you have lived in the chains and captivity of bad habits that have robbed you of your dignity?

Are you in trouble? Fantastic! You are in the perfect position to discover the God who answers prayer! God can give you life without limit and peace that surpasses all understanding. He can give you hope in the darkest night because He is the God who delivers. Call upon His holy name today and find rest in Him!

James 5:14–16
"Is anyone among you sick? Let him call for the elders
of the church, and let them pray over him, anointing him with oil
in the name of the Lord. And the prayer of faith will save
the sick, and the Lord will raise him up. And if he has
committed sins, he will be forgiven. Confess your trespasses to
one another, and pray for one another, that you may be healed."

———————◆◆◆———————

The Bible is a propositional revelation—if you do this, this will happen. In this short passage from James you see several propositions laid out for various audiences. Are you sick? Call on the elders of the church to pray over you, and you will be made well. Have you sinned? Confess your sins and be made whole.

Whatever your need, call upon God and He has promised to meet it according to His riches in glory. However, as powerful as God is, He doesn't answer prayers until they are prayed. Prayer should be your first choice, not your last chance. Stop asking everyone's opinion of what you should do and go directly to the Source of all knowledge, the Creator of heaven and earth. And expect Him to show up Himself!

When a Believer gets in trouble, God doesn't send someone else to check on His son or daughter. He does it Himself! Think of Daniel in the lion's den or the three Hebrew boys in the fiery furnace. The Lord was the fourth Man in the fire. He closed the mouths of the lions. He will do the very same for you!

Matthew 7:11
"If you then, being evil, know how to give good gifts
to your children, how much more will your Father who is in
heaven give good things to those who ask Him!"

———————————

If you were the king or queen of unlimited resources and you saw a ragged, starving child in great need, what would you do? You would tell that child to come to your castle right away. When the child showed up, full of expectation, you would lavish him with gifts until every need was met. You would make sure he had the things necessary to be successful in life, to no longer be hungry or threadbare.

This is exactly what Jesus is trying to do for YOU! Jesus is the King of Glory who has resources that the human mind cannot even begin to fathom. His Kingdom has been built upon streets of solid gold. And of His Kingdom there shall be no end.

If we as mere mortals want to help those in need around us, how much more does our heavenly Father want to do for us? LOTS more! He has written a royal decree to all the people on earth, telling us of His undying love. All we have to do is invite Jesus to be the Lord and Master of our lives and give Him control. He can and will meet your every need.

Philippians 2:9-10
"God also has... given Him the name which is above every name,
that at the name of Jesus every knee should bow, of those in
heaven, and of those on earth, and of those under the earth."

———◆◆◆———

God can break the chains of misery and addiction that enslave you. He will make a way where there seems to be no way. He is God and there is none like Him, not in the heavens above or in the worlds below.

The earth was created by the majestic Word of an Almighty God. In the beginning God said... until there was a perfect world.

The name of John D. Rockefeller will open the doors of every bank; Einstein will open the doors of science; Beethoven will open the doors of any music hall, but the name of Jesus will open the gates of heaven and close the gates of hell.

When you seek the name of the Lord, do it with gusto! Don't be afraid of what your neighbors will think or what your co-workers might say behind your back. When you are in a fight for your life, give it all you've got. Get on your knees and tell the devil to take a hike! He must flee at the Name that is above all names.

Jonah 2:2
"I cried out to the LORD because of my affliction,
And He answered me. Out of the belly of Sheol I cried,
And You heard my voice."

God is greater than the giant you are facing, greater than the burden you are carrying.

You don't have to be in a stained-glass cathedral to communicate with God. Jonah cried out in the belly of a whale and God heard him. Elijah called out in a state of deep depression. Paul and Silas cried out in the middle of a jail cell and walked out with the keys in one hand and a convert in the other.

What's the point? God heard each of them call from a desperate place. God is in charge here. The earth is the Lord's and all those that dwell therein. Your sorrows have not escaped Him. He is not as interested in what you are going through as much as who you are running to. Are you giving God your problems? Are you asking Him for help? Our God is greater!

When you are down to nothing, God is up to something. You cannot sink deep enough that His love cannot find you and pluck you out of the blackest abyss. Do not believe the words of man; trust in God and know that He will hear you in your hour of greatest need.

The Pastor's Blessing

And now may the Lord bless you and keep you. May the Lord make His face to shine upon you and be gracious unto you, giving you His peace. May you walk in the knowledge that our Father, which art in heaven, has all power in heaven and on earth, and that you are His child. His angels go before you and behind you. Heaven is your home. You are destined for greatness—to live as royalty in the eternal kingdom of God. Do not be confounded by this life, but rejoice that your name is written in the Lamb's Book of Life. Hallelujah to the King!

Proverbs 14:34
"Righteousness exalts a nation,
But sin is a reproach to any people."

God will have the last word. He is not wringing His hands over the ungodly, those who choose to make their own path in life. He laughs at the wicked, knowing the day of judgment is coming. He is not in heaven saying, "Let's make a deal." He is saying, "This is the deal."

If someone in your life is playing the role of antagonist, know that greater is He who is in you than he that is in the world. Jesus said that He was persecuted and ridiculed by men when He walked the earth, so if you are also being ridiculed by those around you, know that you are in good company. Square your shoulders and look up! Your redemption draweth nigh.

Where does your help come from? The Lord! If we repent of our sins as individuals, as households, and as a nation, we will come to a greater knowledge of Him. The Bible says to seek first the Kingdom of God. If you are looking for a big change in your life, ask for forgiveness and then make your request known. The Lord is faithful to answer when we call.

2 Corinthians 4:8-9
"We are hard-pressed on every side, yet not crushed;
we are perplexed, but not in despair; persecuted,
but not forsaken; struck down, but not destroyed."

---

*T*rouble is an asset—every improvement you've ever made is because of it.

Look at it this way. Your antagonist is your helper, shaping you into a stronger person today than you were yesterday. Trouble sharpens your wit, improves your skill, and transforms your spine into steel. Don't run from it! Face it head-on, and rejoice at the opportunity to become an overcomer!

A diamond is a lump of coal, made great under pressure. This lump of worthless coal endured intense pressure in the bowels of the earth until its carbons were so tightly compacted that all it could do was reflect the glorious light of day when its opportunity came to shine.

What are you doing with your life? Are you going to remain a lump of coal, or are you working toward becoming a diamond? Don't whine, but shine! God made you more priceless than any diamond; don't sell yourself short!

2 Timothy 1:7
"God has not given us a spirit of fear,
but of power and of love and of a sound mind."

———— ⋅◆⋅ ————

I have spent much of my life traveling on planes, and during a recent trip I came across a man who was clearly trying to make my blood boil. I knew it was going to be a long ride home when he said to me, "Preacher, I don't believe in Christianity. I think it's a religion of escapism." My answer was very straightforward: "It absolutely is."

People can escape sickness and disease because the Bible says that by His stripes I am healed. I can escape death because he that believeth on Jesus shall never die. Children of God can escape loneliness, for the Bible says that God will never leave you nor forsake you. We can also escape depression because the joy of the Lord is our strength.

The man next to me thought I was finished, but I was just getting warmed up. As followers of the Most High God, we can escape fear because He has not given us a spirit of fear, but of a sound mind. We can escape poverty because it is the Lord that gives us the power to get wealth. He supplies all of my needs according to His riches in glory, so I don't have to want for anything.

We can escape addiction—the Word says whosoever calls upon the name of the Lord shall be delivered. We can escape the pit of hell—if we confess our sins He is faithful and just to forgive our sins. And we all know, whom the Son sets free is free indeed!

Proverbs 3:5-6
"Trust in the LORD with all your heart,
And lean not on your own understanding;
In all your ways acknowledge Him,
And He shall direct your paths."

When you trust in yourself instead of God, you become your own god... and you miss out on all the incredible blessings the one true God has in store for you, things you could never accomplish on your own.

Let me ask you a few questions. Do you have the profession of Christ or the possession of Christ? Do you have religion or righteousness? Have you mastered the ceremony but have no consecration to Christ?

Above all else, He wants you to seek Him in all that you do. Is this easier said than done? Absolutely! But it is so worth it when you see that amazing miracle staring you right in the face. Don't believe in miracles? You will when you need one!

If you are facing a difficult circumstance that you have never seen before, give God a chance. He should be your very first cry in the dark when the night seems so black that you can't see your way out. He can hear you. He can help you. Trust Him and He will turn your life around!

Jeremiah 9:23
"Let not the wise man glory in his wisdom,
Let not the mighty man glory in his might,
Nor let the rich man glory in his riches."

The secret of knowing God is discovered when you know God's purpose for your life. What is His top priority for you? Does God's priority match your own?

Your top priority is not to glory in wisdom, which can become a type of intellectual idolatry. If you trust your own wisdom (or that of those around you) over God's, then you will not seek Him first or be able to know what His will is for your life. How can you give God the glory for your life if you aren't trusting Him to lead it?

Do not glory in riches. Wealth and fame will not bring you peace, and they are fleeting. Only the Prince of Peace can give you the health to sleep soundly through the night. I could relay countless stories of millionaires who were touted as the lead examples of their day... only to be found desolate, destitute, and in the depths of despair years later.

Our God is an awesome God! Living beneath His standard is not what He wants for His children. We are the most important thing on His agenda, and we should put Him in a place of honor: at the top of ours.

Isaiah 52:7
"How beautiful upon the mountains
Are the feet of him who brings good news, Who proclaims peace,
Who brings glad tidings of good things, Who proclaims salvation,
Who says to Zion, "Your God reigns!"

Today is the day to make a difference for Jesus Christ! He has made the total difference for you, sacrificing His life on the Cross so that you might be saved, so that you might have an eternal home with such unspeakable splendor that the half has not been told. Today is your day to shine the light and love of Jesus Christ on your community.

You don't have to stand on a street corner and preach to share the gospel to a dying world around you. Do you know that actions speak louder than words? You have heard that phrase before, I'm sure, but have you ever thought about how it applies to your own life? What do your actions say about you? Do you stand up and speak up for righteousness' sake, or do you remain silent?

Today is the day to tell your lost relative, friend, or neighbor that time is short. Don't wait another day. Soon and very soon, Jesus is coming in the clouds of glory to take us home. Are you ready?

Mark 9:35
"He sat down, called the twelve, and said to them,
'If anyone desires to be first,
he shall be last of all and servant of all.'"

———————

We exist to make a big deal out of God. It is not about self-recognition in this lifetime... or in the life to come. It is about honoring the King of kings and Lord of lords with everything we have to give.

Make each day count! Sing your loudest song and dance like your pants are on fire. We only get one chance to share the love of Christ on this earth. Make yours count!

What talents do you have? Are you a good singer? A good cook? A great auto mechanic, doctor, plumber, musician? Use these God-given talents to honor the Lord. The blessing that you will receive in return will be far greater than what you give away, I can assure you!

We are called to be servants. If you are looking for a crown in heaven, you need to wash a few feet here on earth before the trumpet sounds. Start helping those around you and share the love of the Lord! You are never more like Jesus than when you assume the role of a servant.

The Pastor's Blessing

And now may the Lord bless you and keep you. May the Lord make His face to shine upon you and be gracious unto you, giving you His peace. May you walk in the knowledge that you are His child and He is your Savior. Whatever adversity may come, you and the Lord are greater than any mountain that will stand before you. You have more power than any giant that may be presented to you. No crisis shall overcome you because you are a child of the King. In Jesus' name, Amen!

Jeremiah 29:11
"I know the thoughts that I think toward you,
says the LORD, thoughts of peace and not of evil,
to give you a future and a hope."

---

*P*roclaim a year of joy in your house! Stop being mastered by your past; it's over. Forget your mistakes; they are forgiven and forgotten, buried in the deepest sea, never to be remembered against you again.

If God has forgiven you and forgotten your sin, it is time to move on. Don't allow your past to dictate your future. Have a joyful, wonderful life made possible by the Cross.

Place your hope in the King of kings and realize the incredibly bright future you have coming your way. Hope is God's gift to every Believer. Your gift to Him is the joy you proclaim to those around you, shining His example in every dark corner.

Your life's goal should be to give Him praise and glory in all that you say and do, being a living testimony to the faithfulness of the King. Child of God, you have much to celebrate! Don't give the enemy room to come in and destroy the good works that God has already started in you.

Believe that your future is filled with an abundance of rich blessings that will bring you much peace and happiness. And may Almighty God receive the glory for the good things you will do to share His light and love with those around you!

Psalm 1:3
"He shall be like a tree
Planted by the rivers of water,
That brings forth its fruit in its season,
Whose leaf also shall not wither;
And whatever he does shall prosper."

*W*ith each passing year it might seem that the burden grows heavier, the circumstances become more severe, the difficulties increase on every side. But let me encourage you in the Lord and tell you that God is on your side. He sees you and knows your every need. He doesn't just know the major obstacles you are facing... He knows your EVERY need.

Declare that this year is going to be a year of divine hope, divine prosperity for the church of Jesus Christ. It is time that we stand up and speak up, making our personal petitions known. We do not have to hide behind the woes of a flailing nation or a people who have forsaken the God of Abraham, Isaac, and Jacob.

Today, in Jesus' name, stand up and declare a year of greatness for your family and your loved ones. Lift up your heads and rejoice; it's going to be a wonderful year.

This will be a year of supernatural harvest where souls are saved, captives are set free, and burdens are lifted. Your enemies will be defeated and you will experience a year of great success. As you seek the Lord first, everything you put your hand to will begin to prosper far beyond your wildest dreams.

Ephesians 6:4
"And you, fathers, do not provoke your children to wrath,
but bring them up in the training and admonition of the Lord."

You will either raise your children by the law of God or the law of the jungle. Your children deserve your personal direction—don't let them live their lives without guidance. And don't criticize your children for what they are doing wrong if you have not shown them the path they need to travel. Don't tell them to read the Word of God; read it with them. Don't send them to church; attend with them.

Father, you are responsible for the spiritual well-being of your children. There will come a day when you will answer to God for the decisions you made in raising your children. You will make an account for what you did do, and for what you didn't do. Are your children responsible members of society? Do they love the Lord? If not, you need to make this your TOP priority.

Spending millions of dollars on your children will never make the same impression as spending your time with them. I have seen children attend the funeral of their father without shedding a tear; months later, when the nanny passed, they cried like babies. Don't let this be the memorial you leave. A merciful God sent His Son to die for you! Share the love of the Lord with your children. They deserve the very best!

John 10:27

"My sheep hear My voice, and I know them, and they follow Me."

A book is objective; it is the same every time you read it. But the Word of God is alive. A living thing is constantly changing. The amazing thing about the Word is that while what is inside doesn't change, it changes what is inside of you... for the better. As you read the Word and apply it to your life, you become a better wife, a better husband, a better student, a better employee. Whatever you are doing, as you begin to do it "as unto the Lord," you become a shining beacon of light in an otherwise dark world.

You can hear the voice of the Lord very clearly when you apply the words found in Scripture—as a son knows his father, a servant knows the king, a sheep knows the shepherd.

Once when I was in Israel, I saw a watering hole that was packed with sheep from one side to the other. I knew there was no way those sheep were ever going to separate and head back to the assigned pasture with the shepherd that brought them. It was impossible to tell one animal from the next, they were so tightly woven into a woolen mass. Then the shepherds began to whistle... and each sheep lined up and headed back with the master who brought them to the watering hole.

"My sheep know My voice," Jesus said. If God whistled to get your attention in the crowd, would you be able to hear Him?

Ephesians 4:1
"I... beseech you to walk worthy of the calling
with which you were called."

———————

Do you want to know how you can tell when God is calling you to something? Look at the condition of your life. Is there peace in your heart? If an opportunity is destroying your peace, then it's not right for you.

Listen to God's voice and follow His direction. He doesn't need to get out a magic marker and write on your kitchen wall to make a point. If you "get the feeling" that what you are doing isn't right... STOP! If your peace is destroyed by what's going on in your life, STOP!

Don't follow your feelings; emotions can be toxic. Forego looking for a feeling that has no Scriptural basis. Crucify your feelings and dive into God's Word. Pray for the Lord's direction. Think it out, using the Bible as your compass. Ask yourself hard questions and come up with practical solutions. The Holy Spirit will lead the way, making you ready and worthy of your calling.

Proverbs 12:15
"The way of a fool is right in his own eyes,
But he who heeds counsel is wise."

———————————

God sees the end from the beginning. Think about the direction your life is taking. Where will your choices lead you? Who are you dating? Take charge of your life!

Choices have consequences. Don't wind up one day in a pit of your own making and start pointing the finger at everyone around you. You are today where you decided yesterday to be.

You have the opportunity to live with your hand in Christ's or to make your own choices and live like hell on earth. But once you get to the place you have chosen, don't blame God for the choices YOU made.

Think about Jonah for a minute. He was full of himself and didn't want to hear from God. Did this bother God? Absolutely not! The sun still came up that morning and God sent His messenger (a great fish) to pick up the runaway prophet. After a little swim around the ocean, the fish spit Jonah right out on the beach... right where God wanted him.

When God speaks to you, you can go to the destination of HIS choosing, or He will pick you up in the surf and eventually place you right where He wanted you to be in the first place. Either way, you are going to do exactly what God wants you to do. Take it from me; it is MUCH easier when you choose to follow His lead.

Matthew 7:15
"Beware of false prophets, who come to you in sheep's clothing,
but inwardly they are ravenous wolves."

———◆———

Don't listen to false prophets. If what someone is telling you doesn't match the Word of God, that person is not to be believed. Walk away.

If you think a false prophet has to look or act a certain way, think again! The devil comes to rob, to kill, and to destroy. Anyone who is telling you something contrary to the Word of God is a false prophet! Don't take at face value what someone tells you—question that person according to the facts found in the Word of God!

Who are you listening to? When someone tells you that XYZ is found in the Bible, do you immediately know whether or not they are speaking the truth? Do you know enough about the Bible to be able to defend your beliefs?

When God speaks to you directly, do you hear Him? Hearing is a learned behavior. Babies are born with the ability to hear, but they don't understand what they are hearing. Let me give you an example. If you hear a rattle and you're outside, your brain immediately pictures a rattlesnake. A baby might think of a toy. They can hear, but they don't understand.

When you hear things in your spirit or from a friend or family member, check it out with the Bible. God has a clear message just for you. Are you listening?

The Pastor's Blessing

And now may the Lord bless you and keep you. May the Lord make His face to shine upon you and be gracious unto you, giving you His peace. May you walk in the confidence that your total obedience will bring you total deliverance. God is with you. Whatever is before you will be defeated because the God you serve is the God for whom nothing is impossible! Rejoice and be exceedingly glad that your name is written in the Lamb's Book of Life through the forgiveness of the blood of Jesus Christ. In Jesus' name, Amen!

Luke 1:37
"With God nothing will be impossible."

———◆◆◆———

God is full of grace and truth. He is merciful and mighty, meaning He has no limitations. Try to wrap your mind around that one... NO limitations. As human beings we find it hard to grasp His greatness.

I urge you to remove anything that might limit God and His power from your thoughts. Think about how wonderful your life could be if you stopped limiting yourself, if you stopped painting yourself into a corner and focusing on the mountain of impossibility that surrounds you. What would you try to do if you didn't think you could fail?

God's presence has no limit. You can block out other people, but you can never escape God. You might be able to avoid your mama's calls on a Sunday afternoon, but the Word says that you can go nowhere on earth or in the heavens above or the worlds below to escape God's love.

When you stop and realize how great God is and that He wants the very best for you, it truly is an overwhelming and all-consuming love. We will never be worthy of it, but it is something we must not live without.

God knows your movements before you make them and your words before you say them. Choose wisely, knowing He is only a prayer away.

Psalm 107:20
"He sent His word and healed them,
And delivered them from their destructions."

———— ◆•◉•◆ ————

The Word of God is alive and powerful. It brings peace in the midst of a storm, joy in the midnight hour. The Word gives you the divine inspiration and power to sing "Victory in Jesus" when defeat seems imminent. The victory is yours in the name of Jesus!

When you meet God's conditions, a miracle is the only thing that can happen. When I fill a tray with water and place it in my freezer, it turns to ice. I don't have to pray that God turns it into ice; ice is the only thing that can happen if I leave it there long enough. That is the physical law.

There is a spiritual law that is just as real. When you meet God's conditions, you don't have to keep praying about the outcome. A miracle is the only thing that can happen. God will not fail you. The supernatural will happen. The miracle will appear in due season.

Hebrews 11:6
"Without faith it is impossible to please Him,
for he who comes to God must believe that He is,
and that He is a rewarder of those who diligently seek Him."

You can't have a harvest without seed. Faith is the seed that makes everything in the Word of God work. Have faith in God. Without faith it is impossible to please God, to accomplish His will in your life. Do you have enough faith for God to perform miracles in your life?

You don't have to understand miracles to be a part of one or to ask for one. I don't understand how a brown cow eats green grass and produces white milk and yellow butter, but it happens every day. You don't have to be able to explain God's miracle-working power to experience it. Don't limit yourself by your carnal understanding.

The Bible says to enter the Kingdom as a child. Children enter with complete faith, totally trusting that what you are telling them is the truth, that what you are saying absolutely can and will happen. This is how Jesus wants us to come to Him—as children, to lean on Him and trust Him fully. For without faith it is impossible to please God.

Malachi 3:6
"I am the LORD, I do not change."

———————

God cannot change. He is the same yesterday, today, and forever. His plans stand firm. He is unwavering in His principles and does not adapt to situational ethics. It doesn't matter what I think, what you think, or what the government says. God does NOT change.

There are zero exceptions.

The great thing about this is that what He did for you yesterday, He can do again for you today. Were you sick and He healed you? Was your marriage crumbling and He brought you into an even place? Did He help you through financial struggles last year when the IRS sent you a huge bill?

He is the same. I cannot say that enough. You cannot trust God to help you in one area of your life (watching over your children, for example) and then not trust Him in others (as if helping to heal your broken marriage would be too much). What He has done in the past, He can and will do again. Have faith in God and know that whatever you ask in His name, it shall be done.

2 Chronicles 26:5
"As long as [King Uzziah] sought the LORD,
God made him prosper."

If you don't know what you're looking for, how will you know when you find it? What is success? People think it's just a lucky break or a stroke of genius. But what is success, really? Lots of money? A great physique? Fame?

In the Word of God, success is for everyone. You must believe that you can succeed in order to do so. If your mind can conceive it, you can achieve it!

The Bible is the greatest success manual ever written; it will bring you more success than you can ever imagine. Open the Word today and believe that you are capable of achieving God's very best for your life! You can accomplish anything you set your mind to when God is on your side.

He wants His people to have the best of things in the worst of times. If you will look at yourself through His loving eyes, you will see a cup running over... a life filled with limitless possibilities. Today is the day to start believing that you not only deserve God's very best, but you can have it!

Hebrews 11:1
"Now faith is the substance of things hoped for,
the evidence of things not seen."

———————

Take away hope, and life with all of its fascinating opportunities is reduced to a mere existence. Without hope, life becomes bleak, drab, and joyless. Without hope, life is a burden, a never-ending treadmill of chaos.

People without hope often sink into depression, becoming filled with deep despair. Life turns meaningless because there's no difference from one joyless day to the next.

If you are weary in well doing or life has become overwhelming, you can still have hope as a child of God. If your heart is broken, hope thou in God! If your dreams are crushed, hope thou in God! If the fear of tomorrow has seized you, hope thou in God!

Begin to praise Him for the good things that are on the way, knowing that even if you can't see them from your human perspective, God is still on the throne and good things are coming. Remember, faith is starting out before you know how things are going to turn out.

Ecclesiastes 10:10

"Wisdom brings success."

———◆◆◆———

*C*hampions are willing to do the things they hate, to achieve the things they love. Athletes run wind sprints to achieve the win. They will run the same course over and over again until their technique is perfected. If they want to win, they have to become disciplined in their sport; they have to give it their all.

Are you running the race of life like a well-seasoned champion, or are you just sitting around, hoping that one day you might get close to the finish line? Are you settling for mediocrity? If you are successful, you will learn to do the things you hate, to achieve the things you love.

You pay a price for getting better, stronger, faster. But you pay a greater price for staying the same. In Jesus' name, try something new even if you do it wrong. Success is the progressive achievement of worthwhile goals that fulfill your divine purpose in life.

God desperately wants you to thrive in all that you do, that your life may honor Him. Seek out godly success and know that this will take you much farther than anything you could possibly do on your own!

The Pastor's Blessing

And now may the Lord bless you and keep you. May the Lord make His face to shine upon you and be gracious unto you, giving you His peace. May you run beneath the sheltering wings of the living God. May the Holy Spirit and His purging fire cleanse you from all forms of leaven, so that you are not puffed up but only filled with His presence. May the peace of God that surpasses all understanding be in your house, filling your children and your children's children. We are the property of the Lord of Hosts and want to stand before Him cleansed, sanctified, purified by the blood of Jesus Christ. In the authority of His name, we pray and say . . . Amen!

Philippians 4:8
"Whatever things are true, whatever things are noble,
whatever things are just, whatever things are pure,
whatever things are lovely, whatever things are of good report,
if there is any virtue and if there is anything
praiseworthy—meditate on these things."

Tell me what you believe and I will tell you who you are and what you're willing to do. You become what you behold. Why is video so powerful as a medium? Because it burns an image in your brain, and a picture is easier to remember than what you hear.

This is why the Bible tells us to meditate on things of "good report." What are you filling your mind with? How do you spend your day? Do you sit around watching horror movies, allowing the spirit of death to infiltrate your home? Home should be your sanctuary—a place where your family members can rest as a shelter from the storm, not a place where they are facing unbridled turmoil.

Child of God, He wants us to live a life of limitless blessing. Meditate on His Word and saturate your life with the goodness of the Lord so that you can start reaping Kingdom blessings today, in Jesus' holy name! Turn off the TV and open the Word of God. Find out what it means when He promises that the Word never returns void.

Colossians 3:23-24
"Whatever you do, do it heartily, as to the Lord and not to men,
knowing that from the Lord you will receive the reward
of the inheritance; for you serve the Lord Christ."

Life is God's gift to you. What you do with your life is your gift to God. You can do a lot more than you think you can; you just need the opportunity to demonstrate your potential.

As I have told my children many times, you can do anything you want to do, but you can't do everything. Focus on what you're good at and strive for excellence in all that you do. Work with laser focus. Do what you are good at better than anyone else, and you can write your ticket to success.

You do not have to be the smartest or the most beautiful in order for God to use you. Isn't that great news? But you do have to apply yourself and work hard to be successful. The only place that "rest" comes before "work" is in the dictionary. So roll up your sleeves, and let's get to it!

Song of Solomon 6:3
"I am my beloved's And my beloved is mine."

---

*T*his day is set aside to celebrate those we love. If you are looking for some racy reading in the Word of God, turn to the Song of Solomon and you will find some of the most romantic words ever written.

Sex was God's idea. It is a beautiful thing that allows us to have children and grandchildren who can bless us for years to come. But Valentine's Day is not just for lovers; it is for celebrating the people we love, those who are significant in our lives.

Don't waste another moment. Call, write, or send a carrier pigeon to tell those closest to you how you feel. Let them know how much they mean to you. We are not promised tomorrow, and today is growing shorter.

In life we are shaped by those who love us—and by those who choose not to love us. Don't allow those who cannot love you to come in and destroy the love lavished upon you by others. Focus on those who reflect the light of the Savior in your life. And remember the One who loved you so very much that He sent His only Son to die in your place. That, my friend, is true love.

Philippians 1:6
"Being confident of this very thing,
that He who has begun a good work in you will
complete it until the day of Jesus Christ."

———————◆◆◆———————

*P*roblems can transform your spaghetti spine into steel. They can make you a lean, mean, fighting machine. They can turn mama's little biscuit eater into a soldier for the Cross.

Problems can move a defeated mindset to a confident one that declares nothing is impossible with God. Improvements are most often made as a direct result of a crisis. Have you had a problem this year, this month, this week? Rejoice and be exceedingly glad. Problems are a sign that you are still a part of the human race and that God is still at work in you.

Are you seeking His face on how to resolve that which concerns you most? The rewards you receive in life are determined by the problems you solve, not the ones you create. Ask for God's healing in your broken places, and walk away from the problem causers. God has something much greater in store for you!

Hebrews 6:9
"Beloved, we are confident of better things concerning you,
yes, things that accompany salvation."

The Cross means that what you used to be is over. Let it go in Jesus' name. God never consults your past to determine your future. Losers focus on what they're going through, while champions focus on what they're going to. Your attitude is the first secret on your journey to success. What are you focusing on that affects your attitude?

"I can't" is the brother of "I don't want to." Your attitude is an inward feeling expressed by your behavior, and it is a choice that should never be based on circumstances. It will be different when you decide to make it different.

Your attitude determines the quality of your life and your relationships. It's not what happens to you, but what happens in you that matters. So, make a choice today to be happy, and watch as the quality of your life improves dramatically!

Psalm 118:24
"This is the day the LORD has made;
We will rejoice and be glad in it."

───────◆◈◆───────

There's a difference between "Good morning, Lord!" and "Good Lord, it's morning!" Does your face look like a reprint of the book of Lamentations? If you woke up this morning and didn't see your picture in the obituary column, shout "Hallelujah!"

It's a great day to be alive! Rejoice and be exceedingly glad. God is on the throne and everything is going to be just fine. Pick your chin up and know that the Champion of Calvary is already fighting your battles.

It is adversity that tests your quality. It is the refiner's fire that burns out the impurity and helps you reach your maximum potential. A rubber band is only effective when it is stretched. The tea kettle sings when it is up to its neck in hot water. The kite flies against the wind. God will not fail you! You will always win if you put your faith in God and refuse to quit!

Isaiah 41:10
"Fear not, for I am with you; Be not dismayed,
for I am your God. I will strengthen you, Yes, I will help you,
I will uphold you with My righteous right hand."

———◦◦◦———

*A*ttitude is that fire in your bones that keeps you going or cripples your progress. When my attitude is right, there is no barrier too high or valley too deep; hell has no challenge so great that I cannot defeat it with a water pistol.

As flawed human beings, we spend much of our time fretting over things we cannot change instead of changing the things we can actually control. Don't allow worry to steal your peace.

When I was a boy, my mother used to tell me that crows only pick at the best fruit. Serve the Lord with all your heart, soul, mind, and body and you will have a successful life drenched in the favor of God Almighty.

The Pastor's Blessing

And now may the Lord bless you and keep you. May the Lord make His face to shine upon you and be gracious to you, giving you His peace. May you walk in the absolute confidence that at the midnight hour the best of things can happen to you. God will bring you peace that surpasses understanding, abundance beyond your knowing, and victory you have never seen before. Rejoice and be exceedingly glad. Nothing is impossible to those who believe. In Jesus' name, Amen!

Luke 6:26
"Woe to you when all men speak well of you,
For so did their fathers to the false prophets."

———◆———

I personally have never had to worry about fulfilling this verse—the mail truck is filled with reminders every week of how "well" people are speaking of me! But I don't waste one second of my time concerned with what others think. We are here to honor God in all that we say and do until the time of His return; His approval is the only one that matters in this lifetime and the life to come.

Are you worried about what people are saying about you? You can avoid criticism by not saying or doing anything. But who wants to live a life like that?

You cannot make everyone happy all the time, and when you're busy trying to please everyone else, you are simply miserable. Stop it today in Jesus' name! Rise to the occasion and be what God wants you to be. You will draw closer to your divine destiny while living a life filled with the joy of the Lord!

Proverbs 8:17
"I [Wisdom] love those who love me,
And those who seek me diligently will find me."

Find God in the morning and allow Him to control your day. Don't start your day with stinking thinking but instead make a conscious decision to begin each day with a good attitude. Your attitude will determine your attainments.

In the medical field, for example, doctors will tell you that patients with potentially fatal diseases fare much better during treatment if they maintain a positive attitude. There is much documentation about endorphins and exactly why this occurs, but this medical proof just verifies what the Bible has said all along: "A merry heart doeth good like a medicine."

If we are placing our lives in God's hands, then no matter what life throws our way, we will have a shelter from the storm, a high tower to run into when the seas are raging. Seek God diligently, and the answer you need will come in due season.

Genesis 6:22
*"Thus Noah did; according to all
that God commanded him, so he did."*

---

*P*ersistence is going to the place of your failure and trying again. Have you failed miserably and feel like there is no hope in sight? Are you following God's plan for your life, or are you making up your own rules as you stumble through life?

If you are following God's plan, there is no need to worry. Let me remind you about Noah. He built the ark just as the Lord commanded. No one had ever even seen one drop of rain! Imagine Noah hammering away while his neighbors laugh in his face. But guess who had the last laugh? When the last tiny snail boarded that boat, God sealed the door. And then the rains came.

Noah was persistent. He finished the job that God gave him, even though it didn't make sense in the natural. And Noah's persistence saved his family. If God tells you to do something, just get busy doing it. It could save YOUR family.

Psalm 46:10
"Be still, and know that I am God; I will be exalted among
the nations, I will be exalted in the earth!"

What are you chasing? Who are you chasing? Stop right now!

What do you do when you don't know what to do? Sit down until you figure it out. The Bible says to be still. The answer might be right under your feet but you're so busy running in every direction that you can't see what is right in front of you!

Trust in the Lord with all your heart and lean not on your own understanding. Why? Because human understanding is flawed at best; it is shortsighted. If you are constantly chasing the pot of gold at the end of the rainbow, you don't have time to listen for the small, still voice that is trying to lead you down paths of righteousness.

Before your world implodes, sit down and take a breath! Cry out to your Father, and know that He is listening to your heart. He knows your need before the words ever leave your lips. Give Him the opportunity to intervene. Be still and know.

Hebrews 6:12
"Do not become sluggish, but imitate those who through faith and patience inherit the promises."

———————

$\mathcal{P}$ersistence is a fire in your bones that burns with a white-hot intensity that nothing can put out! It carries you through ridicule, rejection, and reversal, and it doesn't need public approval or a slap on the back. Persistence isn't politically correct, but it gives you the power to say in faith, "Mountain, get out of my way, for nothing is impossible!"

The victory is ours if we persist! The Bible promises us that faith is the victory that overcomes the world.

Persistent people don't hesitate but are bold and daring; they take action. Neither are they controlled by their circumstances or by others.

Nothing great has ever been accomplished without persistence. Don't look at yesterday's mistakes or play the blame game! Know that the victory is already yours; reach out and claim it in Jesus' name!

John 1:12
"As many as received Him, to them
He gave the right to become children of God,
to those who believe in His name."

Our God is the God of the supernatural! He saves you from sin and makes you a new creature. And He is not a respecter of persons. He can save as many as receive Him "from the gutter-most to the uttermost." No sin is too great, no past too checkered that He cannot wash you whiter than snow with the shed blood of His Son, Jesus Christ. By this, the Father brings us into His family, adopting us as His own.

God is a supernatural Healer, a Deliverer in the day of trouble. In your darkest hour, the Lord shows Himself as the light of the world. When your heart is broken, He touches your life and eases the pain; He is the God of another chance! When your dreams are crushed, He brings you great hope and all-surpassing peace. He is worthy of all praise, honor, and glory!

Today is the day to make God your top priority. Open your heart to His complete transformation! He makes every child of His a new creation.

James 4:7
"Submit to God. Resist the devil and he will flee from you."

———————

*H*ave you been knocked down by life's circumstances? Don't give an alibi; give another try. God doesn't sponsor flops and He doesn't manufacture junk. You are not the victim, you are the victor. All things are possible for you.

Has hell thrown the kitchen sink at you? Rise up and fight! Put on the full armor of God and start waging war against the devil. As you get on your knees and resist the enemy, God will begin to bind those things on earth that you are calling out in His name. And when you endure to the end, you will gain your just reward.

As a Christian, you are never going to outgrow warfare. So stand in there and fight like the champion you are, knowing God designed you for victory!

The Pastor's Blessing

And now may the Lord bless you and keep you. May the Lord make His face to shine upon you and be gracious unto you, giving you His peace. May the Lord show you the path to prosperity that begins with honoring Him with the firstfruits of your living and your giving. May you experience a barn-bursting harvest by the authority of God the Father, the Son, and the Holy Spirit. Amen!

Matthew 5:9
"Blessed are the peacemakers,
For they shall be called sons of God."

Where is peace found? Nowhere in the Bible is peace sought as the goal for our existence. Peace is always the consequence of something. The Bible says that the fruit of the Spirit is peace.

Peace is the fruit of reconciliation. Paul said, "Being justified by faith we have peace with God." There can be no peace of mind until there is peace with God. In every human heart lurks a sense of right and wrong and a hunger to do things the right way. If you are in need of peace today, start praying for righteousness in your life. When your spirit gets right with the Lord, you will live as the days of heaven on earth, even in the middle of the most turbulent circumstances.

The Word says He keeps those in perfect peace whose mind is stayed on Him. He is the Prince of Peace. Reconcile yourself to Jesus Christ, and know that He will begin to drench your life in peace like never before.

James 1:25
"He who looks into the perfect law of liberty and continues in it,
and is not a forgetful hearer but a doer of the work,
this one will be blessed in what he does."

When you look in the mirror, what do you see? A countenance full of hope, or one that seems hopelessly lost? As much as you try to be the general manager of the universe, the only thing you can change is you.

If you don't like the person in the mirror, adjust! But please know that you cannot change what you will not confront.

Are you having trouble pinpointing what exactly needs changing? Have you lost contact with yourself? Let me ask you this: How well are you hearing—and heeding—the Spirit? Is your time spent talking with your family members, or are you constantly in front of the TV? Do you meditate on God's Word, or do you spend your free time in the pool hall? Where you spend your hours is a direct reflection of who you are.

Are you always at the office, constantly shunning your responsibilities at home? If you win the rat race, it only means you're the number-one rat. Don't accept a lifestyle that compromises who God wants you to be. Stop living a tired life filled with depression, and start living life to the fullest! Put your hope in God! He is the only One in your life who cannot fail you.

Hebrews 3:1
"Holy brethren, partakers of the heavenly calling, consider the Apostle and High Priest of our confession, Christ Jesus."

In the New Testament, the word "confess" has the same meaning as the Old Testament word "proclaim," which comes from the Latin "to shout forth." Put these terms together, and the meaning is "to shout forth a confession of the Word of God."

This means you have the right to proclaim what's in the Word of God. The supernatural power comes from above; Jesus Christ is the High Priest of our confession. When you confess what is found in Scripture, our High Priest releases His authority to make what comes out of your mouth happen.

If today you are in a struggle, find a Scriptural confession and proclaim it. Jesus, your High Priest, will begin to release His anointing over it and destroy the thing that is attacking you.

Proclaim your freedom from financial reversal! Proclaim your freedom from the problems that plague your marriage! Proclaim blessings over your children! Proclaim joy as a sweet spirit that saturates your home! God has already paved the way for these promises to be yours. Today, start speaking the Word aloud and claim the victory that has already been won!

Proverbs 16:15
"In the light of the king's face is life,
and his favor is like a cloud of the latter rain."

———◆———

The latter rain was the rain that brought forth the fall harvest in ancient Israel. A cloud announced the rain and guaranteed what was to come, but the rain actually produced the harvest, the blessing.

If you are under a dark cloud, this is not a cloud of despair and disappointment but one sent by God announcing that the latter rain is just about to come. Get ready!

This is a cloud announcing that your supernatural breakthrough is on the way. The harvest you've been awaiting is closer than you think. Lift up your head and rejoice! God Almighty is about to bless you with abundance you cannot contain!

Stop doubting that good things can come your way because of your past, because of what your relatives tell you, because of what the enemy has planted in your life. Believe that God can and will bring the latter rain into your life and soak you to the bone with His divine blessing! It's going to happen in Jesus' name!

1 Kings 17:14–15
"Thus says the LORD God of Israel: 'The bin of flour
shall not be used up, nor shall the jar of oil run dry,
until the day the LORD sends rain on the earth.'
So she went away and did according to the word of Elijah;
and she and he and her household ate for many days."

———— ✦ ————

Sometimes getting what you want is not getting what you need. God has promised to meet our needs, not our greeds; and there is a difference. If your children need a ride to school, you can ask God to meet your need. If you're waiting for Him to send you a limousine, you might want to examine your priorities.

Think about the poor widow of 1 Kings 17. She gave her last bowl of meal to Elijah, knowing that she and her son would be left with nothing. And as soon as she offered her last morsels to the prophet, her oil drum began to fill to the rim. The Bible records that the barrel never ran dry again.

What are you doing for the Kingdom? If you are dishonoring God with your life and yet asking Him to provide for you, then you first need to get your priorities straight. Honor God with your living and your giving, and you will see that you do not have room enough to contain the blessings of the Lord.

Psalm 44:3
"They did not gain possession of the land by their own sword,
Nor did their own arm save them; But it was Your right hand,
Your arm, and the light of Your countenance,
Because You favored them."

———◆◆◆———

Many of God's children live with an insecurity complex and can't see themselves as being blessed and highly favored. Sometimes God's children are envious of others who appear to be more blessed. Life seems to be a bowl of cherries for everyone else, but for you, life is the pits; the bird singing outside your kitchen window is a buzzard.

You may feel as if you are doing the right thing, working just as hard as everyone around you. Life appears great for your neighbors but is stressful for you. Where is the favor of God upon your life? Has He overlooked you?

I want you to hear this; It is God's desire to bless you with favor that will knock your socks off! He wants to bless you with blessings you cannot contain! So get ready for good things to come your way. Don't let the circumstances of your life dictate your attitude. God's favor is for life, and no one around you can steal it unless you willingly give it away. Put a smile on your face and be encouraged that today is a great day to rejoice in Christ your Savior!

Psalm 94:9
"He who planted the ear, shall He not hear?
He who formed the eye, shall He not see?"

God is in control. If your prayer didn't get answered the way you wanted it to, don't get discouraged; God has something better in mind for you. Be patient. Learn how to wait upon the Lord.

Remember, good is the enemy of better, and better is the enemy of best. You can't trust God to release what is in His hand until you let go of what is in yours. Trust that He has something wonderful just waiting for you that your human mind cannot even begin to grasp.

Keep praying. Keep watching. Keep waiting. God hears your prayers; He sees your need; He is in complete control, and He knows all. There are three answers to your prayer: yes, no, or wait. If God is telling you to wait, then it means that you are just not quite ready for the amazing things He has in store for you. Trust that in due season your need will be met with a solution so spectacular that when you see it come together, you will immediately know that indeed the Lord had His hand upon you all along!

The Pastor's Blessing

And now may the Lord bless you and keep you. May the Lord make His face to shine upon you and be gracious unto you, giving you His peace. May you live with the expectation that the King is coming and that your primary objective as a Believer is to be a witness to every person that Jesus is Lord, to the glory of God the Father. Let His name be glorified to the nations of the world. Amen and Amen!

Psalm 23:6
"Surely goodness and mercy shall follow me
All the days of my life;
And I will dwell in the house of the LORD forever."

---

*F*avor is not temporary. Goodness and mercy will follow me for how long? ALL the days of my life! Things might be going great in your life right now, and you're still wringing your hands wondering if God's goodness will wear out. Let me tell you something: you ain't seen nothin' yet! God has something so great for your future that you can't even grasp it. That's how awesome it's going to be!

Sit back and rejoice with joy unspeakable and full of glory—a harvest of goodness is yours because of divine favor. The Bible says the Lord will cause blessings to run you over! God looks into the future and sees the destiny He has created just for you. He is so excited about your tomorrow that all of heaven is celebrating the good things that are getting ready to take place in your life.

If your miracle doesn't come through by noon today, take heart. His favor is for life, and blessings are on the way!

Psalm 65:5
"By awesome deeds in righteousness You will answer us,
O God of our salvation, You who are the confidence
of all the ends of the earth."

———————————

If you think you're having a bad day, a bad week, maybe even a bad year... I submit to you that it's not nearly as bad as what Lazarus endured. But God brought him back from the dead and gave him a new beginning. God can do the very same thing for you today. He can supernaturally heal you from the inside out... even if you feel dead inside.

Maybe your life seems meaningless. You have lost all hope. God wants you to take a good look at yourself. What do you see? No matter how bleak the picture, how deep the pain, He wants you to have the greatest comeback of all time. He wants you to enjoy the most exciting life you can possibly imagine. Allow the Master to intervene in your life on every level, and know that He can transform you in the blink of an eye.

Let Him be your confidence. Nothing and no one is beyond the reach of God.

1 Peter 2:4-5
"Coming to Him as to a living stone, rejected indeed by men,
but chosen by God and precious, you also, as living stones,
are being built up a spiritual house, a holy priesthood,
to offer up spiritual sacrifices acceptable
to God through Jesus Christ."

If you have been rejected by friends and family, lied to, cussed and discussed, know that you are exactly in the right place. God puts you in the middle of fiery trials to burn out the imperfections and craft you into a vessel of honor. If you cannot endure great burdens, you will never survive great success.

In the Bible, the one who goes through a great trial is the next one God promotes. If you can't stand fierce criticism, then you will be destroyed by compliments. Am I getting through here?

God has great things waiting for you on the other side of this dark day. Hold on, child of God, and know that God is building you up even as others try to tear you down.

Decide that today is going to be a great day in Jesus' name. In spite of what you see in the natural, God is fighting for you in the supernatural, making you holy and acceptable to Him. The small bumps in the road only prepare you for the moment when you finally reach the mountaintop!

Proverbs 8:32
"Now therefore, listen to me, my children,
For blessed are those who keep my ways."

———————•◦•———————

*Y*ou qualify for the favor of God by absolute obedience to His Word.

The Bible is a book of propositional revelation, meaning that if you do this, God will do that. Do you want to be saved? Then confess with your mouth the Lord Jesus Christ. If you confess... then you will be saved.

Do you want to be healed? If you can believe that all things are possible to them that believe, then you can be healed through the shed blood of Calvary. There is no limit to what you can do with God on your side. As long as you are walking in His plan for your life, God will grant you unlimited favor.

Yes, we all fall short. We all sin. Jesus was the only sinless Man to ever walk the earth. Still, divine blessings can be yours when you follow the commands God has listed very plainly in His holy Word. It is just that simple.

Isaiah 1:19
"If you are willing and obedient,
You shall eat the good of the land."

---

*D*on't let your past control your future. Look at what you're going to; don't focus on where you have been.

You might be in the middle of a great storm, perhaps the greatest storm of your life. Instead of perceiving this as a punishment or a sign that God doesn't love you, see it for what it really is: God using this moment in time to move you to the next level of favor.

Let the winds of adversity blow you higher and higher into the Lord's favor. Let adversity move you from faith to faith and glory to glory. If you're under attack, pack your bags and declare that you are moving on up to the glory and favor of the Lord, knowing that the best is yet to be.

Child of God, when everything around you looks bleak and dark, don't focus on the grim circumstances shrouding your life. Keep your eyes trained on Jesus and you shall eat of the good of the land. After all, the SON shines most brightly within the darkest night!

If you are waiting for the "big reveal," you have to be willing to walk in obedience down the path that takes you there.

Psalm 139:14
"I will praise You, for I am fearfully and wonderfully made;
Marvelous are Your works,
And that my soul knows very well."

———————

What obstacles have you overcome? It is not your position that makes you successful, it is what you have overcome to get to where you are today.

When you were born, the genius of heaven exploded. There will never be another one just like you. Don't limit yourself! There is within you the spark of the divine waiting for the opportunity to rocket into a galaxy of unlimited potential. You were born an original; don't die a cheap copy!

When you arrive at the gates of heaven, you have achieved the ultimate success. But what are you doing right now to show God how much you love Him? What are you doing to honor Him with your life? Are you whining about how bad things look in your tiny slice of the universe? Child of God, look up right now and know that you were born to achieve greatness. Do not settle for second best!

Psalm 43:5
"Why are you cast down, O my soul?
And why are you disquieted within me?
Hope in God; For I shall yet praise Him,
The help of my countenance and my God."

Never rewrite your theology to accommodate a tragedy you are going through. I often hear people say things like, "Pastor, I can't find a godly man/woman so marriage isn't for me." WRONG! God says it's not good for man to be alone. It was HIS idea for you to find someone.

Others make statements like, "The world is a madhouse, so I'm not going to have children." Let me again point to the Word of God, the greatest guidebook known to mankind, which says that children are a heritage from the Lord. If it's in God's Word, it's for YOU. Start praying today that God will meet your need according to His Word. If you want to get married or have children, find the perfect job or continue pursuing your divine destiny, He is simply waiting for you to ask. Nothing is impossible to those who believe.

When God answers your prayer, don't be upset with Him that your spouse isn't everything you wanted. Remember, YOU are the one who made the final decision there. Start praying for God's will in your life and know that He will direct your paths and bring you out to rich fulfillment.

The Pastor's Blessing

And now may the Lord bless you and keep you. May the Lord make His face to shine upon you and be gracious unto you, giving you His peace. May you live in the confidence that you are a child of God. Your past has been washed whiter than snow by the blood of the Son of God. God does not see sin that has been washed in the blood of His Son. Live with all confidence that your future is in the hand of God and no one can take you out of His hand. The Lord is God and there is none like Him, not in the heavens above or in the earth or the worlds beneath. From everlasting to everlasting, He is God. In Jesus' name, Amen!

Proverbs 28:25
"He who trusts in the LORD will be prospered."

———◆———

*H*ope is faith reaching out in the darkness, assured that you will feel the hand of God reaching back on the other side.

As Christians, we rejoice in the hope and the glory of God the Father. Without hope, joy is suffocated. With God, there is hope for a brighter tomorrow. It is the anchor of our soul. Our hope looks at sickness and disease and says (without a shred of doubt), "The Healer is in the house." The hope we find in God looks at the global financial crisis and knows that it is the Lord who empowers us to get wealth.

As David said in Psalm 37, "I have never seen the righteous forsaken or their seed begging for bread." God will plant you by streams of living water, and whatsoever you do shall prosper. Hope thou in God!

Romans 8:25
"If we hope for what we do not see,
we eagerly wait for it with perseverance."

What's the difference between hope and optimism? Optimism hopes for the best without a guarantee. But we have a hope that is guaranteed by the past performances of God. Our provision is found within His promises. And what God has done in the past He can and will do again.

How do I know this? The Bible says that He is the same yesterday, today, and forever. Has God helped you in the past? Then He will help you again.

Remember when the doctor handed you a diagnosis that medical science couldn't cure? That day He was the Great Physician. Remember when you were consumed by depression, unable to see past the grisly circumstances you were facing? He was your song in the night, an ever-present help in the time of trouble. If He was with you yesterday, in your greatest hour of desperation, why can't you believe that He will meet your need again? Do you think God can't handle it? Give Him a try!

Everyone has problems that are beyond our control and might seem hopeless from a human perspective. But God sees us and He hears our prayers. He is simply waiting for us to call upon His holy name. The biggest tragedy in life is not falling down but staying down. Don't take such ownership of your problem that it consumes and defines you. Persevere, and hope thou in God!

Romans 12:19
"Beloved, do not avenge yourselves,
but rather give place to wrath; for it is written,
'Vengeance is Mine, I will repay,' says the Lord."

You will encounter rejection and betrayal by the dearest on earth. During the course of your lifetime you will encounter bitterness and temptation, maybe a deep desire for revenge. You can find yourself embroiled in a hatred that is all-consuming. Maybe today you find yourself feeling the agony of being forgotten by those you have helped the most.

I have great news for you! Through the power of Almighty God, it is possible to move beyond your personal tragedies to reach your divine destiny. It is possible to recover from heart-breaking setbacks, to move beyond pain and devastation and to be re-created by the Lord. He can make old things new again and restore that which the enemy has taken from you.

Do you need a fresh start today? Are you seeking new inspiration? Look to the Friend who sticks closer than any brother, knowing that the battle belongs to Him. Begin to sing a song in the night, because good things are on the way!

Psalm 30:5
"His anger is but for a moment, His favor is for life;
Weeping may endure for a night, But joy comes in the morning."

———————

*T*he favor of God is a powerful, supernatural force that can move mountains of impossibility and make the sun not only stand still but reverse in its tracks. Jesus' name causes demons to tremble and the gates of heaven to swing open wide. So don't ever let anyone convince you that you are worthless, a nobody! You are blessed and highly favored of God, royalty in the kingdom of heaven. The favor of God is my destiny and yours, a destiny shared by every Believer who follows the path of righteousness.

When you understand the favor of God, you can kiss your insecurity goodbye. Don't look at the circumstances—when God says you are favored, it doesn't matter what the outward appearance is.

Remember Joseph? He was thrown in a pit by his brothers and eventually ended up in prison. But the Word records that the favor of God was always upon him.

Stop looking at the pit and start looking at the palace. It's not what you're going through; it's Who you're running to. You are blessed and highly favored of God. You have much to celebrate!

Matthew 5:10
"Blessed are those who are persecuted for righteousness' sake,
For theirs is the kingdom of heaven."

God always compensates you when people oppose you. He can bless you so that the situation that used to intimidate you... you now master. Don't let others' opinions or cruelties define you. Allow God's promises to show you exactly who you are through His eyes.

Are you ready for all of that goodness?

God won't give you something great until you are desperate to have His very best. Can God trust you with favor? Or are you trying to do everything on your own, keeping God on a shelf for special occasions only?

Other people will often envy the demonstration of God's favor upon your life, so don't be deterred by their criticism. Lift your head and square your shoulders. Smile. It will make your enemies crazy. Clap your hands and shout for joy! You are favored by the living God, and the Kingdom of heaven is yours!

Acts 5:29
"Obey God rather than men."

———————

Satan knows that if you, like Joseph, survive the pit and head for the palace, you will shake the world. Satan cannot afford for you to shape the destiny of the world, so he will try to crush you right now... before you are able to make a Kingdom difference.

Satan will find the part of your life that is most vulnerable and attack there. He can pinpoint your weakness and use your fears against you if you aren't surrounding yourself daily with God's promises, putting on the full armor of God.

Yet just as the Lord did for Joseph, He can use for His very best—for YOUR very best—what the enemy means for evil. Satan manipulated the hatred and jealousy that Joseph's brothers harbored against him to push Joseph into the pit; God brought Joseph through the pit and to the next level of spiritual revelation and growth. The brothers unknowingly revolutionized Joseph's relationship with God and gave him more power and favor than ever before.

It is the same with you today. God is using your enemies and obstacles to move you to a higher level of ministry. Don't worry about your circumstances. Good things are about to explode because God is your Father, and favor is born in the womb of obedience. Seek Him first and all of these things will be added unto you.

Exodus 3:8
"I have come down to deliver them out of the hand of
the Egyptians, and to bring them up from that land to a good
and large land, to a land flowing with milk and honey."

God wants you to have the very best—and He always provides for your best. But we don't always believe it.

God sent Moses to lead the Israelites out of Egypt, and even though they were enslaved and desperately in need of someone to help them, their response to Moses was, "Prove to us that God sent you!" It took ten earth-shattering miracles before Moses was free to lead the people out of captivity, through the Red Sea, and into the wilderness. And what was their reaction? "Why did you bring us out here to die?" They romanticized their past so much that they were more willing to return to Egypt and live as slaves than to trust God for the Promised Land.

Today I am telling you to do yourselves a favor and forget the past. It's over! Move on, trusting that the Lord has good things prepared for you!

The Pastor's Blessing

And now may the Lord bless you and keep you. May the Lord make His face to shine upon you and be gracious unto you, giving you His peace. May you walk in your life with this confidence: That you are a child of the King. That your sins have been forgiven and you are liberated from your past. You have much to look forward to in your future—eternal life with God in heaven made possible through the atonement of the Cross. In Jesus' name, Amen!

Luke 4:10
"It is written: 'He shall give His angels charge over you,
To keep you.'"

---

*Y*ou know that you are living inside the will of God through the peace of God that surpasses all understanding. Let this peace rule your life. How does this work? If you don't have peace about what you're doing, walk away. If you don't have peace about the relationships you are in, let them go.

You can either be a people pleaser or a God pleaser, but you can't be both. God is not the author of confusion. If something is contrary to the Word of God or conflicts with what the Holy Spirit is telling you, then pass it by. I have often said, "Some people bless you when they come, and some people bless you when they go!" Don't be afraid to let destructive people walk out of your life.

God has an exact assignment carved out just for you. Find it and live inside of it. This is the only way to truly live a happy and fulfilled life. When Jesus was on the Cross, He had to make a concerted decision to do God's will, so you are in good company. Jesus knew that He would lose the favor of God if He didn't follow the will of God; so He chose to not offend God.

Sometimes following God's will isn't pleasant or easy, but the Word says that we will either offend the world or offend God. I would rather have God on my side any day of the week. Which will you choose?

Romans 10:17
"Faith comes by hearing, and hearing by the word of God."

———————————

Doing God's will brings you to a crisis of belief—a fork in the road that demands you make a decision that will launch you into the next level with God.

After this type of deeply spiritual encounter, you can't live "as usual." Your life will never be the same because you have come to a more meaningful relationship with your Lord and Savior.

Noah couldn't live as usual after building the ark. Neither can you stay where you are and go with God at the same time. You cannot sit on the bank and simultaneously launch out to the deep. You must choose to travel down one path—yours or God's. You have to obey God's voice and move forward, or else you are choosing spiritual stagnation.

You will never have the favor of God upon your life until you choose to pay the price to follow Him. Gaining His favor requires action on your part. Faith is believing that He is who He said He is, and that He will do what He said He will do. Walking in divine favor always leads to a surprise ending in a truly fantastic way!

Genesis 37:19-20
"Then they said to one another, 'Look, this dreamer is coming!
Come therefore, let us now kill him and cast him into some pit;
and we shall say, "Some wild beast has devoured him."
We shall see what will become of his dreams!'"

When things go wrong year after year, you will experience a gamut of emotions, just as Joseph (and many others in the Bible) did: rejection, betrayal, false accusation, bitterness, depression, a desire for revenge, hatred for those who have betrayed you, the agony of being forgotten by those you have helped. Satan will tell you things like, "If you're a child of God, your life couldn't possibly be this messed up." Don't listen! The night of depression is broken as you walk from the prison to the palace to be with the King.

Get beyond your heartbreaking setbacks to achieve your divine destiny. Go from bitterness to blessing, from tragedy to triumph, from devastation to re-creation in the hands of the Master.

Don't let emotions blind you and steal your love, joy, and peace. When you allow things (or people other than Christ) to become your obsession, they own you. And you will never find a true sense of completion until you live out the dream that Christ has placed in your heart!

John 11:40
"Jesus said... , 'Did I not say to you that if you would believe
you would see the glory of God?'"

---

*A*re you feeling down? Maybe life isn't going the way you planned? Remember, comebacks happen when you are reduced to nothing. Why? Because God can reveal and receive the glory when He makes something spectacular out of nothing at all.

Remember when Mary and Martha asked Jesus to come and heal their brother, Lazarus? He was gravely ill and passed away before Jesus arrived. Was it an accident that He didn't come immediately? No, He knew just how sick Lazarus was. The sisters were reduced to nothing, feeling totally abandoned by their Friend.

Have you ever felt like God has forgotten you? Lazarus' condition looked hopeless, but God made something wonderful out of a seemingly impossible situation... and He received the glory. Are you praying for a promotion? A healing? A breakthrough? God's delays are not God's denials; they are blessings disguised for those who will wait in faith. Keep praying until the answer comes.

Joel 2:25

"I will restore to you the years that the swarming locust has eaten."

⸻

You are never too big of a mess for God to redeem. Nothing is beyond His ability to restore. There is no deep, dark pit where God cannot find you and pluck you back out of its depths. He is an all-knowing, all-consuming God who is a great defender of His children.

What have you lost in your past? Has someone hurt you so deeply that you can't seem to get your life back on track? Have you lost yourself, feeling as if you are drowning in the pain of yesterday's agony? Has life left you feeling defeated?

Today you can be set free in Jesus' name and move on to a beautiful tomorrow. Do not let someone else control your future. Do not let an event from the past dictate your "next event."

Whatever you have lost, God can restore it. He can heal you, refresh you, and cleanse you from all unrighteousness. Call on Him today and ask forgiveness for your past, moving on to a breath-taking tomorrow. Yesterday is over. Good or bad; it's gone. Focus on the horizon and the unlimited potential you have through Christ Jesus.

Luke 12:48
"For everyone to whom much is given, from him much
will be required; and to whom much has been committed,
of him they will ask the more."

———————

We have been given much, whether we realize it or not. In that one moment when Jesus laid down His life on the Cross, every Believer was granted a full pardon, trading their filthy rags for robes of righteousness and crowns of splendor.

Maybe this week has been full of trials and challenges for you, but I have great news. At the Cross, Jesus overcame the world, the flesh, and the devil. He holds the keys to death, Hell, and the grave; and HE has the last word. When you feel deflated, focus on the Cross. It is an endless supply of hope and the promise of life everlasting.

Until you find Jesus Christ as your Lord and Savior, you are a slave to Satan. We are either servants of Christ or slaves to the prince of darkness by the daily choices we make. Before you get too depressed about that, remember that deliverance is possible for each of us. Jesus Christ has freed you. From what? From death, from sickness and disease, from the clutches of Hell itself. And, child of God, whom the Son sets free is absolutely, utterly free.

2 Corinthians 4:16
"Therefore we do not lose heart.
Even though our outward man is perishing,
yet the inward man is being renewed day by day."

God wants your very best! He wants to liberate you, completely setting you free from all that hinders you. But you must turn loose of the former things.

Don't romanticize the past. If it was wonderful, forget it. If it was horrible, forget it. Looking back will not help you at all. In fact, it will prevent you from making the most of a future that should be filled with joy unspeakable and glory—glory to the King of kings. How can you have all that when you're busy lamenting what was?

Looking in your rearview mirror will never help you go forward. Neither will staying in Park, worried about the things of this earth. Put your car in Drive and start heading in the direction the Lord is leading you.

Today, I am asking God to shut the door to any bad habits that will subject you to a form of captivity. May Jehovah God take you to the Promised Land, where the joy of the Lord is your portion. May you dwell by rivers of living waters, and may His divine love so utterly saturate your life that those around you can see His light from a distance, like a beacon. May you be a testimony of what someone living in divine favor acts like, talks like, walks like. There is no better way to live, my friend, than as a child of the living God!

The Pastor's Blessing

And now may the Lord bless you and keep you. May the Lord make His face to shine upon you and be gracious unto you, giving you His peace. May you have joy that is boundless; joy that is unspeakable and full of glory. May you have the joy of the Lord that makes rich and adds no sorrow. In Jesus' name, Amen!

Romans 12:2
*"Do not be conformed to this world, but be transformed
by the renewing of your mind, that you may prove
what is that good and acceptable and perfect will of God."*

---

*I*t has been said that insanity is doing the same thing over and over again and expecting a different result. Most of us, however, want progress only if we can have it without change.

I would tell you today, without reservation, the only thing you can control is YOU! Don't talk about changing the world until you look in the mirror and change the person you see in the reflection.

Most people choose to change, not because they see the light but because they feel the heat. Don't wait until you are neck-deep in hot water to make the necessary adjustments in your life. God is reaching His hand toward you, just waiting for you to make the smallest effort of faith... and reach back.

He is a God who never fails no matter how long your storm has been raging. Trust Him today to bring you into His perfect will and grant you total peace... not that the world gives, but that only comes from above!

Exodus 4:6-7

"Furthermore the LORD said to him, 'Now put your hand in your bosom.'... And when he took it out, behold, his hand was leprous, like snow. And He said, 'Put your hand in your bosom again.' So he put his hand in his bosom again, and drew it out..., and behold, it was restored like his other flesh."

———————

God wants to lead you to your own personal Promised Land, but let's be honest... you don't have 40 years to get there. God controls everything—He has all power in heaven and on earth—and He says that He wants YOU to have the absolute best every single day of your life.

So what are you waiting for?

God sent Moses to get the Israelites out of Egypt. And after years of waiting for someone to save them from a life of misery, they demanded that Moses prove God had really sent him. Moses did so by placing his hand in his coat and coming out with leprosy (an incurable disease at that time), then placing it inside his coat a second time for total healing.

God will strategically place people around you to lead you to the place of total fulfillment through Jesus Christ. He will lead you in paths of righteousness for His namesake. Don't question those He sends when they come speaking a godly message. Just obey Him. A lack of obedience will only delay (or negate) the blessing. Open your ears and get ready to hear what the Father has in store just for you!

Hebrews 12:1
"Let us lay aside every weight, and the sin which
so easily ensnares us, and let us run with endurance
the race that is set before us."

Don't mount your pity pot and get bitter. Don't drown in the sewer of despair and desperation. Wash the mud off your face and get back in the race! This year is going to be God's year in your life!

Get over what Satan has done to you in the past. Lift your head and proclaim that THIS will be your Jubilee Year!

Turn loose of your resentment and anger. As long as you hang onto those, you are imprisoning yourself and giving your enemy the key. Throw off what binds you in Jesus' name and claim the total victory!

That medical report you just received from your doctor means nothing to you. Whatever you are lacking, give it to God and watch how He will reach down and meet your every need. He is in complete control! He has promises for every Believer—a place of freedom from the past, a place unencumbered by fear of the future, a place full of love, joy, and peace.

1 John 4:4
"You are of God, little children, and have overcome them,
because He who is in you is greater than
he who is in the world."

———————

*L*ife with Christ is full of divine health: mentally, physically, and spiritually. In this place your giants are instantly defeated at the mere mention of Jesus' name.

Second Samuel talks about putting your foot on the neck of your enemies. Why? When your foot is on your enemy's neck, this is a sign of total and absolute victory! There is no question who won the fight!

Anyone who is attacking you for no reason is your enemy, Biblically speaking. My prayer is that this year God will give you the ability to put your foot on the neck of your enemy. You are more than a victor through Christ Jesus! You can defeat the giant in your life by calling on Jehovah God in your hour of need.

God doesn't want you to win halfway; He wants you to gain the total victory, to have the absolute power. You and God determine your future, not someone else. May your future be saturated with the favor of God as you give up those things that are holding you back and rise to the destiny that He has for you... the destiny of a champion!

Mark 11:24
"Therefore I say to you, whatever things you ask when you pray,
believe that you receive them, and you will have them."

---

*I*f the Bible had only this one verse, it would be the best book on planet earth. This verse says that you can talk to God, ask Him for anything at all—in faith believing—and He will give you the desires of your heart.

Prayer is the greatest adventure we mortals could ever have, and is among our most powerful weapons. When you discover the awesome power that God has given you with this industrial-strength tool, your prayer life will never cease.

In ancient Israel, the high priest would petition the Lord on behalf of the people. But the veil was torn in two from top to bottom as Jesus cried out, "It is finished!" With those three powerful words, we were each given the opportunity to approach God the Father ourselves. Think about the power behind that option... speaking directly to the Creator of all things.

As you walk through the highways and biways of life, remember that God is ready, willing, and able to meet your every need. He owns the cattle on a thousand hills and numbers the hairs on your head. He is all-knowing, all-powerful, an ever-present help in times of trouble. Call on His holy name and get ready to shake the foundations of the earth!

Psalm 23:3
"He restores my soul; He leads me in the paths
of righteousness for His name's sake."

When America's founding fathers were writing the Declaration of Independence, they reached an impasse. Benjamin Franklin asked them to pray together so that they might, as a group, reach a mutually beneficial decision. After the prayer was uttered, the Declaration was written and America was born.

Regardless of what our Congress says today, America is still one nation under God. He holds the stars in His hands and the hills in balance. He is Jehovah God, the Great I AM.

When things look bleak and you are at a point where giving up looks like the best alternative, be still. Pray and ask God for His direction. He will lead you along paths of righteousness.

Child of God, you are never alone. At the mere mention of Jesus' name, demons tremble and angels are put to flight. If you are searching for an answer to a big problem today, look no farther! You serve a big God who is ready to help you move heaven and earth at a moment's notice. All you have to do is ask!

Psalm 14:1
"The fool has said in his heart, 'There is no God.'"

———◆◆◆———

God is from everlasting to everlasting. He is the Great I AM. And He is coming again with power and great glory.

Still, many do not believe in His existence. The Word of God calls them a fool. If you have unsaved loved ones, please share the Word with them. Take them to church. Call our prayer line. Today is the day to share the salvation plan of Jesus Christ from sea to shining sea.

The greatest lie that the devil tells us is that we have plenty of time: Time to tell people about Jesus. Time to repent of our sins. Time to live a righteous life. But nothing could be further from the truth. None of us is promised tomorrow.

No man knows the hour or the day. Not one more thing needs to happen for Jesus to return to this earth. With everything I have, I urge you to GET READY! The King is coming again very soon, and the church will be called to meet Him in the air. Give your heart to Jesus and follow Him today. You simply cannot afford to be left behind when the trumpet sounds!

The Pastor's Blessing

And now may the Lord bless you and keep you. May the Lord make His face to shine upon you and be gracious unto you, giving you His peace. May you see the victory that God has for you in your immediate future. The valley that you're now walking through will bring you into the sunrise of God's tomorrow. The favor and the blessing of the Lord will explode in your life because He will give you the desires of your heart. In Jesus' mighty name, Amen!

Psalm 62:5–6
"My soul, wait silently for God alone, For my expectation
is from Him. He only is my rock and my salvation;
He is my defense; I shall not be moved."

———◦———

The Civil War was the most bitter and divisive war in our history. Abraham Lincoln, as a stated fact, was the greatest president in the history of America. He preserved the Union in an hour when it seemed an impossible task.

When everything around him made throwing in the towel look easy, Lincoln fought to give birth to the Emancipation Proclamation. Calling Congress in to pray for this bill to be passed, America saw for the very first time that all men should live with the same freedoms regardless of the color of their skin.

Just as Lincoln refused to be moved from his convictions, you should never compromise your theology to fit your circumstances. Instead, look your problem in the eye, square your shoulders, and declare that you are more than a conqueror in Jesus' name!

Matthew 6:6
"You, when you pray, go into your room,
and when you have shut your door,
pray to your Father who is in the secret place;
and your Father who sees in secret will reward you openly."

---

*W*hy pray? The Word promises that if we pray God will not only hear and answer, but He will reward us openly. This means we don't need to pound our chest to broadcast how great our need is. We can simply leave our problems with the Master and let Him take care of us as He sees fit. You don't need to be Shakespeare in order to get your message across either. Some of the most powerful prayers that I have ever prayed go exactly like this... "HELP!"

But in order to be a successful Christian, you must develop a strong prayer life. Without it, you are a poster child for the prince of darkness, leaving yourself open to fear, doubt, and all forms of calamity. My mother always said, "More prayer, more power. Much prayer, much power."

If you aren't already, begin praying over and with your children, and pray with and for your spouse. It will revolutionize your home! If you want the power of heaven and earth to stand beside you night and day, develop a prayer life that is second to none, and God will begin to open the heavens and pour out blessings you can't contain.

Matthew 5:7
"Blessed are the merciful, For they shall obtain mercy."

God's mercy is covenantal loyalty in action. Throughout Scripture are promises that His mercy is renewed each morning. God loves mercy.

This kind of loyalty and compassion begins at home and should be encouraged in our churches. We should then take mercy out into the streets with us, to our jobs, our neighbors, to those who are hurting and in need of our help.

The church without loyal mercy is a fraud. It becomes a house of legalism, nothing more than the religious keeping a set of rules made by man rather than God. If you are not currently in a church that is 100 percent loyal to the Word of God—refusing to edit or delete those parts that make people uncomfortable—you need to find a new church as soon as you can! Look for a place that preaches the uncompromised Word of God. For this unadulterated message, there is absolutely no substitute!

Job 22:27
"You will make your prayer to Him, He will hear you."

———◆———

We were created as free moral agents. This means that you were designed to make decisions (both good and bad) of your own volition. Yes, God has a perfect plan for us, and yes, we often royally blow it. But the good news is that God does not give up on us. His mercy endures to all generations.

He has given us the amazing gift of prayer, a tool we can use to reach Him at any time, night or day. The One who holds all power in heaven and on the earth has promised to hear us when we pray—promised in His Word that what we bind on earth is bound in heaven and what is loosed on earth is loosed in heaven. But God will not answer until we ask. The initiative lies with each one of us... not God.

The Lord will not get involved in your life until you start asking for His help in prayer. Does He want your very best? Yes, He does. Does He already know what you need? Yes, He does. But He is waiting for you to surrender your need to Him. And there is no greater time than right now!

Psalm 119:105
"Your word is a lamp to my feet And a light to my path."

Certainly we are living in a world that needs the Word of God to light our way each and every day. It is milk for babies and meat for men. The verse that spoke to you during last year's marriage crisis can give you peace in your current financial struggle.

Each verse of the Bible comes alive as you read it and acts as a healing balm to your soul as you apply its sacred promises. It is the guidebook by which you should live your life and the best gift you can give any friend. It never returns void.

Children who are taught early in life to read the Word understand that when circumstances slap them in the face, this is where they need to turn.

The Lord is a very present source of help in our time of struggle, but how do we know that unless we do as commanded and meditate on His Word day and night? In order to be equipped for the battle when it comes, we must hide these precious words in our heart. If you are not reading Scripture on a daily basis, I encourage you to start forming this habit today. There has never been a better time to arm yourself with the Word.

Proverbs 10:22
"The blessing of the LORD makes one rich,
And He adds no sorrow with it."

———◦◆◦———

$\mathcal{I}$ love this verse. It says that God wants us to have great blessing, and with it—no sorrow. I love this because it clearly explains that there is no downside to being blessed of God, and we don't need to apologize for having His blessings showered on us. He is a rewarder of those who diligently seek Him.

Many people around the world who are wealthy by worldly standards are miserable. They have never come to understand the favor of the Lord. Favor doesn't always mean you have the most expensive house on the block; it means whatever house you live in is filled with the love and blessings of God Almighty. God's favor will add immeasurable happiness to your life because He is the one who commands the blessing.

Do you feel hopelessly lost and nowhere close to receiving a torrential downpour of heaven's riches? It only takes God a moment to move you from the pit of despair to the pinnacle of success. No matter how tragic the circumstances that surround you, He can take your life and turn it into a thing of beauty. Give the sorrows to Him, and get ready for your cup to overflow!

Isaiah 45:2
"'I will go before you And make the crooked places straight;
I will break in pieces the gates of bronze
And cut the bars of iron.'"

---

*P*rayer doesn't need proof, it needs practice. God is as close as your next breath. He has promised to never leave you nor forsake you. This means that when the dearest on earth have turned their backs on you, God sees. He knows your pain. And He wants to set things straight.

If you want to make a difference in your day, begin each morning with prayer. As soon as you start to pray, God releases His angels to meet your every need. Then get ready! Great and mighty things are about to happen!

Prayer is the weapon that God has given His children to wage war in the heavenlies. Put on the full armor of God and make it a great day. Satan is a defeated foe who has no power over you as a child of God. He cannot stop you when God is on your side. Run to the One who calmed the raging seas with three simple words: "Peace, be still."

If you feel like you've hit more bumps than usual on the road of life, look to the face of God! He has promised to lead you down a path that will grant you the greatest possible success. If you need Him to make your crooked places straight, call on His name, then leave the driving to Him!

The Pastor's Blessing

And now may the Lord bless you and keep you. May the Lord make His face to shine upon you and be gracious unto you, giving you His peace. May you climb the mountain with the full expectation that God's answer is before you. Though you have prayed for the answer and it has not come, please know that God's delays are not God's denials. The answer will come. You will receive heaven's best because your Father in heaven desires to give you the best of things. Now rejoice and be exceedingly glad, for everything your heart desires is just before you. In Jesus' name, Amen!

James 5:16
"The effective, fervent prayer of a righteous man avails much."

———◦❖◦———

The tragedy of our modern-day society is not unanswered prayer but unoffered prayer. God knows your every thought, need, and desire, but He is waiting for you to ask for great things. When you call on His name, do you ask God to help you find an umbrella for the storm ahead, or to help you build an ark? When you pray in faith believing, expect mighty things to happen.

The Word says all we need is faith the size of a mustard seed to move a mountain. Does the circumstance you are currently in look like a mountain of impossibility? Pray in Jesus' name. Have faith that what you are asking God for, He can and will do.

Speak to the mountain with total authority and watch as the things in your life begin to line up with the Word of God. You will start to gain favor among God and men. This doesn't mean that you will have sunshine every day, but it means that the Son will shine in your life and light your pathway. You will have the best of things in the worst of times as you trust the Savior to lead you in paths of righteousness.

God is ready to remove the mountain of impossibility in your life if you will only ask.

Matthew 16:18
"On this rock I will build My church,
and the gates of Hades shall not prevail against it."

The church is here for restoration, for lifting up those who have fallen. Be merciful enough to help someone in need with a spirit of meekness.

Loyalty says, "Let's restore him. Let's forgive him." Loyalty goes the extra mile even when no one is watching. It is the picture of the prodigal son as the father comes out with a robe in pursuit of a new life through forgiveness. You are not righteous if you are not loyal.

Many times we hold others to a higher standard than we do ourselves. But as Christians, we should set the standard so high that the world wants to know how to have what we have. Today, pour your love into someone as if you could never get hurt. Don't be afraid to love because someone hurt you in your past. It's a new day, and God is on your side!

2 Corinthians 1:20
"All the promises of God in Him are Yes, and in Him Amen,
to the glory of God through us."

There are more than 3,000 promises found within the Word of God. Your daily provision comes directly from these promises, which hold the golden key to open the gates of heaven and close the gates of hell.

When you are needing a spiritual breakthrough in your life, call on the mighty name of Jesus Christ. He will give you a promise within the Scripture that will bring you out to rich fulfillment. When God gives you a promise, hold onto it. Rest on it, knowing that in due season this prophetic word for your life will be fulfilled. It will probably not be done on your schedule, but when God deems the time is right, your promise will be completed.

It isn't difficult to have faith in a God who never fails. What is faith? It is reaching out in the darkness and knowing that you will feel the hand of God reaching back on the other side.

Galatians 6:14
"God forbid that I should boast except in the cross of our
LORD Jesus Christ, by whom the world has been crucified
to me, and I to the world."

The Cross is the central theme of the Bible. Without it you have nothing. But the beauty of the Cross is that it is an open invitation for "whosoever will." Jesus died on this Cross as a scapegoat, to redeem us of our sins. He took on our filthy rags so that we could be afforded opportunities that only the grace of God can provide. All we have to do is accept this gift, accept His love, accept Him as our Savior.

Once we meet Jesus at the foot of the Cross, our sins are washed away and our name is written in the Lamb's Book of Life. There is no symbol or theme more powerful in the life of a Believer than Calvary's Cross. God loved you so very, very much that He sent His only Son to die in your place.

You are a designer original; don't live like a cheap knockoff! Make today your best day! Give it your all in everything you say and do. Live a life full of confidence, knowing that the Lamb of God who takes away the sins of the world is rooting for you every second of every day. Don't listen to the negative things the world has to offer; keep your eyes focused on the Cross.

Matthew 23:14
"Woe to you... hypocrites! For you devour widows' houses,
and for a pretense make long prayers."

———◆———

Did you know that pretense in prayer can keep you from hearing God? Let me give you a simple tip that could potentially revolutionize your prayer life: Don't pray a lie. Now, wasn't that easy?

If your life is falling apart, don't pray long-winded, vain prayers that are meaningless: "Lord, thank You for the victory. My marriage is dead. I have 27 bill collectors on my front lawn. My son is in jail and my daughter just left home to marry the village idiot. Yesterday my car was repossessed while I was at the grocery store. Thank You for this victorious life."

NO! NO! NO! God knows your circumstances. Try this: "God, don't You see this mess I'm in? Help me! I rebuke the financial curse. I pray for salvation for my son, and I rejoice in the victory that You will provide as I seek Your will for my life!" God wants to meet your need, so tell Him what you really need, and get ready to receive the true victory in Jesus' name!

Romans 6:18
"Having been set free from sin,
you became slaves of righteousness."

———◆———

*A*re you saved but not free? Many people are controlled by the people around them or by religious rules—false doctrine that they've been taught their entire lives. I'm going to make it very simple for you: If it's not found in the Word of God, toss it out! You have no use for it in your life.

If manmade rules could pave the way to heaven, then Jesus died in vain. Look to the Cross!

The Cross delivers you from arbitrary rules for obtaining righteousness with God. It erases your past and gives you a future full of promise. You don't need anything but the Cross—the blood of Jesus Christ—to be made whole and totally set free from any form of bondage. Period.

Some of you might fear what the future holds or still harbor guilt from the past. Today, in Jesus' mighty name, and by His sovereign grace, you can be supernaturally set free. Let your past be gone. Leave behind every failure. The Cross has set you free!

Revelation 12:11
"They overcame him by the blood of the Lamb and by the word of
their testimony, and they did not love their lives to the death."

Child of God, get a vision of this: living your future in absolute victory, enjoying divine health, thriving in a life of financial abundance, and watching your enemies being defeated one by one. Today, in Jesus' name, declare that if God is for you, who can be against you?! The Bible promises that you will be given back seven times what the enemy has stolen from you.

Put the enemy on notice that God is in control of your life, of your children, and of your marriage. No weapon formed against you shall prosper. Your marriage will be healed in Jesus' name. Your business will become a huge success. You will be released from the pain of your past and the guilt of yesterday. Move from tragedy to triumph, because whom the Son sets free is free indeed!

Repeat this proclamation and be set free:

In the name of Jesus, and by the blood of the Cross, I'm free from the guilt of the past. In the name of the Lord Jesus, I am free from the spirit of condemnation. There is therefore now NO condemnation to those who are in Christ Jesus. I'm free by the blood of the Cross and God's amazing grace. I'm free by the blood of the Lamb and the word of my testimony. And today I am testifying that the Lord Jesus is my Savior. The victory is mine. Good things are coming because Christ paid the price at the Cross through His precious blood. Hallelujah to the Lamb of God!

The Pastor's Blessing

And now may the Lord bless you and keep you. May the Lord make His face to shine upon you and be gracious unto you, giving you His peace. May you be free from the fear of the past, looking forward to the joy of tomorrow. May every controlling thing in your life be destroyed, and may you be completely controlled by the spirit of God and the love of Christ. Let this day be the first day of the rest of your life... a day filled with love, joy, and peace in the Holy Spirit. In Jesus' name, Amen!

Psalm 91:14
"Because he has set his love upon Me,
therefore I will deliver him;
I will set him on high, because he has known My name."

———◆———

*H*ave you been criticized by others? Let's be honest, who hasn't been criticized in their lifetime? Let me teach you a very simple yet powerful lesson that will help you develop the mindset of Christ: Jesus did not criticize the adulteress who was caught in the act. Rather than condemning her for her sin, He loved her in her sin so that He could win her from her sin.

Don't go around telling people how bad they are, or they will shun you. And don't accept undue criticism (criticism that isn't constructive) from others. We are called to a higher purpose and must not lower ourselves to a lesser standard.

The message of the church is not "Who can we put down?" but "Who can we pick up?" Not "Who can we turn out?" but "Who can we bring in?" Not "Who can we ridicule or condemn?" but "Who can we bring to the Cross?" Bring those whose dreams have been crushed and point them to Calvary, to the Author and Finisher of our faith. Jesus will give anyone a brand-new beginning and make life beautiful again.

Mark 7:13
"[You are] making the word of God of no effect through
your tradition which you have handed down.
And many such things you do."

When Jesus healed the blind man on the Sabbath, the Pharisees appealed to their tradition, which stated that no one could heal on the Sabbath. Guess what? Jesus did it anyway! He mixed spit and dirt together and laid hands on the blind man regardless of the objections, seeking the Kingdom first.

Here is the trouble with doing things "because we have always done it that way." There was a young wife who always cut her ham in half when preparing her annual Christmas feast. She would first cook one half in her gourmet oven, and then the other... just like the women in her family had done before her. One day her husband asked why she did it this way, since it took longer. When the young lady asked her grandmother why this was their tradition, her grandmother said, "Honey, when I was your age, I only had a pot big enough to cook one half of the ham at a time."

Don't be afraid to do something because someone tells you not to. If what you are doing lines up with the Word of God, GO FOR IT! Don't let anyone slow you down.

Hebrews 4:12
"The word of God is living and powerful, and sharper than
any two-edged sword, piercing even to the division of soul and
spirit, and of joints and marrow, and is a discerner of
the thoughts and intents of the heart."

The Word of God is such a powerful weapon that, when spoken out loud, it makes demons run for cover. If you are looking for victory in any area of your life, I encourage you to start reading the Bible out loud. Read the promises of God, believing that He can and will deliver you in your day of trouble. No mountain is so high and no valley is so deep that the hand of God cannot reach down and snatch you out of harm's way!

The Bible is God's blueprint for our lives. You can have what this book says you can have. You can do what it says you can do. You have no limits as a child of God.

Whatever you are looking for to fill that gaping hole in your life, child of God, pray and ask Him to bring it to pass. Call upon the Lord and you shall have whatever you ask in His name. His Word promises that.

We can achieve the impossible when we are holding God's hand and He is walking us down the path toward our divine destiny. With Him, nothing is impossible!

Proverbs 3:1-3
"My son, do not forget my law, But let your heart keep
my commands; For length of days and long life
And peace they will add to you. Let not mercy
and truth forsake you; Bind them around your neck,
Write them on the tablet of your heart."

Want to read something that will make your life long and happy? Read the Word. It will be health to your navel (the connection between the child and the mother) and marrow to your bones. Marrow is the inside of the bone cavity where blood cells are produced, giving life to the physical body. The word marrow is often used to signify strength and vitality.

In other words, the Bible is the source of life—the thing that revitalizes every part of your being... heart, soul, mind, and body. The health of your spiritual life directly affects your physical life.

How can you have a healthier body? Write Scripture commands on your heart. Dive into the Word with such intensity that it becomes second-nature to you... so that when the storm hits, you don't have to fumble around searching for a verse to meet your need; you already have written the words on your heart.

God's mercy is from everlasting to everlasting. As we seek His face for our lives, He is faithful and just to supply our physical and spiritual needs so that we can live to the full here on earth before we join Him for all of eternity.

Ephesians 3:20-21
"Now to Him who is able to do exceedingly abundantly
above all that we ask or think, according to the power
that works in us, to Him be glory in the church by
Christ Jesus to all generations, forever and ever. Amen."

Whose power works in us? His power. If you have ever experienced the power of Jesus Christ as it saturates your life, there is no mistaking it.

As human beings we were designed to crave the majesty that is Him, and there is nothing that can satisfy us like His presence.

When you are in the presence of God, you know without a doubt that He is speaking directly to you, and often through you! There is no greater power in heaven or on earth than that which comes directly from the throne.

Are you sick in your body? Call upon the Name that is above all other names! Is your marriage in trouble? Ask Him to be the Way Maker. Are you lacking in your finances? He owns the cattle on a thousand hills. If you are in need, He says to try Him and see that He will do such great things, you won't be able to contain the blessings raining down on your life.

I challenge you today to ask Almighty God to touch that part of your life that is broken and in desperate need of repair. He is the God who cannot fail, and He will answer when you call.

Romans 12:12
"Rejoicing in hope, patient in tribulation,
continuing steadfastly in prayer."

---

*E*xpect the goodness of God to become a routine part of your life if it's not already.

Nothing about God is ordinary or routine, but knowing that His supernatural goodness is just waiting to rain down on your life should become the norm. He wants you to have His very, very best!

God has a specific plan that was tailor-made just for you—a divine destiny with boundless potential. His plan contains blessings that you cannot contain and the unlimited favor of God.

Look up and fully expect Him to meet your needs above and beyond your wildest dreams. What He has in mind for you is more valuable than priceless diamonds and sweeter than ice tea on a hot summer day. It just doesn't get any better than the favor of God!

Rejoice in the hope that is Jesus Christ. Rejoice knowing that ALL things work together for good. Just because you are in the middle of your darkest day does not mean that God doesn't see you. He knows exactly where you are and what you need. Continue praying; continue being patient, and heaven's best will come your way!

Psalm 42:5
"Why are you cast down, O my soul?
And why are you disquieted within me?
Hope in God, for I shall yet praise
Him For the help of His countenance."

If you don't know what to do, be still and place your hope in God. Have faith that He is working behind the scenes on your behalf, for what you see in front of you is just the very tip of the iceberg.

Lift up your head and lift your heart. Satan is a defeated foe, and the victory is already yours. Just reach out and take it!

Without hope life is bleak and joyless, and without any song. Without hope life is meaningless. But not for those who trust in the Lord! Every Believer has hope for tomorrow, hope for a supernatural breakthrough, hope for divine healing for your body, hope in the knowledge that your prodigal son or daughter can come home, hope that God can send someone special into your life if you're single... hope that is absolutely unlimited because we serve an awesome God who knows no bounds!

The Pastor's Blessing

And now may the Lord bless you and keep you. May the Lord make His face to shine upon you and be gracious unto you, giving you His peace. May you walk in the freedom that God has given to every one of us... the freedom to reach your divine destiny personally, spiritually, physically, professionally—on every level. May God cause you to reach the highest point because it is your destiny in the Lord as an heir and joint-heir with Jesus Christ. In Jesus' mighty name, Amen!

Genesis 12:1, 4
"Now the LORD had said to Abram:
'Get out of your country, From your family And from
your father's house, To a land that I will show you...'
So Abram departed as the LORD had spoken to him."

———◆———

Sometimes God takes you out of your comfort zone, asking you to get up and do what you've never done before, or to give up what you currently have in order to obtain something even greater. But you have to be willing to surrender what you hold in hand—to trade better for best. He may even ask you to put some things down so that you can reach for the crown He has designed just for you. When Abraham took the journey into the unknown, he gave up his right to choose the best of the land... and gained his full inheritance.

If God takes someone or something out of your life, let them go. Don't drag them back in! God is trying to bring in something (or someone) that will bless you and not hinder you. God is your Protector and Provider, and when someone poisonous is in your life, He will let you know.

Let them go. Even if they are your best friend, let them go. God cannot use you unless you are focused on Him. He cannot use you if you are listening to someone else's voice instead of His.

Don't be afraid to try something new. If God tells you to do something, move forward with confidence, knowing that untold blessings have been set aside just for you.

Romans 1:16
"I am not ashamed of the gospel of Christ,
for it is the power of God to salvation
for everyone who believes."

———————————

*T*he Bible is the living, inspired Word of God; an anchor when inexplicable trouble is raining down on your life like a relentless thunderstorm. Its message is the power of God unto salvation, the good news that we all need to hear on a daily basis.

How did your day begin? If you began with some Bible reading or a word of prayer, you have covered your day with supernatural power. You are armed and ready to face the day, no matter what the enemy throws your way!

In our society, it is absolutely necessary to face each and every day wearing the full armor of God. Spiritual warfare is a way of life for every Spirit-filled Believer. That's just a fact.

The full armor should be as important to you as putting on physical shoes before you walk out the door to work. And a rich helping of prayer first thing in the morning should be like choosing a delicious plate of huevos rancheros over cold, sugary cereal—it's just the obvious winner to begin your day!

There's no substitute for a strong start, because you never know what the day will hold. God is your safety net—a very present help in times of trouble. Begin your day with Him, knowing that the two of you together can handle whatever comes your way. Our God is able!

Psalm 103:17
"The mercy of the LORD is from everlasting to everlasting
On those who fear Him,
And His righteousness to children's children."

---

*H*ope for the Believer is based on the evidence found in the Word of God. If He has done it in the past, He will do it again.

The Bible says He is the same from everlasting to everlasting, never changing. I know people who change their look so often that sometimes you don't even recognize them when you see them in the grocery store! That will never happen with God. He is always the same.

Did He help you with last year's marriage or financial crisis? Did He bring your lost child home or heal you from a disease that medical science deemed incurable? If He has done that in the past, why don't you believe that He will do the same again? Do you think God has run out of miracles or mercy? Hardly!

My hope is anchored to the never-failing promises of God. When you are facing adversity, search the Word of God and He will give you a promise to fit your problem. I'm not talking about placing your finger in the middle of your Bible when it flops open. I'm talking about inviting God into your problem and asking for Divine wisdom. Ask Him to give you His promise for your situation.

I call it the three P's: if you have a Problem, open the Bible and find God's Promise that will lead you to His Provision.

Colossians 1:9
"[We]... do not cease to pray for you, and to ask that
you may be filled with the knowledge of His will
in all wisdom and spiritual understanding."

---

*P*rayer is not getting God ready to do your will; it is getting you ready to do God's will. It is the vehicle that gets you where you need to go, exactly when you need to be there—the door to wisdom and understanding.

Prayer invites God to intervene on our behalf—binding in the supernatural realm what we bind on earth. Get Him involved, ask your friends to pray too, and start moving heaven and earth until His perfect will is complete in your life. Don't be afraid to think big either. We serve a big God!

He is so big that I don't hope God heals; I know God heals. I don't hope for a better tomorrow; I know a better tomorrow is coming. I don't wish for wisdom; I know He supplies it.

When the trumpet sounds, we will be out of here in the blink of an eye. It will happen just that fast! Until that day, I will place my trust in God, knowing that He walks with me every step of the way.

Don't leave things to chance; leave things to God! His ideas are so breathtaking that most of them have not yet entered into the minds of men.

Joshua 1:9
"Have I not commanded you? Be strong and of good courage;
do not be afraid, nor be dismayed,
for the LORD your God is with you wherever you go."

Where are you in the fight of life? No matter your place, I have great news and a recipe for total success! Be bold, be of good courage, be strong—for the Lord your God is with you!

Before you even knew there was a problem, the victory was already yours. His angels are surrounding you, preparing your way. They are your rear guard. The power of the Holy Spirit is living within you. Lift up your head and rejoice! Great things are on the way!

Don't focus on what you see happening around you; focus on the One who surrounds you with His everlasting mercy and grace. If you concentrate on the raging waves that threaten to suck you under, you will surely drown. When you concentrate on the One who commands, "Peace, be still!" you will walk hand-in-hand with your Savior right over your problems until you come to dry land on the other side of the shore.

Until the day of His return, Jesus will complete the good work He started in you.

Proverbs 9:10
"The fear of the LORD is the beginning of wisdom,
And the knowledge of the Holy One is understanding."

———— ◆ ————

Would you like divine guidance so accurate that you could make decisions with the wisdom of Solomon? Decisions that would cause the prosperity of God to explode in your life? In your relationships? In your business?

Would you like guidance from God that produces peace of mind, self-confidence, divine health, and joy unspeakable? Would you like to reach your highest potential?

Child of God, this is very easy for you to have right now. I'm not talking about something you must wait to gain after entering the pearly gates. Today is the day to start gaining divine wisdom, and it's probably much easier than you think.

No matter what your background is, where you live or work, or the kind of car you drive, God wants you to have a life without limit! All you need to do is begin to seek His face. Saturate your life with His Holy Word, knowing He can guide you in the way everlasting.

Once you turn your life over to the Lord, it will become a thing of such unbelievable beauty that everyone around will want what you have: the joy of the Lord that makes rich and adds no sorrow.

1 Thessalonians 5:23
"Now may the God of peace Himself sanctify you completely;
and may your whole spirit, soul, and body be preserved blameless
at the coming of our Lord Jesus Christ."

———————

You are three people: your body, your soul, and your spirit. Through the body, you relate to the world with your five senses. Through the Spirit, you relate to God and His guidance for your life. Through the soul, you decide which you will obey—the flesh or the Spirit. This is where decisions are made.

This morning when you woke up, perhaps you might have thought to yourself that you wanted a dozen doughnuts for breakfast. Then you got on the scale and decided maybe that wasn't the best idea. This is your conscience telling you that your flesh is wrong. While the doughnuts are tempting, they are not the best choice.

God wants you to walk in the Spirit and enjoy the life you were intended to have, a life of favor and grace. When you make decisions today, listen to your Spirit and know that this still, small voice is God leading you in the direction your life needs to take so that you may prosper in all things.

If you follow where the Holy Spirit leads, you will never take a wrong turn.

The Pastor's Blessing

And now may the Lord bless you and keep you. May the Lord make His face to shine upon you and be gracious unto you, giving you His peace. What we have left at Your altar, Lord, may we never carry it on our shoulders again. Every burden lifted. Every yoke destroyed. Every chain broken. Every enemy defeated. Every need supplied. Every request answered. You are a God who is all-sufficient in the midst of our insufficiency. We give it all to You today, God, and declare that we are set free. For whom the Son sets free is free indeed! Amen!

Psalm 37:7
"Rest in the LORD, and wait patiently for Him;
Do not fret Because of him who prospers in his way,
because of the man who brings wicked schemes to pass."

———◆———

*I*n the past I have asked the Lord, "Why do Your children miss Your will so often, and why do they suffer so needlessly? Why can't they reach their divine destiny, standing in the winner's circle and prospering like King Solomon?"

And God answered me very clearly. He said that He knows how to help you find your healing, how to find streams of living water in the desert of your days, how to find the husband or wife you are seeking, the finances your family needs... He knows!

He will guide you with His all-seeing eye if you will only look to Him long enough to get a clear signal. Leave your own will aside, let go of the flesh, and listen to the voice of the Lord as He gently guides and provides.

If you will be still, just for a moment, God will take you by the hand and lead you down the path of rich fulfillment.

Ephesians 2:8
"By grace you have been saved through faith,
and that not of yourselves; it is the gift of God."

———————

*A*djust your feelings to fit the facts. You are saved, made holy, and sanctified by faith in the Lamb of God.

Don't allow Satan to control you via your feelings. Your emotions can be toxic, completely detrimental to your success. And Satan will use whatever he can get ahold of to control you, to destroy you. But I have great news! Faith is the victory that overcomes the world, the flesh, and the devil. And you are an overcomer through the shed blood of Jesus Christ!

Everyone has a bad day now and then. But once you get down, do you stay there? Or do you start singing a song of praise and asking God to saturate your day with His peace and His joy? Don't allow the circumstances that you are in right now to dictate your mood, good or bad. Circumstances come and go, but true joy comes from the Lord.

God is good. He is faithful and full of grace. With God on your team, you can charge the gates of hell with a water pistol and come out victorious! You are saved and redeemed by the blood of the Lamb! Don't allow negative emotions to consume you. You have too much going for you to be controlled by toxic emotions and temporary circumstances!

James 4:3
"You ask and do not receive, because you ask amiss,
that you may spend it on your pleasures."

———————

Today I want to challenge you to transform your attitude from "I can't" to "I will" by the grace of God. Your Father in heaven desires to give you the very best of things, and you need to start anticipating this in order to receive heaven's best for your life!

Have you ever noticed how, when you expect the worst, that is exactly what happens? So stop expecting the cloud in the middle of your parade. You were born for greatness!

Start asking God to saturate your life with blessings and you will begin to receive them. The Bible says that you have not because you ask not. God has unlimited treasure at His disposal, just waiting to be gifted to you at the right moment, and you're walking around with your fingers crossed, saying, "I hope something good happens for me today." That, my friend, is a defeatist attitude.

God is saying, "Stop it! I've got something special for you. Ask, and I will open the windows of heaven and bless you with blessings you cannot contain!"

When you start gearing your mindset toward the positive—what you CAN do, what you CAN achieve, what you CAN be in Jesus' name—you will completely transform your life overnight. You will be amazed at how easy it is to do when you start making the conscious decision to receive God's very best!

2 Corinthians 9:8
"God is able to make all grace abound toward you,
that you, always having all sufficiency in all things,
may have an abundance for every good work."

The will of God will never take you where the grace of God cannot keep you. His grace IS sufficient. It might not look like it today from a worldly perspective, but focus on the message found in the Cross... a message of life-altering, grave-shattering abounding hope, grace, and mercy.

While we are here on earth, we all have trials and tribulations. No one gets by without them. Your neighbor may tell you how perfect her life is, but guess what? It's not. You cannot walk through this tumultuous journey called life without receiving some type of battle scar.

When you focus on God and your priorities are aligned with His, it doesn't mean you won't suffer; it means that you will find Him right beside you, to comfort you in your hour of need, even if you are walking through the valley of death. The Bible promises us that. He is as close as the mention of His name.

And, Oh, what a reward we will receive one precious day! Are you ready to wear the crown that God is designing with your name on it? Guess what? No one wears a crown in heaven who didn't carry a cross on earth. Your cross was personally built for you by God, to develop in you the character He desires.

As He molds you and makes you into something beautiful, reach out and help those around you who are struggling. Do good to them, no matter your circumstances. God has a purpose in mind for whatever situation surrounds you. And remember... His grace abounds.

Hebrews 9:22
"According to the law almost all things are purified with blood, and without shedding of blood there is no remission."

———◆———

Without the Cross it is impossible to be saved or delivered. The blood of Jesus Christ makes salvation possible.

Let me ask you a question. "If the Cross was taken out of your life, out of your thoughts and speech, would people be able to tell a difference in you?" If the answer is "no," then this is the year to dig deeper into the Word and begin building a stronger relationship with Christ. Or maybe you just need to begin building a relationship with Christ. In that case, there is no time like the present.

What does the Cross do for you? It can fill you with joy that is unspeakable, hope that is real, peace that surpasses all understanding, confidence that is unlimited—and grant you eternal life... just for starters. That sounds pretty good, doesn't it?

Lay your pain, your sin, your agony, your past, your everything at the foot of the Cross and find a new life in Jesus Christ. If you haven't been walking with Him like you know you should, there's no better time to start than today!

Proverbs 11:28
"He who trusts in his riches will fall,
But the righteous will flourish like foliage."

———— ◦ ◈ ◦ ————

God's favor can make you the envy of the nations. When you have the favor of God, you can do with great ease what others cannot. You can climb to the divine destiny God has created just for you because you can believe in things other people cannot see.

When you are favored of God, there is no limitation for you. The Word promises us that He will take the wealth of the wicked and place it in the hands of the righteous, that you are the head and not the tail. He wishes above all things that you prosper, even as your soul prospers.

This means, don't envy the new car your neighbor has or the perfectly tailored suits you always see him wearing. Child of God, what you have is far more valuable than earthly riches. The favor of God is upon you. If you got out of bed this morning and your name isn't in the obituaries, you have something to shout about! You still have time on this earth to give glory and praise to your heavenly Father!

Don't ever wish to be someone else. God didn't make a mistake with you. Your neighbor who looks so put together on the outside has his own battles to fight; don't covet them. Your favor was tailor-made just for you. Wear it like a suit of armor as you face every day, a fearless warrior ready to do battle in the name of the Lord!

Ephesians 2:9
"[It is] not of works, lest anyone should boast."

No one on earth can comprehend the atomic power of the blood of Jesus Christ. This blood gives us the ability as mere mortals to do far above and beyond what we could ever think or imagine on our own, both in the personal and spiritual realms.

The blood of Jesus Christ is like kryptonite to Satan. The Bible tells us that we can ask for healing by the stripes that were on Jesus' back; that the shed blood of Calvary's Cross completely redeemed us from sickness and disease.

Whatever battle you are fighting today, call on the name of the Lord and pray for the shed blood of Christ to cover your family. You may not know where they are or what they're doing, but God does. And in their greatest hour of need, He can wrap His mighty hand of protection around them and save them from the worst evil imaginable. Our God is that powerful!

We are not saved by the good works we do or our church membership. We are not saved by religion or ritual. We are saved simply by the holy blood of Jesus Christ and given the opportunity to enter the pearly gates and walk on streets of gold forevermore. Buddha can't offer that. Mohammed can't offer that. Only Jesus Christ can grant eternal life.

If you are ever in doubt about what to pray, plead the blood of Jesus Christ over yourself, your friends, your family members, those who need to find the Lord. When you do, all of Hell trembles. Demons must flee. Yokes are broken. Captives are set free. And all of heaven rejoices!

The Pastor's Blessing

And now may the Lord bless you and keep you. May the Lord make His face to shine upon you and be gracious unto you, giving you His peace. May you be set free at last from everything in your past that has tormented you, from everything that the prince of darkness has tried to place upon you. Cast your burdens at the base of the Cross and walk away free. For whom the Son sets free is free indeed. In Jesus' name, Amen!

Psalm 118:6
"The LORD is on my side; I will not fear.
What can man do to me?"

*A*re you walking through a trial right now? Can you feel the fiery challenge licking at your heels? Congratulations! You are one step closer to the perfectly designed destiny God has crafted for your life.

As I have told my congregation many times, the only people who have no conflict in their lives are in the cemetery. If you are a breathing organism, you will have conflict. This doesn't mean you need to live in fear of what life or other people will throw your way next. Exactly the opposite is true. When something comes your way, give God thanks that you are in the perfect position to hand Him your problem... and then move aside and allow Him to fight your giants. As a child of God you are more than a conqueror!

Do not fear the rejection of others; the Lord is on your side. Don't fear sickness and disease; they were conquered at the Cross. Do not fear financial ruin; God owns the cattle on a thousand hills. Do not fear what tomorrow holds, for you know Who holds tomorrow. Do not fear death; He holds the keys to death, hell, and the grave. You can walk in total victory because you are a child of the King. Trust Him; He's got this!

Psalm 119:58
"I entreated Your favor with my whole heart;
Be merciful to me according to Your word."

Goodness gives me what I don't deserve. Mercy spares me from what I do.

God's favor is for life; it's not simply a temporary fix to a bad day. If you are wondering when the goodness of the Lord is going to end, here's your answer: Never. So stop worrying about something that will never happen.

Have you ever noticed how most of the things you worry about don't happen anyway? Worry is like a rocking chair. You can rock back and forth until you work yourself into a frenzy, but it will never take you anywhere.

Sit back and relax; God has it all under control. You ain't seen nothin' yet! Rejoice with joy that is unspeakable and full of glory—God will cause His blessings to overflow us, just as He promised.

If today is a bad day, don't think His favor isn't shining upon you. Know that it is, and start living life to the fullest in Jesus' name!

Zephaniah 3:17
"The LORD your God in your midst, The Mighty One, will save; He will rejoice over you with gladness, He will quiet you with His love, He will rejoice over you with singing."

The essence of the word joy ("gladness" in this verse) literally means "dancing" in Hebrew. This is saying that when God looks on the destiny He has for you, He gets so excited about your tomorrow that He begins to dance.

Think about that visual for a moment. The God who created heaven and earth is so excited about the things coming your way that He is celebrating in your honor. He is ecstatic about YOUR future. And if God is that excited, it's time you joined the party! Start focusing on the positive.

When I was a child, we sang a song in church that talked about counting our blessings one by one. Don't ever let the devil take that away from you. Don't minimize your blessings! Many people thank God for the great things He has done but then conclude with, "But what have You done for me lately? What great thing happened to me in the past 30 minutes?"

God is not looking for whiners! He's looking for winners!

If you are sitting around your house recounting all the bad things of the past and anticipating the worst, you won't enjoy the blessings when they come. They will pass you right by because you were too busy focusing on the wrong things. Focus on the Lord, and know that He will turn your mourning into dancing.

1 Samuel 16:7
"The LORD does not see as man sees; for man looks at the outward appearance, but the LORD looks at the heart."

———◆———

I have said this from the pulpit many times: God does not call the equipped, He equips the called. Don't worry about what things look like on the outside; God is still in control. He sees your heart and knows your every thought. While others might reject you for your outward appearance, God says, "That is the exact person for this mission. Get ready, because it's going to be epic!"

Remember David, the small shepherd boy? He went out and faced the giant while all of the big, strapping warriors from the land were sucking on Maalox tablets and crying. They were trained men in top physical condition... and then here came David with only a slingshot and a sack lunch for his brothers. Yet God had this assignment for David, so he equipped the lad for the fight.

Keep your heart right with God, and never fear the harsh words spoken by those around you. David's brothers mocked him as he declared that he would go out there and take on the giant alone. And think of Noah. He built an ark when no one on the face of the earth had ever seen one drop of rain. Despite the taunts coming from his neighbors, Noah just kept on building, one board at a time. And then the rains came.

God sees your heart and hears your cry. Trust that He is working all things together for your good, and listen for the still, small voice that will lead you to your appointed destiny. And then... get ready for the victory!

Ruth 2:15-16

"When she rose up to glean, Boaz commanded his young men, saying, 'Let her glean even among the sheaves, and do not reproach her. Also let grain from the bundles fall purposely for her; leave it that she may glean, and do not rebuke her.'"

———◦◦◦———

*H*ave you heard the story of Ruth and Boaz? You probably know that the widowed Ruth pledged her loyalty to Naomi, her mother-in-law... "Where you go I will go." She then headed out to the fields to work.

In ancient Israel, the corners of each field were intentionally left unharvested so that widows and orphans could easily gather grain to feed their families. One day as Ruth was gathering grain for herself and Naomi, Boaz saw her. Wanting to know who Ruth was, he did a little digging and found out all that she had done to help her mother-in-law (which was well beyond what was required in those days). Boaz was so taken with Ruth that he told his workers to let her glean where others did not go and to intentionally let additional grain fall from the gathered bundles. All she needed to do was pick up the abundance and take it home. The Bible calls these bundles "handfuls on purpose."

This is what God wants to do for YOU. When you walk in His will, seeking His face, He wants to richly bless you by giving you handfuls on purpose.

Malachi 3:10
"If I will not open for you the windows of heaven
And pour out for you such blessing
That there will not be room enough to receive it."

God in heaven is your Kinsman-Redeemer through Jesus Christ. He doesn't want you to live a lifestyle of scrounging for what is left over. He doesn't want you to have just enough to meet your needs. He wants you to have more than enough—the very best.

Think of yourself holding a pitcher of water in one hand and a drinking glass in the other. While others might prefer to just deposit a few drops of love and human kindness in your cup, God wants to take the pitcher and continue to pour water into your glass until it is filled to the brim and running over. That is the kind of love, the kind of abundance, the kind of blessing that He wants us to receive on a daily basis.

He is Jehovah Jireh, the Lord your Provider. Today He is telling you to lay your needs at the foot of the Cross, knowing you are covered with the mantle of Christ in every area of your life.

With Him as your Kinsman-Redeemer, you are completely set free from every form of bondage! Get ready for the fullness of the Lord to drench your life completely, to refresh you anew, and to bring you blessings that you never even thought possible.

John 4:24
*"God is Spirit, and those who worship Him must
worship in spirit and truth."*

When you get a great promotion at work, what is the first thing you do? When you are finally able to buy that brand-new car or move into your dream home, who do you thank? Do you go out with your friends to celebrate, or do you take time out to thank the One who sends every good and perfect gift?

Remember this: the gifts of God should never become more important than the God who gives the gifts.

Oftentimes we get so swept up in the goodness of God that surrounds us that we forget to honor the One who is blessing us. But there should never be a day that we don't praise God for His amazing grace, His love, His blessings, and His mercy that endures to all generations. He is so good and so faithful. What have you thanked Him for today?

I challenge you to stop and express your gratitude for the many blessings in your life: a warm home to live in, food on the table, healthy children, a good job—and the list goes on. Dedicate this day to thanking God for the many things we so often take for granted... for He inhabits the praises of His people.

The Pastor's Blessing

And now may the Lord bless you and keep you. May the Lord make His face to shine upon you and be gracious unto you, giving you His peace. May God bring a new love and a new harmony to your family. May this harmony be filled with a peace, love, and joy that is supernatural. On a daily basis we invite the presence of God into our homes to fill us and renew us so that we might be a living testimony of Your love, mercy, and grace. In Jesus' name, Amen!

Genesis 39:21-23
"The LORD was with Joseph and showed him mercy,
and He gave him favor in the sight of the keeper of the prison.
And the keeper of the prison committed to Joseph's hand all
the prisoners. ...The keeper of the prison did not look into
anything that was under Joseph's authority, because the LORD
was with him; and whatever he did, the LORD made it prosper."

Do you remember the story of Joseph and his beautiful coat of many colors? His brothers were jealous and threw him in a pit. Then he went to prison for something he didn't do and eventually ended up in the palace. This was a long trip over several years, but the Bible records that with every step of his journey, Joseph found favor with both God and man. Yet there were some days where, to the human eye, things didn't look so favorable.

Your life might be a lot like Joseph's. Things on the outside might not look so blessed and highly favored, but God promises that His favor is for life. Favor doesn't mean you drive the newest car or live in the biggest house on the block. It means that you serve a great big God who will never leave you nor forsake you. It means that He sees your needs and meets you right where you are... and He loves you in spite of yourself, flaws and all.

When people around you begin noticing God's favor on your life, they aren't all going to celebrate with you. Jealousy is a very real emotion that humans express in many ways, none of which are very attractive or godly. But rest assured, God is using this small bump in the road to move you to the next level of favor with Him.

Keep your chin up and know that when God's favor rests on you, you will live as a favored son or daughter, even amid challenging circumstances.

2 Corinthians 4:17
"Our light affliction, which is but for a moment, is working for us a far more exceeding and eternal weight of glory."

God has given you a dream, a vision for your future. Maybe your dreams now seem like a distant illusion that will never come to fruition. Your hopes have been shattered and your heartache is beyond measure. Perhaps you have been rejected by the dearest on earth. You have lost your hope for the bright future that once seemed attainable and have completely let go of your dream, settling for second best.

Let me encourage you with a word from God today. He can restore to you what the enemy has taken. In one moment, He can return to you a lifetime's worth of heartache and defeat. It can happen just that fast!

The darkest hour is always just before the dawn, and your change will come when it seems most impossible. Get ready! You are about to experience a complete breakthrough that will be as the latter rain, making your future years better than the former.

1 Peter 1:6
"In this you greatly rejoice, though now for a little while,
if need be, you have been grieved by various trials."

When God places you in the middle of a trial, He puts you there for a little while to burn out your imperfections so that you can become a vessel of honor to Him. If you cannot endure great burdens, you will never survive great success.

And you might as well smile while you're walking through the valley, because your attitude in the trial will determine just how long you stay there. Are you interested in wandering around that mountain for 40 years? Use the valley as a time for God to restore your soul, to reveal Himself to you in a very real way, to learn the things that you won't learn anywhere else.

The people who are most successful in life are the war-torn and battle-scarred, not the chubby little babies whose parents never disciplined them. They are the lean, mean fighting machines who have weathered the storm and lived to tell about it.

God uses the challenges in your life to develop within you something that will honor Him and bless others. So rejoice, and face the challenges of this day head-on, choosing to be made better, not bitter. Our God is able!

Numbers 6:24-26
"The LORD bless you and keep you; the LORD make His face shine upon you, and be gracious to you; the LORD lift up His countenance upon you, and give you peace."

What is a blessing? It is the imparting of the supernatural power of God into a human life by the spoken word of God's delegated spiritual authority.

In ancient Israel God commanded the high priest to speak the blessing over all Israel. Once the blessing was spoken, God poured out His unsearchable riches over the land. The spiritual authority in a home is the father. If the father is absent, then the mother is the spiritual authority. A father or mother can bless the members of his or her household by the power of Almighty God. Parents can literally give the angels an assignment to watch over their children and to keep them safe in all their ways.

God has given us the authority to use His power to supernaturally release the blessings of God upon our friends and family. Do not let this precious gift go to waste!

You were born to be blessed! Not because you deserve it, but because God is your Father and He chooses to bless you with blessings you cannot contain.

Luke 17:6
"The Lord said, 'If you have faith as a mustard seed,
you can say to this mulberry tree, "Be pulled up by the roots and
be planted in the sea," and it would obey you.'"

———— ✦ ————

Because of the triumph of the Cross, you and I have been saved by the blood of Christ. Because of this great triumph, demons tremble when you mention Jesus' name.

When life knocks you to your knees, you are in the best position to pray—strategically aligned to reach out to the One who even the winds and waves obey. You can command all of heaven and earth by simply asking God the Father to intervene on your behalf.

Just ask! Don't be shy! Start talking about the power of the blood and watch as every demon in the county flees. The precious blood of Christ gives life to your prayer and to the proclamations you claim based on the promises found in God's Word. Without exception, the Word of God never returns void.

What are you asking God for today? What good thing will you proclaim in Jesus' name? Know that whatever you ask in faith believing, you can have because of the precious blood that was shed for you on Calvary's Cross.

Job 10:12
"You have granted me life and favor,
and Your care has preserved my spirit."

———————

Many of God's children live with an insecurity complex and can't see themselves as being blessed and highly favored. While life might be a bowl of cherries for their relatives, it's always the pits for them. If they inherited General Motors, someone would outlaw cars.

It might seem as though God has overlooked you, and you are asking, "Where is the favor of God in my situation?" I want you to hear this: It is God's desire to bless you with favor that will knock your socks off! He wants to bless you with blessings you cannot contain.

Your circumstances might not look favored, but don't let the conditions of your life determine whether or not you continue to seek God's will and accept His favor. Rise up each morning and say, "By the power of Almighty God, I am a child of Almighty God, blessed and highly favored!"

Satan is not worried about what you will do for the Kingdom if he can preoccupy you with a seemingly endless parade of problems. Some might be large, valid issues. But stay focused on the Prize. When you focus on the problem, then the problem consumes you. When you stay focused on Jesus, He fills your days with laughter and your bitter midnights with song.

Don't let Satan steal your joy and rob you of your peace. Life is simply too short for that! Enjoy each day as if it was your last, and know that God is still on the throne and everything is going to be alright!

Romans 8:37

*"In all these things we are more than conquerors
through Him who loved us."*

The day Jesus died on the Cross looked like a day of total defeat, when in fact it was a day of total victory! From a human perspective, it looked as if the enemy had won. The soldiers were mocking Him. His robe was torn and sold. The sky was gray and dismal. All hope seemed lost.

What appeared to be utter defeat was actually the portrait of sheer victory on a grand scale that the world had never before seen. That was the day you and I were set free from death, hell, and the grave, from sickness and disease. It was the day we were liberated from the chains of the past, from addiction, from every kind of hindrance that would defeat us in our daily lives.

On this day, Jesus descended from the Cross into the bowels of the earth and shook His finger in the face of the prince of darkness. He gave us all authority, on earth and in heaven. No matter what we ask for in His name, we can now have it because of the complete victory that was won on the darkest day the earth has ever known.

Think of the chains that bind you today and then look in the mirror. You are now face-to-face with your worst enemy. Yet the person you see in the reflection has been completely liberated, set free to live a life of abundance. Calvary made that possible! Today, whatever chains have shackled you to the past, whatever controls you and manipulates your life, keeping you from enjoying the goodness of the Lord... let it go in Jesus' name. You are more than a conqueror. Live like it. Act like it. Think like it. That is what Calvary did for you!

The Pastor's Blessing

And now may the Lord bless you and keep you. May the Lord make His face to shine upon you and be gracious unto you, giving you His peace. May you so walk in the Word of God that it brings the love, joy, and peace of God to you, to your spouse, and to your children. May your days be filled with health and prosperity because the blessing of the Lord is upon the righteous. In Jesus' name we pray and ask, Amen!

James 1:6
"Let him ask in faith, with no doubting,
for he who doubts is like a wave of the sea
driven and tossed by the wind."

———❖———

*D*o you have a special need in your life today that only God can meet? Have you let the people around you fill your mind with doubt, telling you that your need is too great or that someone like you doesn't deserve to be helped in such a fantastic way? Know that Satan is the author of lies, and he will use whatever methods he can to destroy your peace and minimize your faith until you feel like a battered boat tossed about in the sea.

Ask God and He can and will meet your need, period. End of story.

God has big plans for you! Don't settle for anything less. You can be exactly what God wants you to be—forgiven, loved, and purified by the blood of Jesus Christ. When God has set a dream in your heart but those around you are calling your goals too lofty, square your shoulders and tell them that you can do ALL things through Christ!

Stop focusing on the chaos and the crowds. Don't listen to the chatter. Be like the deaf turtle who won the race when everyone on the sideline was shouting that he would never make it. He just kept plugging along as if they had said nothing. You do the same. Ignore the fools who want to cause you nothing but strife, and get busy making God's dream for your life a reality!

Psalm 119:2
"Blessed are those who keep His testimonies,
who seek Him with the whole heart!"

———◆———

When you're thinking life has defeated you, begin to pray and seek the Lord's face. He will point you in the direction you need to go. He will never leave you nor forsake you. And He will work things in your favor as you learn to lean on Him.

Are you going round and round in circles? Today is the day to get off the merry-go-round and actually start steering toward success in your life.

When you get behind the wheel of your car, don't turn on the radio. Don't talk on your phone. Listen for the voice of the Spirit!

If God is trying to gently place you on the path of His choosing, the road less traveled... you have to be willing to listen and be led. Tune out the distractions and focus on the Source of every blessing that has ever come your way. He promises to go before you, like a guide on an Alaskan hike. You want to walk right behind Him, in His immediate footsteps, so you don't make any fatal errors. You want to go exactly where He's leading, and do as He says. This is the way to life!

Colossians 4:2
"Continue earnestly in prayer,
being vigilant in it with thanksgiving."

Just as your parents often told you "no" to ensure your safety as a child, God sometimes does the same thing for His children.

Why does God tell us "no?" Let me ask you something. Have you ever been to the mall and seen the child who is wandering around the department store, tearing everything up in his path while his parents shop for hours? Do you enjoy being around that kind of behavior? I know I don't.

It's the same with us. If God gives us everything we ask for and never disciplines us, we turn into spoiled brats. We destroy ourselves because we know what we want, but what we want isn't always what we need. God is too wise to make a mistake and too loving to be unkind. He sends us what we need, as soon as we need it.

Which means our prayers aren't always answered instantly. The Bible tells us to be diligent in prayer and to persevere until the answer comes. That is one of the building blocks of faith—hanging in there until we have an answer. The answer may be "no." Sometimes God has to trim the branches on our tree for us to reach our full potential... especially if we repeatedly stunt our own growth by making foolish choices. Regardless, don't throw in the towel if God hasn't responded by lunchtime; He is working on something great!

Deuteronomy 30:19
"I call heaven and earth as witnesses today against you, that I have set before you life and death, blessing and cursing; therefore choose life, that both you and your descendants may live."

I have great news for you today! The same blessings that were spoken throughout the Old Testament can be imparted today... in your home and over your children. It is very easy to release the unlimited power of Jesus Christ upon your life and the lives of those you love. Boundless blessing can begin to infiltrate your home immediately—you don't have to wait for your eternal reward to reap the benefits of being a Christian.

No power in hell or on earth can conquer the unleashed power of God upon your life, and once you understand the difference it can make, you will not want to live another moment without it. You might be saying, "Pastor, I don't even know where to start or what to say!" That's just perfect, because the Word of God is filled with promises and blessings from cover to cover. All you need to do is open it up and read it aloud. Begin proclaiming the goodness of the Lord in your home. As you speak the Scriptures out loud, every demon trembles and every angel rejoices. As you continue speaking, you are literally inviting the Holy Spirit to come into your home and take over.

If you want to dramatically impact your life, start speaking straight from the Word of God and blessings will begin to roll over you like a Mack truck! You don't have to understand everything about Scripture or be a theologian to receive the benefits. When you use your voice to release the blessing, a tidal wave of abundance is all that can happen!

Psalm 42:11
"Why are you cast down, O my soul? And why are you
disquieted within me? Hope in God; for I shall yet praise Him,
the help of my countenance and my God."

*D*o you feel hopeless? Is your life spiraling into a seemingly endless black hole of depression, guilt, fear, or uncertainty? The unprecedented goodness of Almighty God can give your life a brand-new meaning, a brand-new direction.

Each and every one of you were born with a blessing that is just waiting to be poured out upon your life. No one can accept your blessing or take it from you unless you give it away. Square your shoulders and believe that you indeed deserve to partake in the richness of Jesus Christ. You deserve to be blessed beyond measure as a child of the King. Make a change for the better and get ready for your life to be saturated with joy.

Someone in your past may have convinced you that you were unworthy. For better or worse, our lives are shaped by those who love us and by those who refuse to love us. To live a rich and full life, you must leave the pain of the past behind and move forward. Easy to say and hard to do, but God loved you so much that He sent His only Son to die in your place, and that is more than enough reason to celebrate!

Don't live in the past. Take responsibility for the role you played in whatever piece unraveled and ask forgiveness for it. Then be set free to move forward. But remember this: you cannot change what you will not confront! You have the ability through the power of the blessing to revolutionize your life, so what are you waiting for?

Psalm 147:5
"Great is our LORD, and mighty in power;
His understanding is infinite."

---

*T*he world will tell you what you can and can't do, what is socially acceptable, what is politically correct. There are rules for what you can say, what you can wear, how you must act in social settings so as not to offend the sensibilities of those around you. There are limitations on the limitations and fine print for the fine print.

But with God there is NO limit... ever. He is our great supply, faithful to meet us right where we are—on the mountaintop or in the valley, celebrating the biggest victory of our lives or sitting with us in the wreckage from a devastating storm.

When people tell us something cannot be done, we know that THEY do not set the limits for what WE can accomplish by God's might. Only the Lord sets the parameters for His children—and the Word says no good thing will He withhold from those who diligently seek Him.

Today, know that nothing is impossible for you! Start out with confidence, heading straight for the finish line, because God will help you trudge through each and every mile if you will hand Him the reins and let Him take control.

John 16:33
"These things I have spoken to you, that in Me you may
have peace. In the world you will have tribulation;
but be of good cheer, I have overcome the world."

Are you having a bad day? A bad week? A bad month? Rejoice by choice! Don't look at your circumstances, but look to the One who can control them.

Right now, this instant, you can have total, all-consuming peace in your life, no matter how out of control things might be. The world didn't give you this peace, and the world can't take it away. You can give it away, but no one can take from you what you don't give them.

You can choose to saturate your life with God's peace even when all hell is breaking loose around you. Happiness is based on your circumstances, but true peace comes from the Lord. You don't have to be happy to have peace in your life.

No matter what challenge you are facing, know that God sees you right where you are, and everything is going to be alright! How do I know that? Because His eye is on the sparrow, and the Bible says that you are much more important to Him than the birds of the air. He knows the number of hairs on your head and collects your tears in a vase. Nothing goes unnoticed by Almighty God! And yes, He sees you right smack dab in the middle of your firestorm. Will you allow Him to take control and lead you to safety? Invite the Prince of Peace to rule and reign in your heart today!

The Pastor's Blessing

And now may the Lord bless you and keep you. May the Lord make His face to shine upon you and be gracious unto you, giving you His peace. May you live this day knowing that God is in absolute control of everything that's going on in the universe. He can control every detail of your life, but you need to release Him to be the Lord of your life. His Lordship will bring to you green pastures and still waters, answers and solutions where now you have only questions and problems. God is a good God, and He is awaiting the chance to make your life a thing of great beauty. In Jesus' name, Amen!

Genesis 9:13
"I set My rainbow in the cloud, and it shall be for the sign
of the covenant between Me and the earth."

What is a covenant? The Bible, the inspired Word of God, is a book of absolute covenant. The God we serve is a God of covenant. What He says, He will do. Israel belongs to the Jews forever because of a covenant promise.

Have you ever been driving down the highway as a brightly colored rainbow peeked through the clouds on the other side of your wet windshield? That remarkable array of colors is God's billboard, announcing that after thousands of years, He is still true to the covenant He made with Noah. The rainbow is the eternal symbol of God's vow that He will never again flood the earth.

In the New Testament church we have the covenant of blood where our sins are forgiven because of the Cross. When Jesus Christ was our scapegoat at Golgotha, His shed blood paid the debt that we owed. It was a debt that only He could pay as the only One who ever lived without spot or wrinkle. He was and is the Lamb of God, slain from the foundations of the earth. He is from Everlasting to Everlasting. And His Word is truth.

God never breaks covenant with His people. If you are looking to have a deeper relationship with Him, examine your covenants. Are you a covenant keeper or a covenant breaker? If you have broken your word in the past, you can come to the Cross and ask for forgiveness, starting anew this very hour.

Psalm 103:1
"BLESS the LORD, O my soul;
and all that is within me, bless His holy name!"

Do you believe in miracles? Sooner or later you will face a crisis that you can't manage on your own. It will be a circumstance that will crush your life like a giant wave rushing over a child's sandcastle. You will one day need a miracle from God to touch your life. Perhaps this miracle will mean the difference between life and death.

Rest assured. Our God is able.

I want you to know that God can infuse your life with peace, joy, and hope. He has promised us joy unspeakable and full of glory if we will only invite Him into our lives.

Our God is a miracle-working god. In Genesis, God breathed into a handful of dirt and created everything in the universe. If you don't think that's a miracle, head out to your backyard and see how far you get with a handful of dirt.

A speck of His glory set the sun to flame. The next time you are at the beach watching the waves crashing all around you and the noonday sun glimmering against the sandy beach, remember this: He holds the seven seas in the palm of His hand and calls the stars by name. Nothing is too big for our God!

Jeremiah 29:12-13
"You will call upon Me and go and pray to Me,
and I will listen to you. And you will seek Me and find Me,
when you search for Me with all your heart."

Keep on praying until you hear from heaven. God always answers prayer. He tells us yes, no, or wait. You might not like the answer He gives you, but He will always respond to your request.

The New Testament church was born in Acts in the Upper Room during 10 days of prayer. I know that might sound a little extraordinary by today's standards, as most preachers would get laughed out of the building if they hosted a prayer meeting for more than an hour! But at this earth-shattering Upper Room prayer meeting, there were 120 people in attendance.

This was a national event, where a group of Believers literally shook the rafters until everyone was completely saturated by the presence of the Holy Spirit in that place. They weren't afraid of what the people around them thought; they were crying out to Abba Father with every fiber of their being and waiting upon the Lord.

If you want to have New Testament power, you need to do the same thing! Pray until God Himself sends you the answer. Don't wait for your neighbor's advice, your mother-in-law's idea, your friend who stuck her finger in the Bible and came up with a new verse for you. NO! Listen and wait upon the Lord. He alone holds the key to your ultimate success. Wait upon the Lord and be of good courage. He will direct your path and strengthen your heart!

Matthew 6:14
"If you forgive men their trespasses,
your heavenly Father will also forgive you."

Forgiveness and restoration should be distinguishing marks of those who love the Lord. The world will always be bent on punishment and further disgrace when someone falls; the people of God are called to react differently—to forgive as we have been forgiven, and to seek to serve.

What are you doing to show that you belong to Christ? Are you leading other Believers by example? Do you turn the other cheek when someone mistreats you, or did you throw a fit because someone parked in your sacred spot in the church lot on your way into the Sunday morning service?

What are you doing to help a brother or sister in need? If you are not living as Christ did, God cannot use you. He only uses servants. They are His salt.

Isaiah 26:3
"You will keep him in perfect peace, Whose mind
is stayed on You, Because he trusts in You."

———◦◉◦———

Jesus didn't die on the Cross so He could condemn us. He came to save us and grant us the peace that surpasses understanding as we navigate life's roads to the inexplicable splendors of heaven. The half of what we will see upon our much-anticipated arrival has not even entered our minds. But until that day when we meet our Savior face-to-face, we must continue to stay the course.

We were never promised a primrose path on this earth. We were, however, promised that in Him we could find peace. If we will seek Him, Jesus will carry our burdens no matter how great our load and make a way where none seems to be. He knows our end from the beginning.

What do you need to trust Him with today? Take it to the foot of the Cross and leave it there. Don't carry part of the problem back home with you. Leave the entire burden with God, knowing that He will not only meet your need but give you sweet rest in the valley.

Psalm 145:19
"He will fulfill the desire of those who fear Him;
He also will hear their cry and save them."

———

What does favor look like? The Bible says the blessings of the Lord make rich and add no sorrow, yet there are lots of very wealthy people in the world who do not possess true joy because they equate happiness with their earthly possessions. But the world can't supply happiness. And thankfully, it can't take away true happiness—the joy that comes from the Lord.

When God showers you with blessings, there will be no mistaking the Source. His presence saturates the room and satisfies your desires. Yet so often He is our last resort. Why don't you try asking Him first the next time you feel empty or discouraged? He longs to commune with you and satisfy you with Himself.

The favor of God surrounds your life each and every day. Stop surveying your circumstances to see if your life "looks" favored. Your problems were solved, your needs were filled, your enemies were outnumbered—even before the troubles began. Have confidence that as you trust God, He will provide. Your blessing is on the way!

1 John 4:8

"He who does not love does not know God, for God is love."

———◦◦◦———

Certainly you want to show the love of the Lord to everyone, but when you start to build the infrastructure of friends that surround you on a daily basis, make good choices. Surround yourself with kind-hearted, loving people.

Do they love the Lord? Do they show this love to others? Are they constantly looking for ways to serve the Kingdom, to reach out to those in need? Remember, the greatest of all is the one who serves.

As for your own heart, be willing to love others who are different than you. Maybe you know people who don't attend the same church or wear the same style of clothing you deem appropriate... love them anyway. God does!

Strive to be the blessing, and when someone needs to leave, don't sweat the small stuff. God is taking you to another level without them. If God is taking them out of your life, let Him. He has something wonderful in store for you if you will simply give Him the lead. You can't fulfill your divine destiny holding onto someone who is detrimental to your spiritual health. If they must go, let them go. But keep striving to show the love of the Lord to those around you. In this way we represent Christ.

The Pastor's Blessing

And now may the Lord bless you and keep you. May the Lord make His face to shine upon you and be gracious unto you, giving you His peace. May you feel the love of God and learn to live within His limitless love for you. May you come to know and understand that God so loved the world that He gave His only begotten Son, so that your life could be one of perpetual peace and joy that is unspeakable and full of glory. In the name of the Father, the Son, and the Holy Spirit, Amen!

Revelation 21:5
"Then He who sat on the throne said,
'Behold, I make all things new.'"

———— ·•◈•· ————

*I*t is never too late to get a fresh start! The Bible contains many stories of people who failed miserably and were given another chance by God. And really, at some point or other in our life, we ALL need a fresh start.

Have you heard of David, the shepherd boy who killed Goliath? Read through the Psalms and you will learn about his many escapades, along with those of others. Problems are a part of life. Challenges are here to stay. Mistakes are made by everyone. But guess what? God is waiting to give your life the jumpstart you need to move in a fresh, new direction!

Are you tired of the way things are going right now? Would you like to have the ultimate makeover? Today is your day to be blessed by God!

Don't let those around you label your life as "over" or "useless." God created you in His very own image with an exact purpose in mind. Ask Him today to re-ignite the fire of your life and point you in the direction He has for you. Great things are on the way!

2 Chronicles 13:5
"Should you not know that the LORD God of Israel
gave the dominion over Israel to David forever,
to him and his sons, by a covenant of salt?"

What is a salt covenant? In the Bible salt always represents loyalty, a word that is lost in today's vernacular. The salt covenant is one of loyalty. God intends for His children to be loyal to Him, to keep His covenants, just as He has been loyal to them. He also intends for them to keep their vows to each other.

"Covenant" is defined as the ability to remain faithful even to your own hurt. This means that once you give your word, no matter how difficult it becomes, you honor your word to the party with whom you made the covenant. Everything that is permanent or important in the Word of God is sealed by a covenant between two parties.

Marriage is an example of a covenant relationship that involves loyalty. If you have been married for five minutes, you understand how this works. You may have even exchanged salt during your wedding ceremony as a visual demonstration of your loyalty.

Are you true to your word? Or are you a covenant breaker? If today some of your relationships are broken and your heart is bruised, I encourage you to make them right. Forgiveness is one of the greatest gifts heaven has given us, and it's something that can revolutionize your life in an instant. Forgive those who have hurt you, so that you can uphold your covenants.

2 Thessalonians 3:16
"Now may the Lord of peace Himself give you peace always in every way."

---

*P*eace is not the absence of conflict but the presence of God no matter the conflict.

When I was a young boy, we had a pair of hound dogs that hated each other. Any time they were left alone together, they would go at each other until there was no fight left in them. So you see, peace is not always the absence of conflict— sometimes we're just too tired to fight!

Maybe you're having a tough day or perhaps you are in the fight of your life. Know that God has not forsaken you. YOU matter to Him, right down to the last hair on your head and every tear in your eye!

Everyone in this life will face trials. As long as you're still breathing, obstacles will come your way. Just remember: if God can bring you to it, He can bring you through it. Don't run from a problem in fear, but face it head-on, knowing if you're on God's team, you can defeat any enemy. No matter how enormous the challenge, don't worry about it. Put your trust in Him.

When we ask Him to take our problems as His own, He will saturate our lives with peace.

Psalm 37:3
"Trust in the LORD, and do good; Dwell in the land,
and feed on His faithfulness."

Trust God. You may not always get your way, but He will work things together for your very best in the long run.

Sometimes the very best answer for us is "no," whether we want to believe it or not. Because while we are face-to-face with the moment we are living in, God sees the entire picture... not just the tiny snapshot that we see from our human vantage point.

Before my daughter was married, she dated a young man who was a good man. However, I knew that she would not fulfill her divine potential if she were to marry him. I began to pray and ask God to supernaturally bring into her life the man who would not only honor her for the beautiful lady that she is, but who would be a good father to her children and permit her a lifestyle that allowed her to successfully continue working in the ministry. I had faith that God would deliver in time, and today all of the things that I prayed for have come true.

God is not a respecter of persons. What He did for me, He can do for you. Begin a prayer journal and write down the things you would like for Him to do in your life—the areas you would like for Him to supernaturally touch. What places need supernatural intervention and inspiration?

Make a prayer list and start sending your petitions to the throne room of God. He is waiting. Then, mark the dates beside your requests and have faith that in due season, the Lord will answer your prayer.

1 Peter 4:12–13
"Beloved, do not think it strange concerning the fiery trial which
is to try you, as though some strange thing happened to you;
but rejoice to the extent that you partake of
Christ's sufferings, that when His glory is revealed,
you may also be glad with exceeding joy."

---

*H*ave you tried and failed? Remember, the tea kettle sings its very best song when it's up to its neck in hot water.

Planes fly against the wind; boats move against the tide. Life can often be a struggle. But how could you know the taste of sweet victory if you never faced a single battle? How could you know the strength of an all-powerful Savior if you never needed saving?

The challenge you are facing today can be handed over to God and used to bring you to a higher level of learning, a deeper level of commitment. God isn't punishing you by allowing your trials, but He is watching to see what you will do in the middle of the shark tank. Will you trust Him to save you, or will you wait until you see Jaws headed your way before crying out for help?

When you ask God to send you a lifeboat in the middle of the ocean, don't be surprised when it shows up! When you pray specifically for something and it becomes a reality, you can be sure that God was diligently working behind the scenes to meet your every need. Thank Him for the victory!

Lamentations 3:23
"[His mercies] are new every morning;
Great is Your faithfulness."

———————————

Wouldn't you love to wake up every morning and feel you had a brand-new lease on life, with the old mistakes and yesterday's bad habits simply falling aside for a fresh start? Doesn't that sound great? You can have that through Jesus Christ! His love for you is never-ending and His mercies are renewed each and every day!

Today, take the time to see yourself as God sees you... as a mirror of His own image. He designed you to be a little lower than the angels, with the royal blood of heaven flowing through your veins. He loves you so much that He has strategically carved out a plan of absolute perfection to meet your every need. Not just a few of your needs, but every single need you will ever have before you even know it exists. Think about that for a minute.

Have you had a hard week? Wake up tomorrow morning knowing that you can have a fresh start in Jesus' name! Wipe away the past, knowing that God can wipe your slate clean and set the captive free in a New York minute. It can happen just that fast. Today is the day to celebrate the faithfulness of Jesus Christ in your life. There is no substitute for Him.

Romans 8:31
"What then shall we say to these things?
If God is for us, who can be against us?"

---

*E*mbrace the fact that God is on your side. And if He is on your side, you are destined for total victory in Jesus' mighty name. You will never face an enemy that is stronger than God, and you will never know defeat when you have Him as your Commander-In-Chief. He is the Alpha and Omega, the First and the Last. He knows how things will turn out even before you start out.

What would you accomplish today if you knew that God was standing right beside you and you could face any giant? Well, then, get busy! He is your Defender and Protector, and He has promised to defend you. Your enemies will come at you one way and flee in seven different directions. What Satan means for evil, God can and will use for your good.

There is no problem you will ever face that He cannot handle... if you will only trust Him with it. He is our Redeemer but also the Lily of the Valley. Let His sweet aroma flow into your life and saturate you with joy, peace, and confidence that the battle belongs to the Lord and the victory has already been won!

The Pastor's Blessing

And now may the Lord bless you and keep you. May the Lord make His face to shine upon you and be gracious unto you, giving you His peace. May you walk in the divine destiny that God has given to you, down paths of righteousness. May Jesus Christ be both Savior and Lord in your life, and may you come to fulfill your divine purpose. May you as a parent be a righteous example to your children, that they in turn may grow and teach their own children the ways of the Lord. And may our nation be healed by the leadership of the father in the home, sharing the love of Father God first at home and then with others. In Jesus' name, Amen!

Psalm 136:1
"Give thanks to the LORD, for He is good!
For His mercy endures forever."

———————

The things and people of this life may not always be trustworthy, but God's love will never fail us! When the dearest on earth have rejected you, have left you behind, have done unspeakable things... God's love is there to surround us in the midnight hour. There is no place we can go to escape it, no hole too dark or too deep where He cannot reach us with His outstretched arm.

When those around us disappoint and wound us, we must stop looking around for support and look up. Remember, the One who holds the universe in the palm of His hand sent His only Son to die just for YOU! God's love is immeasurable, more all-consuming than the relentless tide that overtakes the sandy beach.

Are you struggling through the greatest crisis of your life? Thank the Lord that His mercy endures forever. Thank Him that He will see you through to the end, bringing you out to rich fulfillment. Are you celebrating the greatest victory? Thank Him still. No matter where you are in your life, it is never a bad day to praise the Lord. He delights in the praises of His people.

Whatever life sends your way, His love surrounds you. He is from everlasting to everlasting. Be still and know that He is God, and that He loves you so very, very much!

John 14:6
Jesus said to him, "I am the way, the truth, and the life.
No one comes to the Father except through Me."

Jesus Christ is "the way, the truth, and the life." What does that mean? Follow Him and you will never go wrong. Forget about what your neighbors (or relatives) are saying. Remember how Noah's neighbors made fun of him as he built the ark? Noah certainly had the last laugh there.

Cling to the Bible and saturate yourself with the truths that are found within its sacred text. Dare to make your life the best it can be with the help of Almighty God. The Bible and human history reveal stories of dreamers who changed the world by acting on their God-given dreams—people who dared to imagine the impossible regardless of what those around them said.

Joseph dreamed his way from the pit to the palace. Moses took up God's vision to liberate the Jewish people from Egyptian bondage. Daniel dreamed his way into the knowledge of his country's future. Abraham Lincoln's dream ended slavery in America.

What is your dream? Today, know that you can make it a reality because God has called you to it. What He brings you to, He will bring you through. So stop looking at all the reasons why you can't accomplish your goal and start moving toward the prize that God has in store for you in Jesus' name.

Psalm 38:15
"In You, O LORD, I hope; You will hear, O Lord my God."

———⊰•⊱———

$\mathcal{D}$on't lose hope. It is always too soon to throw in the towel. When you are down to nothing, God is up to something so great, you can't even imagine the effects it will have on your life.

Does everything around you look bleak? This is the perfect time for God to step in and take over. He has not promised us that life would be a pleasure cruise, but He has promised that if we place our hope and faith in Him, He will be there to carry us through the storm.

Are you having a bad day? Praise the Lord! Are you facing financial reversal? Praise the Lord! Is your marriage in crisis? Praise the Lord! No matter what you are going through, no matter how bad, lift up your voice in praise and faith. He will hear and respond, granting you His all-surpassing peace, making a way for you that is knock-your-socks-off miraculous.

Turn that frown upside-down and know that as you begin to praise the Lord, He will saturate your soul with a peace and joy that the world didn't give and the world can't take away!

Isaiah 55:8-9
"'My thoughts are not your thoughts, Nor are your ways
My ways,' says the LORD. 'For as the heavens are higher than
the earth, So are My ways higher than your ways,
And My thoughts than your thoughts.'"

When we pray and ask God for something, He doesn't always answer on our timetable. Sometimes He says "yes," sometimes He says "no," and sometimes He says "wait." But we continue to seek His will for our lives.

He is the Alpha and Omega who sees the beginning from the end, the Bright and Morning Star. Give Him the opportunity to work something in your life that is so fantastic, you have no doubt that it was Divine intervention.

Are you facing a giant today? Does it feel like if you don't win the victory in front of you, it could alter life as you know it? Do all that you know to do and then stand upon the promises found in God's Word. Ask God to take over. When you follow His mandates, you are in the right position for Him to intervene on your behalf. He can turn your problem inside out and bring a resolution so complete that your human mind cannot begin to grasp the awesomeness of His plan. Not until you live through His answer will you see it was so complete that it covered every tiny detail of your problem. We serve an awesome God!

Our human resources are so incredibly limited. Why would we want to hold God to our standards? Seek His face and thank Him for the answer that is already on the way. He has the perfect solution already lined up!

James 1:12
"Blessed is the man who endures temptation;
for when he has been approved, he will receive the crown of life
which the Lord has promised to those who love Him."

If good things come to those who wait, then great things are in store for those who are willing to persevere to the end.

Is today one of those days where throwing in the towel looks really good? Tie a knot in the end of your rope and hang on. Child of God, we are not promised that every day will be a walk through the rose garden of life, but we are promised that, as the Friend who sticks closer than any brother, He is the one to call on in our hour of great need.

Christ endured the Cross. He endured the temptation to call 10,000 angels to rescue Him from the worst kind of torture any human could possibly imagine. That is how great His love is for you and for me. What are you enduring today? Know that a crown of life awaits those who are willing to finish the race!

Don't get sidetracked! Don't let Satan throw you off your game. If he can send you a problem big enough to deter your focus from the Lord, then he has won the battle. No matter your challenge, stay focused on the Cross. It will be the moral compass that will guide and provide, leading you down the narrow path to life everlasting.

1 Corinthians 3:6-7
"I planted, Apollos watered, but God gave the increase.
So then neither he who plants is anything,
nor he who waters, but God who gives the increase."

———◆◆◆———

*B*e encouraged and don't give up on your tomorrows. Accept the good plan God has for you—a plan filled with hope, purpose, blessing, and increase in every area of your life! And when the blessing comes, know that your heavenly Father sent it.

When we do our part, God does His. He has promised to meet our needs according to His riches in glory. Call upon His mighty name and know that all of heaven rejoices as your ashes are turned into absolute beauty. No matter how shattered or broken your life might be, He can heal your heart and gently place the pieces back together in Jesus' name.

Ask the Master today to intervene on your behalf. Your beautiful transformation is only a breath away!

Deuteronomy 28:12
"The LORD will open to you His good treasure,
the heavens, to give the rain to your land in its season,
and to bless all the work of your hand."

God has great things in store for your future! No matter what might be happening today, or how bleak the horizon might look, He has already lined up a new beginning. Weeping may endure for the night, my friend, but JOY comes in the morning!

New friendships are on the way. New opportunities that will enrich your life are just around the corner.

There is no limit to the treasures God has awaiting you if you will seek His face and get ready to receive them. Expect His abundance to rain down on you like a thunderstorm in a barren desert. This is what God wants to do for you. He wants to exchange the filthy rags of yesterday for a beautiful coat of many colors, blessing you beyond your wildest dreams. He wants to wash you whiter than snow.

Your life might not feel like a miracle-in-the-making from where you stand today, but be confident that as you heed God's will, His plan will unfold. Seek first the Kingdom. As you follow God's lead, He will transform your life into something that is absolutely breathtaking.

The Pastor's Blessing

And now may the Lord bless you and keep you. May the Lord make His face to shine upon you and be gracious unto you, giving you His peace. May you walk in the confidence that you are a child of God; your tomorrows are going to be filled with joy, peace, and accomplishment beyond anything you can possibly imagine. You are living in the Kingdom of Glory where Jesus Christ is Lord. In Jesus' name, Amen!

Psalm 113:3
"From the rising of the sun to its going down
the LORD's name is to be praised."

———— ◆ ————

Take time today to kneel in worship to the King of kings and Lord of lords. Whatever is going on in your life, good or bad, it is always a good day to praise the Lord. He is worthy of our highest praise.

Praise can elevate you to a place of complete worship and allow the Holy Spirit to begin working in you and through you. Sing to the Lord a new song. The lyrics of a song can say in just a few lines what it takes a sermon 30 minutes to relay. Let the Holy Spirit saturate your very being to the core as you sing praises to Jesus' holy name. There is nothing like that deeply sacred moment when you feel as if the Lord is standing right next to you, hanging on your every word!

Give Him the opportunity to begin a good work in your life, to bring an answer your way, or to turn your sorrow into dancing. He is alive and well, sitting on the throne of grace, waiting to hear from you. When you don't know what to say or where to start... PRAISE HIM! You can't help but have a great day when you do. Praise keeps you from focusing on the negativity that could surround you and helps you place your gaze where it should be: on God.

Come before the Lord today and give Him praise for the blessings in your life and for the ones that are on the way. Taste and see that the Lord our God is good!

Deuteronomy 31:6
"Be strong and of good courage, do not fear nor be afraid
of them; for the LORD your God, He is the One who goes
with you. He will not leave you nor forsake you."

⸺◆⸺

It is not what others say about you that defines you. It is what God says that defines you.

When people are rehearsing the parts of your past that God has already forgiven you for, don't let anyone paint you into someone that you are not. You have been set free in Jesus' name. God is good, all the time. His mercies endure to all generations. There is no need for you to live under the shadow of a lie.

If you allow people to control your life, you will live a miserable existence. This is not the joy-filled life that God has in mind for you. He can silence your enemies and send them packing. There is no need for you to live under a dark cloud created by misguided fools.

Square your shoulders and hold your head up high! God has great things in store for you. He believes in you. He wants your very best. He goes with you around every turn. Expect His blessing and know that His favor is yours, no matter what others are saying.

Wait on the Lord and be of good courage! You were created to do great things for the Kingdom!

Philippians 4:19
"My God shall supply all your need according to
His riches in glory by Christ Jesus."

No matter what you are facing, Jehovah Jireh can shine His light on your problem and make it vanish as He meets your every need. Are you up against something so enormous today that you don't even know where to start? Does the problem seem insurmountable? Give it to God! He is the one who calms the storms with three simple words... "Peace, be still!"

You may have a million-dollar problem on your hands, or you may have a five-dollar need. Whatever it is, give it to God. He has promised to supply ALL your needs according to His riches in glory. There is no limit to His resources. Give Him the opportunity to reach down and touch your life.

Do you need healing? Call on His name. Do you need a financial miracle? Call on the name of Jesus! Is your marriage struggling? He can make all things new again. Call on Him today and get ready to receive a barn-bursting answer to your problem!

He is a God of power and might! Call on His majestic name, realizing He will meet your need so completely that things you didn't even know you needed will be taken care of!

Deuteronomy 23:5
"Nevertheless the LORD your God would not listen to Balaam,
but the LORD your God turned the curse into a blessing for you,
because the LORD your God loves you."

———— ◆ ————

Don't waste your time worrying about what everybody does to you or what mean-spirited people say about you. Instead, spend your efforts on how you respond to them. Don't let the enemy come in and attack your thought life. If he can strong-arm you into obsessing over negative things, he has won the battle.

Choose life over death, blessings over curses. Make a conscious decision to look for the beautiful, the priceless, the uplifting.

Move beyond the chaos of the day, the bad news report on the television, or the fact that your least favorite relative is moving in with you for the entire summer. God is good! He is faithful! He loves you! Focus on the great things He has done, for He can and will do those things again—and even more!

God didn't bring you through last year's financial crisis only to let your marriage fail this year. Our God is able and willing to bless you. Set your sights on what you can do through His power, and it shall be done in Jesus' name!

Genesis 1:26
"Then God said, 'Let Us make man in Our image,
according to Our likeness.'"

———

You were created in God's image, a little lower than the angels. He didn't create you to be average. He doesn't want you barely scraping by. You were made to excel in all things, to honor Him in all you say and do, to share the love of Christ with those who are hurting.

Don't settle for second best, and don't let anyone around you try to kick you down the ladder of life! You are an heir and a joint-heir to the Kingdom that will never end. You have everything going for you and nothing to be ashamed of! You can leave your faults at the Cross as you ask the Father for complete forgiveness.

If you have gotten off course, that's okay. Sometimes we have to change our course in order to go in the direction God has for us. Be open to change. Be sensitive to what the Lord is telling you. Know that God has something better waiting in the wings, and that through Him you have a limitless future.

Whatever you get up and do today, do it with all you have, as if unto the King. He has charged us to live with excellence as an example of what His children can accomplish here on earth. Make the very best use of today and let the light of God's love shine so brightly that all those who come into contact with you will want His light too!

Matthew 5:45
"He makes His sun rise on the evil and on the good,
and sends rain on the just and on the unjust."

———— ◆·◈·◆ ————

Life is not fair, but God is. All the forces of darkness cannot stop God's plan for you. It was set in stone before time began. As human beings, we can choose to deviate from God's plan for our lives, but He has charted a very specific course that takes us down the path to our divine destiny. All you need to do is listen and obey. No matter what challenges you are facing, just keep putting one foot in front of the other.

Don't give the enemy any room to sneak in with fear or doubt. Don't fret over what others are saying. Stay the course. God will take care of the rest.

Miracles and tragedies occur in every life. Move beyond the tragedy and dwell on the good, the positive, the gifts that God so liberally doles out. Don't look at how great your neighbors have it and become filled with envy. Trust that even when you feel like you're drowning, God is up to something great, diligently working on your behalf to make something absolutely amazing transpire in your life!

Psalm 26:11-12
"As for me, I will walk in my integrity;
Redeem me and be merciful to me.
My foot stands in an even place;
In the congregations I will bless the LORD."

———◦◆◦———

God is not asking us to do what is easy or popular with the "in" crowd. He is asking us to do that which is right, that which brings Him honor and glory. He wants us to be a witness to those around us, a witness of His redeeming grace and love.

God has promised to bring us to an even place, guiding us to where the joy of the Lord abounds. In this place His presence surrounds and insulates you, even in the middle of life's greatest storms, like a soft, warm blanket on a cold winter's night.

Prepare for the storms before they hit. Saturate your life in the Word of God; memorize His promises; sing praises to the King. When you end up face-to-face with tragedy or conflict, you can then call all of these great promises to mind and find both infinite comfort and a song to sing, just as Paul and Silas did in their jail cell.

You can learn how to bless the Lord in and out of season, come rain or shine, for God is full of mercy and love. He says, "This is the way; walk in it." Continue in integrity, and when your feet hit the floor every morning, you will be filled with unshakable joy and peace.

The Pastor's Blessing

And now may the Lord bless you and keep you. May the Lord make His face to shine upon you and be gracious unto you, giving you His peace. May you walk in the confidence that your life will be victorious and beautiful with God's help. Nothing is impossible to you because of Him! You are numbered among the righteous because of the blood of the Cross. In Jesus' name, Amen!

Galatians 6:9
"Let us not grow weary while doing good,
for in due season we shall reap if we do not lose heart."

---

*M*ake the journey, and don't quit until you've arrived! God has something spectacular in mind for your life. You might be in a dark spot right now, but once He reveals the beauty of the entire painting, you will see for yourself the masterpiece He has created in you. Don't give up!

The Mona Lisa is one of the most remarkable and well-known works of art in the world today even though it is very small in size. What if you were a fly stuck in the black paint of that portrait? Would you still think it was a masterpiece? No. Because from your vantage point things look pretty bleak. But when you step back and see the entire painting, it is a thing of rare beauty. This is how God sees you. You are a prized masterpiece to the Master Painter.

The path you are traveling right now may take you down a long and twisted highway. Know that where He is leading is where you were destined to go. Do not lose heart. Your reward is just around the corner if you faint not.

Mark 10:44
"Whoever of you desires to be first shall be slave of all."

———◆◆◆———

Serving is a very powerful thing. When you have a pure motive and you're reaching out to help others, there is something very powerful about that action. It sends a message to the world that God is using you for His good.

Maybe you are helping someone who can never fully appreciate what you're doing. Perhaps you are assisting someone who can never in any way repay your kindness. That is the very best kind of servanthood. God sees; do not grow weary in well doing.

God wants to be a blessing through you, but He also wants to be a blessing to you. When you reach out to those around you in their hour of need, God takes note. When you least expect it, He will use someone to touch your life in a very real way... when you need it the most. That is when you know the Holy Spirit is working on your behalf.

Don't bother keeping tally of your good works; just continue serving those whom God allows to cross your path. Do it as unto the Lord, aware that the greatest among us is the servant of all. Man may look on the outside, but God sees your heart!

Psalm 20:4
"May He grant you according to your heart's desire,
And fulfill all your purpose."

———————◆———————

Place your desires before God. Pray about them and trust Him to give you the desires of your heart if and when they are what you need. For example, maybe you're praying for a husband. You see a man in front of you and he looks like the perfect "10." From the outside, he is everything you ever wanted! God, however, sees further down the road, where the man who is the exact person for you will be waiting.

Have patience and believe that God is working to bring the perfect mate your way at just the right time. In His time especially, good things come to those who wait. He is also faithful to bring you what you actually need—not just what you think you want–if you ask Him to supply the desires of your heart according to His will for your life.

Have you ever purchased something at the last minute because it was right by the checkout counter and looked really wonderful while you were waiting for your groceries to be rung up? This is called an impulse buy. God doesn't want you to have an "impulse buy" mate. He wants you to marry the one who will allow you to fulfill your divine destiny and reach your greatest potential. His plan can and will bring you to a place of completion.

Ephesians 4:24
"Put on the new man which was created according to God,
in true righteousness and holiness."

Today you might be looking for a new beginning in your business, your marriage, maybe even your family relationships. Perhaps you need a total recovery in your health, or a miracle to survive. God knows your situation, and He wants you to know that He deeply loves you. He has not forgotten about you; He is still on the throne, large and in charge. And everything is going to be alright. His eye is on the sparrow, and I know He's watching over you and me.

Would you like to experience a new beginning?

First, start by forgetting the past. If you have asked for forgiveness, God has already forgotten about your sin or mistake; you should too. Forgiving yourself for your errors can completely set you free from a bondage that could destroy you. Move on.

Second, you must be willing to change. You can't have God's best until you are willing to let go of what is only good. Trade good for better and better for best.

Finally, write down your goals. A life without goals is like a ship without a rudder. If you have no specific destination, any road can get you there. Plan your work, and work your plan. Once you start making these changes, God will work in you and through you until you are totally renewed.

Deuteronomy 5:33
"You shall walk in all the ways which the LORD your God
has commanded you, that you may live and that it may be
well with you, and that you may prolong your days in
the land which you shall possess."

---

*A*re you aimlessly wandering through what seems like a desert? Does God seem far away? Perhaps you don't feel like He hears your prayers anymore.

I can assure you that God does indeed hear you, and He wants to outrageously prosper you in all things. Did you hear that? He wants to prosper you far beyond what you think you deserve. Don't listen to the "grace killers" in your life who keep bringing up your past mistakes and claiming you don't deserve God's very best. Yes, you do!

God wanted what was best for Israel, but they spent 40 years wandering the desert, looking for the Promised Land. This was a trip that should have taken 14 days. Think about that—a two-week trip took them four decades! Why? Because they refused to let go of what they left behind in Egypt and walk in His ways.

If you want to live a successful, progressive life, you cannot do so without change. When you want what you've never had, you need to be willing to do what you've never done. God longs to lead you to your own promised land. Just walk with Him and listen when He calls. You don't want to waste 40 years trying to reach your divine destiny. Embrace what God has stored up for you. The best is yet to come!

Matthew 7:21
"Not everyone who says to Me, 'Lord, Lord,'
shall enter the kingdom of heaven, but he
who does the will of My Father in heaven."

---

*F*avor is found in obeying the will of God. The secret to living a successful life is finding out what God wants you to do and then doing it.

How can you know His perfect will? If you read the Bible, all of life's major decisions have already been made for you.

For example, who should you marry? The Bible says we are not to be unequally yoked, so the answer is simple: marry a Believer. How do you get ahead in life? First, get started. Then, move forward. The Word says that diligent hands bring wealth.

The Bible has a promise to fit every problem. If you will dive into the depths of Scripture, the peace of God will surround you like a comforting embrace.

What should you think about? The Bible says whatsoever things are just, lovely, and of good report. Your thoughts, words, and actions become habits, so choose them wisely.

When making decisions that will impact your life, consult the Word of God; it never returns empty and it will never lead you wrong. If you have headed down a pathway that dead-ended in destruction, TODAY is the day to seek the Father's will for your life. It is never too late! God's grace is greater than all your sin, and His arms are open wide!

2 Corinthians 12:9
"He said to me, 'My grace is sufficient for you,
for My strength is made perfect in weakness.'
Therefore most gladly I will rather boast in my infirmities,
that the power of Christ may rest upon me."

When a ship is sinking, it sends an SOS in hopes that rescue will come. Our SOS in the ocean of our infirmities is "G-R-A-C-E." It is God's strength, not ours, that delivers us from drowning in the waves of guilt and shame, fear and failure, illness and ruin.

Grace is the unmerited favor of God. It is an ocean without a shoreline whose depths are unknown. God's grace is endless, a healing source of life-changing waters that have never been charted because it knows no boundary.

Do you need a touch from the Lord today? Do you need saving from a storm or deliverance from a shipwreck? His grace is sufficient! Stop trying to do things in your own strength and let God take over. In our weakness His strength proves itself to be perfect!

The Pastor's Blessing

And now may the Lord bless you and keep you. May the Lord make His face to shine upon you and be gracious unto you, giving you His peace. May you walk in the confidence that as you live by the principles of diligence, God will bring you before kings and people of authority. You will prosper and be well, exceedingly abundantly above all that you can ask or imagine, because you are practicing the principles of righteousness. God will lead you and guide you into the breakthrough you've expectantly awaited. In the authority of Jesus' name, Amen!

Jeremiah 31:34
"From the least of them to the greatest of them,
says the LORD... I will forgive their iniquity,
and their sin I will remember no more."

---

*G*race will set you free from the tyranny of the past. Did you fail? Did you make a mistake and now you can't forgive yourself? Have wrong choices stained your life?

Ask God's forgiveness and experience His amazing grace! Then forgive yourself. Live, love, laugh, and be happy! God is a God of new beginnings. He has buried your sin in the sea of forgetfulness, never to be remembered against you. Get on with your life!

Stop letting your past haunt you or dictate your future. If yesterday was an epic failure, release it. If it was the best day of your life, release it. Your future is unlimited by the grace of God.

Galatians 1:10
"Do I now persuade men, or God?
Or do I seek to please men? For if I still pleased men,
I would not be a bondservant of Christ."

———◆———

Grace will set you free from the tyranny of other people. Perhaps today you are being held hostage by the foolish opinions of others or their unreasonable demands. Don't let someone send you on a guilt trip when you are following the will of God. Once you get on that ride, it's hard to get off!

Regardless of what you do, someone's going to blame you for something. You cannot please everyone all the time. That's just a fact. Every family and every church has people I like to call "grace killers." Rather than letting them decide your life, consult God. He already has a plan in place for you.

Don't become a prisoner to the performance trap either. You will never earn the approval of others by what you do. Just give that up right now! Don't make people your lord and master. You will either be a people pleaser or you will be a Father pleaser. Which do you want to be?

I can guarantee you that pleasing God will make your life a much more peaceful place.

Galatians 5:1
"Stand fast therefore in the liberty by which
Christ has made us free, and do not be
entangled again with a yoke of bondage."

In the United States, this is the day that we celebrate our freedom... freedom that our men and women have fought for and defended for centuries. To these select souls, I salute you and I bless you in the name of the Lord. You are what makes America great—the land of the free and the home of the brave.

There is another freedom for Christians—a kind we can use to forgive others. It comes through the grace of God.

This grace not only forgives you but allows you to be set free from the bondage in your own life to forgive others. No matter how miserably you have failed, God's grace is greater.

It is my prayer that the revelation of God's grace explodes in your soul and gives you love, joy, and a peace that surpasses all understanding! The freedom you can experience through His grace is like no other. It can break the chains that bind you and give you a new vision for tomorrow that is filled with hope. Forgive others. Forget your past. And learn to love yourself, seeing yourself as God sees you... as a priceless gem.

Psalm 34:18
"The LORD is near to those who have a broken heart,
And saves such as have a contrite spirit."

———————

*G*od is asking you today: Is there anyone reading this who has a broken heart? Are you lonely? Have you been forsaken by the dearest on earth? Have your dreams been shattered? Is your family in crisis? Your marriage dying?

Christ and His amazing grace is the answer.

His unlimited grace can be applied to any area of your life that needs His healing touch. Is your heart broken? Let the balm of Gilead flood the cracks and make you whole. Are you lonely? He is a companion to widows and orphans and the Friend who sticks closer than any brother. Are your dreams shattered? He can give you a brand-new dream and supply you with the resources to accomplish every step as He has ordered it.

His grace is without end, and available for the asking.

Micah 6:8
"He has shown you, O man, what is good;
And what does the LORD require of you
But to do justly, To love mercy,
And to walk humbly with your God?"

***

We are called to act justly, love the unlovable, show mercy to the merciless, forgive the unforgivable. Would you be able to show mercy to someone who tormented you?

The first outward demonstration of grace is mercy! Simply stated, if you have no mercy, you are not a Christian. The Bible says blessed are the merciful, for they shall obtain mercy. If you want to receive mercy, then guess what? You have to give it!

Satan could care less how much you sing the old songs of the church just as long as you sing them with a snarl on your lips and bitterness in your heart. When Satan takes the mercy out of your conduct, he has effectively killed the Christian spirit within you.

Christianity without mercy is just another cult. It is like a tree that bears no fruit or a well that has run dry. If you want mercy to rain down in your life like a flood, today is the day to start offering it to those who have hurt you most. You will be surprised at how this one gesture will completely set you free!

Proverbs 28:13
"He who covers his sins will not prosper,
But whoever confesses and forsakes them will have mercy."

Sin is a cancer. You either get the cancer or the cancer gets you. It is a crimson stain that can only be removed by the blood of the Cross.

Today is the day to be free of the sin that controls your very existence. Maybe you aren't even aware of it, but if there is sin in your life, you need to confess it before God the Father.

If you want God to be merciful to you, come clean before Him. It's not because He doesn't already know what you did. He knows. But what you don't confess to Him, He will shout from the rooftops. His Word promises that.

God is waiting for you to fall before Him and ask forgiveness. This puts you back in the race toward the prize of your high calling. Sin can no longer stand in the way of your blessing!

Psalm 80:3
"Restore us, O God; Cause Your face to shine,
And we shall be saved!"

$\mathcal{I}$ have good news for you: the King of Glory is looking for you!

He wants to restore your good name, restore your fortune, restore everything the enemy has tried to destroy over the years. He can wipe away every tear from your eyes and give you a new song.

Don't fear the future, for you know Who holds the future. Don't fear death, because Jesus came that you might have life and have it more abundantly. He is the Way, the Truth, and the Life. Fear not disease, for He is the God who has healed you in the past and He can certainly heal you again.

He is only a whisper away when you need Him! Call on His mighty name and wait for Him to shine on you. Whatever has been taken from you, He can return it many times over. Get up and proclaim that this is the day the Lord has made. Our God will save!

The Pastor's Blessing

And now may the Lord bless you and keep you. May the Lord make His face to shine upon you and be gracious unto you, giving you His peace. May the Lord open the windows of heaven and bless you financially. May you live according to the dictates of God's Word. For it is the Lord who gives you the power to get wealth, and He will be faithful to you as you are faithful to Him. In Jesus' name, Amen.

Isaiah 65:16
"He who blesses himself in the earth Shall bless himself in
the God of truth; And he who swears in the earth Shall swear
by the God of truth; Because the former troubles are forgotten,
And because they are hidden from My eyes."

---

*D*id you fail last year? I mean, just miserably fail? I have a word from heaven for you today: Turn it loose! Don't get bitter; get better! Get up and dust yourself off! Wipe the dirt off of your face and get back in the race!

Turn loose of last year's bitter memories, last year's mistakes. Turn loose of the rejection that has tried to shove your life off course. Turn loose of habits that shackle you. Turn loose of emotions that shame you. Turn loose of your resentment toward other people. Turn loose of your bitter divorce or business failure.

God has a future filled with abundance just waiting for you. He wants you to have the freedom that is only found in Him. To experience wealth untold and joy unspeakable. To enjoy divine health and live in a land where your giants are defeated.

Today, give up those things that are enslaving you and start living as if your past is behind you—because in His eyes, it is! His truth is your blessing.

James 1:17
"Every good gift and every perfect gift is from above,
and comes down from the Father of lights,
with whom there is no variation or shadow of turning."

———— ◆ ————

*A*re you afraid of change? Afraid to let go of what you are firmly grasping and exchange it for what's in God's hand?

If you allow our steadfast God to mold you and make you into something spectacular, change can be a wonderful thing. It will bring you blessings as well as lead you closer to your divine destiny.

Remember, it took one day to get Israel out of Egypt, but it took 40 years to get Egypt out of Israel. They were not big fans of change, even though God had wonderful gifts awaiting them—gifts that could be trusted.

If your mantra is, "No, I was born this way; it is what it is"... then you might want to start rethinking things a bit. Get out of the rut you have placed yourself in. A rut is just a grave with both ends kicked out of it! Change direction and head north! Try something new, even if you do it wrong. Open your heart to heaven's gifts. Life will get a whole lot more exciting when you let God bring you to a new place.

Matthew 6:33
"Seek first the kingdom of God and His righteousness,
and all these things shall be added to you."

*H*ave you ever known someone who is always on the go? It seems like they are doing great things, and then you realize they are just moving in continuous circles? Maybe some of your relatives are like that. Maybe you are. If so, don't confuse motion with progress. Don't be the constant traveler who never arrives at his destination.

Stop for a minute. Regroup if you need to. But always seek God first. Find out where He wants you to go, and then start out on that road. If you feel like the one you are traveling is challenging, be aware that the enemy attacks anyone God has chosen to promote. And warfare always surrounds the birth of a miracle.

Spiritual warfare is a way of life for the Believer, so strap on the full armor of God and head straight for the enemy. With God on your side, the victory is already won.

If you feel hopelessly lost, or if your life isn't going in the right direction, just stop. Ask God to chart your course anew, and then begin walking down the path He desires. Your life will become a thing of beauty that will give you a deep sense of fulfillment all the days of your life.

Matthew 6:9–10
"In this manner, therefore, pray: Our Father in heaven,
Hallowed be Your name. Your kingdom come.
Your will be done On earth as it is in heaven."

A prayerless Christian is a powerless Christian. I don't care how busy you are, you must make time in your life for prayer. It is the greatest power tool you have in your spiritual toolkit, because whatever you ask the Father for here on earth is done in heaven. The powers of hell cannot prevail against the power of prayer.

Prayer, however, is not sending God to do your will. Prayer is preparing you to do God's will.

No matter the size of your need, the best way to approach it is by asking God to take charge. Request that He take the lead, and watch as the challenge dissipates before your very eyes. God can take your tragedy and turn it triumphant! He can hand you a victory so complete that those around you will want it too!

Our God is able, but He is waiting for you to give up your feeble attempts to handle all your own problems. Hand them over to Him and allow Him to work on your behalf. Your human resources are limited; God's are limitless. If you have a need today, simply lay it at the feet of the King and receive heaven's answer.

John 8:36
"If the Son makes you free, you shall be free indeed."

I want this year to be your Year of Jubilee! I want your life, your marriage, your home to experience an explosion of divine joy! I want your harmful habits to be broken, and for this to be your breakthrough year.

Allow God into your life and your home and watch as He intercedes on your behalf, opening the windows of heaven and pouring out untold blessings. Let this be your best year ever!

Stop your self-defeating habits and negative thoughts. You can have the best of things in the worst of times. You can do all things through Christ who strengthens you.

Change that thing in your life that is holding you back, and be set free in Jesus' name. This is your year to shine, to enjoy the immeasurable favor of Jesus Christ! Don't stop until your dream has become a reality!

Lamentations 3:22
"Through the LORD'S mercies we are not consumed,
Because His compassions fail not."

———————

What area of life do you need God to begin supernaturally blessing? Where do you need an extra measure of His mercy? His compassion? His covering and faithfulness?

Speak the words out loud. Begin to meditate on Scripture and watch what a great work God will do in your life. Speak with authority, knowing that blessings are already on the way, released the moment you invite God to come in and take over!

You were chosen by God, and if you are following Him, you are favored by God. He wants to bless you with His unlimited grace and boundless love. The Word says "no good thing will He withhold from those who diligently seek Him." Seek Him now. Tell Him your need. His tender mercies are already on their way because our God never fails.

Matthew 21:21
"Jesus answered and said to them, 'Assuredly, I say to you,
if you have faith and do not doubt, you will not only do what
was done to the fig tree, but also if you say to this mountain,
"Be removed and be cast into the sea," it will be done.'"

Today God is telling you to trust Him with the thing that concerns you most, the part of your life that needs supernatural healing. God already knows your need, but He is waiting for you to entrust it to Him.

How can you not rely on a God who never fails to do the impossible? He is ready, willing, and able to meet your every need. He is the God who makes a way when there seems to be no way, the One who makes His people rich without adding sorrow.

He is the Great I AM, the Alpha and Omega. There is no shadow of turning in Him. What He says, He does. Do you have a need today that you think is too great to ever be met? Stop thinking with your human limitations and call upon the One whose grace knows no bounds.

Call upon Him and believe that ALL things are possible in His mighty name. He sees your heart that is breaking, your child who is hurting, your marriage that is suffering. Give Him your burden, and know that when you lay it at His feet, in faith believing, the mountains of impossibility will be removed.

The Pastor's Blessing

And now may the Lord bless you and keep you. May the Lord make His face to shine upon you and be gracious unto you, giving you His peace. May God your Father go before you and give to you richly and abundantly, according to your obedience to His financial principles. May you become the envy of the world because of the abundance God gives you, for you are His child. The royal blood of heaven is flowing in your veins. You are somebody! Lift your head and square your shoulders! You are a part of the eternal Kingdom of God, and your tomorrows are filled with joy because of the power and majesty of God our Father. In Jesus' name, Amen!

Mark 9:23

"All things are possible to him who believes."

———————

Stop saying, "I can't," and start saying, "I will." Nothing is impossible with God.

"Pastor, you don't know the people who are coming against me!" I have heard this many times, and I will tell you that we serve the Name that is above every other name. He is all-powerful and all-knowing. With God on your side, you are guaranteed to come out on the other side a winner!

I will tell you a true story about a mother who asked me to pray for her son. She wanted the gang in her part of town to allow her son to leave their membership without killing him. I told her to invite the gang leaders to her house. She did. I told her to tell them that her son was off limits; that he was a child of the living God who was protected in his going out and his coming in. She did. The gang leaders laughed in her face.

But her son left the gang anyway. We continued to pray over him, for his protection. And within just a few weeks, the men who were planning his demise were killed in the streets. Were these random acts of violence? Absolutely not!

Don't ever underestimate the power of a praying mother—or the ability of Almighty God!

Zechariah 3:4
"Then He answered and spoke to those who stood before Him,
saying, 'Take away the filthy garments from him.'
And to him He said, 'See, I have removed your iniquity from you,
and I will clothe you with rich robes.'"

If you made a bad decision in the past, stop beating yourself up over what you can't change. It is dirty laundry. Get clean and get moving.

See yourself as God sees you. You may be an imperfect vessel in the hand of the Master Potter, but He can take your flaws and transform them into matchless beauty with endless potential. He can remake your mind, body, soul, and spirit into something gorgeous beyond imagination. Behold, He makes all things new!

Only yield to the Spirit's leading. Be willing to make necessary changes. Learn to live without regret, without limitation. Live without saying, "If only..." Exit the emotional grave you have created for yourself and live to the full. Laugh and be happy! God designed you to enjoy life, not to suffer in misery.

Today, declare that whatever is holding you back is OVER. In Jesus' name, take off yesterday's filthy garment and burn it, and put on the robes of royalty instead! Today is a new day, meant to be lived His way.

Matthew 6:19
"Do not lay up for yourselves treasures on earth,
where moth and rust destroy and
where thieves break in and steal."

———— ◆ ————

*W*hen your back is to the wall, you have three choices: You can be a pessimist, an idealist, or a realist. The idealist may be two million dollars in debt, but that infomercial will convince him he can buy and flip the advertised real estate and reverse the curse in an hour. Get serious!

The pessimist is Chicken Little—the sky is always falling in his world. How dreary!

The realist sees that he can't afford his car, so he sells it and rides the bus.

Choose to see things as God sees them. A nice car with an inflated payment is not worth forfeiting your house or marriage.

Don't sacrifice the gifts God has given you for the things of this world. There is nothing like laying your head on your pillow at night with a clear conscience. Don't trade that for any cheap trinket or negativity the enemy might try to distract you with. Enjoy the sweet peace that can only come from God above!

Matthew 16:19
"I will give you the keys of the kingdom of heaven,
and whatever you bind on earth will be bound in heaven,
and whatever you loose on earth will be loosed in heaven."

When life becomes a battlefield, choose to fight until the victory comes. Don't run from the problem; attack the problem head-on.

Whether your fight is physical in nature—which we have seen on American soil with 9/11 and certainly around the world during various catastrophes—or a spiritual battle, begin to wage war in the heavenlies. When you pray and seek God's face, He sets His angels to flight on your behalf. What you bind on earth is bound in heaven. Have faith that when God is in control, no enemy can defeat you.

Are you under attack? That's great! A time of personal attack is the perfect time to make a personal comeback.

As soon as you begin to pray, the power of heaven is unleashed. When you pray, ask God for things that will put your enemies in a tailspin. He is able to do this and so much more. Your greatest enemy was defeated at Calvary. What you see on a daily basis is nothing compared to the battle you have already won through Him.

Start saying prayers that are full of raw meat and gunpowder. Put the devil on notice; don't be shy! You are a child of the King! The battle belongs to Him and the victory is yours in Jesus' name!

John 14:13
"Whatever you ask in My name, that I will do,
that the Father may be glorified in the Son."

Today, I want you to be set free from anything that is holding you back. There is great power in the spoken word, and I want you to say the following prayer out loud, filling in the blanks according to your own personal needs.

"Satan, I tell you in the mighty name of Jesus Christ, and by the power of His blood, that you are a defeated foe. I command you to get your hands off of my _____ [marriage, children, physical body, finances, business, spouse]. I am the property of the Lord Jesus Christ. Through His shed blood, the victory is mine. In Jesus' mighty name!"

Know that when you pray in faith believing, whatsoever you ask will be yours according to the will of God. When you start praying like this, the devil will leave you alone and find someone else to pick on.

Remember David and Goliath? The small, untrained shepherd boy defeated the giant. He walked right up to his greatest problem and said, "I come to you in the name of the Lord." When you confront your problems in this fashion, you are guaranteed the victory!

Psalm 34:8
"O, taste and see that the LORD is good;
Blessed is the man who trusts in Him!"

———————

Are you willing to accept God's very best for your life? Sometimes what God knows is best for us differs from our idea of where we want our lives to go. Sometimes our lives take us down the road less traveled. We must be willing to give up some things, to make changes in our lives, in order to inherit God's fullness, His blessing, and His favor. Change isn't always a dirty word. When God sends it your way, don't resist. Just obey.

God created us to depend on Him. Our stubborn flesh would lead us in one direction, but God's plan takes us on a far better path filled with untold riches and the goodness of the Lord. If you don't know where to turn, ask God to send you a new dream. He will not only give you the dream but help you fulfill it.

God is looking for people who want His best, a special people holy and separated unto Him. Turn loose of the things of this earth and gain the crown of eternal life. Anything you are asked to give up will be so worth it in the end! Let go and let God take over!

Acts 2:17
"'It shall come to pass in the last days, says God, That I will
pour out of My Spirit on all flesh; Your sons and your daughters
shall prophesy, Your young men shall see visions,
Your old men shall dream dreams.'"

———◆———

*H*ave you stopped dreaming your dream? Dreams are the golden ladder by which we ascend to heavenly places, the mountain peaks of vision that we climb to view the promised land that God has given us. Our dreams are the lanterns by whose light we pass safely through the darkest valley, the inner flames that strengthen us to fight through the darkness in our day of adversity.

Columbus' dream brought him to America. Edison's dream brought us out of the darkness. The Bible is full of dreamers and men of great vision. Dreams do not come with an expiration date. It took Joseph 13 years for the dream of his brothers bowing down to him to come true. Don't give up, even if you are still waiting!

Divine dreams come from God, not other people. People have opinions. I have built every one of my churches because of a divine dream. I experienced extreme resistance from others, but that didn't stop me for one second! Divine dreams are sustained by divine favor. It is a gift from God regardless of what those around you say and do.

When you find the favor of God in your life, expect it, protect it, and respect it. The favor of God is a precious thing. Allow God's dream to take root in your soul.

The Pastor's Blessing

And now may the Lord bless you and keep you. May the Lord make His face to shine upon you and be gracious unto you, giving you His peace. May you cast your every burden upon Him, for He careth for you. Your enemies have been defeated. Your mountains have been removed. The Lord your God is the Father of the universe. Rejoice and be exceedingly glad, for you are His and all things are yours, saith the Lord unto His church.

John 3:30
"He must increase, but I must decrease."

———— ◆ ————

*J*ohn the Baptist gave this quote meaning. As soon as I empty myself of my own will, my huge ego, and my pride, God will be able to use me for His glory. But I must empty myself first.

Are you searching for a miracle today? Don't remind God of how lucky He is to have you and all your vast talents. Deny yourself, take up your cross, and follow Him. We are clay in the hands of the Master Potter. Clay doesn't talk back to the potter and say, "Hey! You're molding me the wrong way!" Clay is nothing.

God compares us to clay in the Bible. He is encouraging us to stay on the spinning wheel while He removes the imperfections from our lives. When He is finished molding, you will be a masterful piece of art, a thing of beauty that will bless the world for the rest of your days.

Let God have His way in your life and complete the good work that He began in you.

Zechariah 4:6
"'Not by might nor by power, but by My Spirit,'
Says the LORD of hosts."

---

*P*rayer is not a beg-a-thon or a dissertation by which to send God out to run your errands. Prayer is getting you prepared to do God's will. Once you are living within the will of God, you will be surprised at the amazing things that start happening.

Prayer releases supernatural power into your life. Don't just think about the things you would like to improve, pray about them. Pray until you put things into action. There is nothing more exciting than watching as God's plan for your life unfolds. It is something beyond spectacular, and a great reward for those who faithfully seek Him.

God is just waiting to hear from you, so call on His name and give Him the broken pieces of your life. Prayer can shatter the shackles of misery that are binding you, keeping you from enjoying the abundant life that is the inheritance of every Believer. This doesn't mean your life is Fantasy Island every day, but it means that you can have the peace of God, which surpasses all understanding regardless of what is taking place around you.

Prayer can break controlling habits that are destroying your life; it can renew your hopes and dreams. It can give you a song in the night when everything around you makes no sense at all. Pray without ceasing and your life will be completely transformed from the inside out.

Proverbs 18:21
"Death and life are in the power of the tongue,
And those who love it will eat its fruit."

---

*A*re you looking for a breakthrough in your life today? There is power in the spoken word. If you are looking to move heaven and earth, say these words out loud:

"Through the blood of Jesus I am redeemed. All my sins are forgiven. Through the blood I am justified and made righteous, just as if I'd never sinned. I am sanctified and made holy. I am set apart to God.

Through the blood of Jesus I have boldness to enter into the presence of God. I am free. I am victorious. I have been redeemed and made whole. In Jesus' mighty name, I give Him all the praise for what He will do in my life today. May this year be the best year of my life. May I bring Him honor and glory in all that I say and do, and be a light to those around me. Amen!"

When Satan begins to remind you of how awful your life is, plead the blood of Jesus Christ over every area of your life, every doorpost of your home. Give what you have to God and He will protect you as His very own.

Psalm 32:5
"I acknowledged my sin to You,
And my iniquity I have not hidden.
I said, 'I will confess my transgressions to the LORD,'
and You forgave the iniquity of my sin."

———————

*A*re you spiritually alive but not really free? Are you bound by something in your past that you can't forget or let go? Let me tell you something. If you will confess it, Christ will forgive it. Once Christ forgives you, move on. You cannot live a productive life if you're always looking behind you.

Maybe you are bound by fear. Jesus said more than 350 times in the Bible, "Fear not." You don't have to fear death; He is the Resurrection and the Life. You don't have to fear sickness and disease; He is the Great Physician. You don't need to fear the past; it is forgiven and forgotten.

Apart from God's grace, we humans don't have the ability to forget our sins. But God does. He both forgets and forgives, and washes you whiter than the purest snow.

I don't know what tomorrow holds, but because He holds tomorrow, everything is going to be alright. Forgive yourself for your past and expect tomorrow to be a brand-new day in Jesus' name. God has already covered it!

Psalm 34:10
"Those who seek the LORD shall not lack any good thing."

———◆·◆·◆———

*D*oes something in your life today seem insurmountable? No matter how tough your problem looks, the God we serve is a giant killer. He knew what your problem would be long before you got out of bed and life smacked you in the face. And He already has the perfect answer in mind for you, if you will only seek His face.

He can raise the dead. He can heal the leper. He can bring to you the miracle that you are seeking. It's time for you to quit looking at the setbacks you've endured and recognize that God can do the impossible, restoring all that has been taken from you.

He can restore to you in one day what has been stolen over decades. If you need to start anew in your life and regain what the enemy has taken, tell God about it. He is more than able to slay the giants that stand in your way before the sun sets today.

Stop carrying a load you were never meant to bear and hand it over to your heavenly Father so you can receive His riches. He will not withhold any good thing from you!

Genesis 16:13
"You-Are-the-God-Who-Sees."

———————

$\mathcal{F}$ight the good fight of faith! We are more than conquerors through Christ who strengthens us! No matter where you've been, or the tragic circumstances that currently engulf you... God sees. On your best day, God sees. On your worst day, God sees.

Don't ever think you're not important to Him. When the three Hebrew boys were thrown into the fiery furnace, they cried out to God. Did He send someone else to comfort them in their hour of desperation? No! He showed up Himself as the fourth Man in the fire.

It is the same for you. When you are facing an exhausting trial, all you need to do is call upon His mighty name and He will be right there, waiting to meet your need. He can and will touch the part of your life that seems impossibly broken, to grant the need that can make you whole again.

Call on His name and know that He is the God who sees, ready to supply your every need according to His riches in glory.

Proverbs 17:22
"A merry heart does good, like medicine,
But a broken spirit dries the bones."

What kind of attitude did you wake up with this morning? A positive attitude gives you power over your circumstances instead of your circumstances having power over you. Think about that for a second. Are you driven by your emotions, or do you wake up and say, "This is the day that the Lord has made. I will rejoice and be glad in it?"

Any medical doctor will tell you that the patients who are truly sick (I'm talking about terminal illness, not the flu) always respond better to treatment if they have a good attitude. There are many medical reasons for this, but the Bible said it first: "A merry heart does good."

God's plan is for you to live a life filled with joy. That's not to say that every day will be a carnival ride, but even when you're in the valley, God is standing right beside you, ready to fight your battles for you. If that doesn't give you a reason to shout, I don't know what will!

The Pastor's Blessing

And now may the Lord bless you and keep you. May the Lord make His face to shine upon you and be gracious unto you, giving you His peace. May you walk with the confidence that you can live in total victory. Your past cannot destroy the present, and you cannot control the future. God is almighty! His angels are beside you. He's walking with you through the fire. Have confidence that this day is a new beginning in Jesus Christ. Amen and Hallelujah!

Psalm 121:1–2
"I WILL lift up my eyes to the hills—From whence comes
my help? My help comes from the LORD,
Who made heaven and earth."

———————————————

*O*ur God is an awesome God! If you woke up this morning and didn't see your name in the obituary column, it's time to jump out of bed and praise His name. You were given the gift of one more precious day! And whatever you are facing today, know that God is your help, full of faith and truth! There is no problem so great that He cannot solve it.

He is the Conqueror of death, hell, and the grave. The stripes on His back took away our sickness and disease. Know today that the Lion of Judah is roaring for you! Look to Him; He is faithful to meet your every need.

When the world is in a state of complete chaos and those around you are shrinking back in fear... stand firm. Child of God, lift your eyes toward heaven and know that your answer awaits, for our Redeemer lives!

Mark 12:30–31
"'You shall love the LORD your God with all your heart, with
all your soul, with all your mind, and with all your strength.'
This is the first commandment. And the second, like it, is this:
'You shall love your neighbor as yourself.' There is no
other commandment greater than these."

———◆———

The Cross is where Christ brought us all together, the greatest portrait of God's love. Golgotha is the hill that forever bonded every person regardless of size, shape, or color! We are brothers and sisters in Christ with no room for hatred. His act of love knit every soul together as one, across every time zone and era, in every tiny corner of the globe.

Loving someone doesn't mean you have to agree with everything they say and do. Love them and let God judge them. And show them the difference Christ's love can make in the life of a Believer. If you don't act any differently than the wife abuser down the street, how is your neighbor going to ever have the opportunity to see Christ's love in action?

Love God first. Love your family. And demonstrate the love of the Lord to those around you. There is no greater challenge than to show someone love who doesn't deserve it. But that was exactly where we were when Jesus went to the Cross and died for us. Not one of us deserved it. Yet God in His infinite mercy sent His only Son to die anyway.

Now, don't you think you can love your neighbor who waters his grass on the wrong day of the week?

Psalm 40:8
"I delight to do Your will, O my God,
And Your law is within my heart."

———————

*E*very Christian wants more power with God, but this is not possible without being under spiritual authority. Jesus was powerful on earth because He was under the authority of God the Father, obeying His Father's will, not because He was under His own authority doing whatever He pleased.

Picture Jesus in the Garden of Gethsemane. Jesus knew that He was going to be crucified, and He said these words, "O My Father, if it is possible, let this cup pass from Me; nevertheless, not as I will, but as You will." And with that statement He gave Himself to be our Redeemer, because this was His Father's will. This was the desire of His spiritual authority.

Sometimes in life, God sends us down a path that takes us out of our comfort zone. If you will follow His lead, He will lead you to experience His goodness, bringing you into a deeper relationship with Him and blessing you beyond your wildest dreams.

Philippians 4:6
"Be anxious for nothing, but in everything by prayer
and supplication, with thanksgiving,
let your requests be made known to God."

———————

*O*ur forefathers did not seek to appease the enemy when faced with a potential threat. Appeasement is defeat on an installment plan.

Has your life become a high-stress zone? Do you consistently feel defeated? Pray! Are you surrounded on every side by enemies you never saw coming? Are you desperate for a personal victory? Pray!

The only way to land on your feet is to get down on your knees! As you pray for your own needs and the needs of your loved ones, God can and will begin to move heaven and earth. When you ask God to intervene on your behalf, the battle then becomes His.

Your prayer doesn't have to be long and drawn out. God doesn't want to know if you have a PhD in prayer techniques. He wants to know that you are calling on His precious name in your hour of need and handing the problem over to Him.

Stop worrying about what's happening around you and do something about it. Make your requests known to God!

Matthew 9:20-22
"Suddenly, a woman who had a flow of blood for twelve years
came from behind and touched the hem of His garment...
Jesus turned around, and when He saw her He said,
'Be of good cheer, daughter; your faith has made you well.'"

If you are looking for a major breakthrough in your life, today is the day to ask! God has given you all power in heaven and on earth if you will only submit to spiritual authority and request His help.

Authority is given; it is never assumed. Can you feel God's anointed power in your life? Do you want more of it? As a Believer you have absolute power over many things, such as sickness and disease.

The Bible gives examples of people who were healed simply because they reached out to Jesus and had faith that He would do what they asked. Jesus is still in the healing business today. He is the same yesterday, today, and forever. So, if He made the lame to walk and the deaf to talk, He can certainly heal you. Do you have some rare and aggressive affliction? Did the doctor just hand you a "fatal" diagnosis for which man has no cure? Perfect! As the Great Physician, Jesus has the answers when medical science fails.

Have you just received the worst news of your life? Rejoice by choice! You are in the ideal spot for God to touch you, making you whole again. Reach for the hem of Jesus' garment and receive your divine healing in His mighty name!

Ephesians 6:12–13
"We do not wrestle against flesh and blood, but against
principalities, against powers, against the rulers of the darkness of
this age, against spiritual hosts of wickedness in the heavenly places.
Therefore take up the whole armor of God, that you may be able to
withstand in the evil day, and having done all, to stand."

———————

What are powers and principalities? These are spiritual powers in the heavens. Don't believe in things you can't see? Let me ask you a question: "Do you use electricity?"

What you do on the ground in prayer controls what happens in the heavens. The Word of God says this. All you need to do is ask in Jesus' name and have faith the size of a mustard seed to watch the mountains of impossibility move in your life. If you don't think this will work, I challenge you to give God a chance. Our God is an on-time God, and He is faithful to the last jot and tittle.

Put on the whole armor of God and plan to defeat any enemy. There has never been a servant of God in the history of the world who was disappointed at calling upon the Lord in his or her hour of need. You will not be the first.

Have you prayed once and nothing happened? Pray again! You don't eat a great meal on Monday and then just give up eating until the weekend comes. You eat until your hunger is satisfied and then you come back and eat again. Pray until your hunger is satisfied, until your need is met. Fight to win! Don't give up until God gives you His answer.

John 17:17
"Sanctify them by Your truth. Your word is truth."

———◆◆◆———

Submission to God is absolute. Obedience to human authority is relative, depending on whether or not what they're asking of you aligns with God's Word.

If you are in a church service and the preacher is calling himself a prophet, proclaiming a "word from the Lord" to the congregation, be very careful. Weigh every word coming out of his mouth against the Word of God. If it doesn't line up with the Bible, then completely disregard it. The preacher is either ignorant or practicing witchcraft!

Because your submission to God (and His Word) is absolute, to speak against God's delegated authority brings the wrath of God upon your life. But if someone in authority is telling you something contrary to God's Word, ignore them. God will take care of them in the end. The best thing for you to do is just walk away. There is no point in arguing with this kind of ignorance. It runs deep.

How do you avoid being ignorant yourself? Study the Word with diligence. Then you'll know when you hear something that doesn't align with it, or that is outside His will for His children. The Bible says to hide His Word in your heart so you won't sin against God.

Once you know and apply the Word to your life, it will provide you with promises that enrich every aspect of your being, encouragement in the darkest night, and truths that can set the prisoner free. So what are you waiting for? Start diving into the Word today. The pages of that Book will transform and liberate you like no other.

The Pastor's Blessing

And now may the Lord bless you and keep you. May the Lord make His face to shine upon you and be gracious unto you, giving you His peace. May you walk in the knowledge that you are His and He is yours. You are His child, redeemed by the precious blood of His Son. With Him, nothing is impossible! In the name of the Father, the Son, and the Holy Spirit we receive your richest blessing, Amen!

Matthew 7:8
"Everyone who asks receives, and he who seeks finds,
and to him who knocks it will be opened."

I choose to live a life of blessing because Jesus my Savior redeemed me at the Cross. All who have accepted Him were adopted as sons and daughters of the living God and granted instant access to the Father. In ancient Israel you had to go before the high priest and ask him to bring your petitions to God. NO MORE! Today, any Believer can enter into His unmistakable presence with just a few words.

God is not a respecter of persons. If you seek Him, you will find Him. If you ask, He will answer. It doesn't mean you will love the answer, but He will answer. He has endless resources and can touch your life so completely you will almost forget you ever had a problem.

Instant access means that God's people can have the best of Him in the worst of times. He wants to fight your battles and see you prosper in good times and bad, even as your soul prospers. He is the God who cannot fail, no matter how grim the circumstance!

Follow His plan for your life. He will fulfill you richly.

1 Thessalonians 5:18
"In everything give thanks; for this is the will of God
in Christ Jesus for you."

---

*Y*ou may be walking through great tragedy... Jesus Christ is alive and well and everything is going to be alright. It might not seem like things could ever be the same again, but hold on! Good news is just around the corner. Weeping may endure for a night, but joy comes with the dawn!

If you are having the best day of your life, thank God for it. If you are still alive and healthy enough to get out of bed, thank God for it. If yesterday you faced the biggest giant you have ever encountered, thank God that His answer is on the way.

Amid circumstances that are difficult and beyond your ability to contain, remember that God sees you and is working things out in your favor. Today there might be storm clouds on your horizon, but hold on. We were not promised that every day would be resplendent perfection, but we were promised that His promises are true and that He can perfect whatever thing concerns us most. When you don't know what else to say, repeat this out loud:

"Bless the Lord, O my soul, and all that is within me bless His holy name! Thank You, Lord, for Your blessings on me! Thank You for loving me! Now use me for Your Kingdom so that I might be a blessing to others."

Psalm 63:3

"Your lovingkindness is better than life."

———◆◆◆———

Today is the day to begin proclaiming the Good News in your home, in your workplace, in your community. Why? Because OUR GOD REIGNS! He is the God of the good days, and the God of the bad days. He sees the tears on your pillow at night and hears your heart when you cry out to Him.

When you feel lost and alone, He is El Shaddai, the God who sustains and blesses us even though we don't deserve the rich blessings of the Kingdom. He is all-knowing and all-powerful. Jesus is alive and sitting at the right hand of God the Father, just waiting to overflow your home with His lovingkindness.

Today, the peace that surpasses all understanding can be yours. Whatever is concerning you, leave it at the Cross! Claim your blessing. Seize your victory. Move on to a bright tomorrow with nothing holding you back.

Those around you might live in lack, but you will live in the palace of the King. Your needs will be met, and whatsoever you ask shall be done in Jesus' name. You are blessed and highly favored!

2 Corinthians 5:7
"We walk by faith, not by sight."

---

*Y*ou are a child of God, declared righteous through faith in Jesus Christ. At some point in your life you will discover that the only way to truly live is by faith. You can keep banging your head against the same brick wall, or you can ask God to miraculously supply the perfect answer you need when no solution is in sight. He is the God of the impossible, the Way Maker.

Walk by faith and not by sight. Trust in the Lord with all your heart, and shut out any distractions that would lead you apart from what God is doing in your life. Focus your love and attention on Christ, your Redeemer. Soak in the Word of God and listen to His voice. Pray in faith, believing that when you ask, you will receive. When you seek, you will find. When you knock, the door will be opened to you.

What happens when you put water in a freezer? It freezes. What happens when you put that same water on the stovetop and crank up the heat? It boils. God is just as reliable. The only thing that can happen when you pray in faith is for your prayer to be rightly answered, at the right time.

You are precious to God, created for His glory. He is acquainted with all your ways and has laid His hand of blessing upon you. Don't sell yourself short. My prayer is that the God who gave you life will show you the divine path for which you were created. Once He does, follow it without deviation and realize the rich blessings of the Kingdom as they rain down upon your life.

Luke 12:3
"Whatever you have spoken in the dark will be heard in the light,
and what you have spoken in the ear in inner rooms
will be proclaimed on the housetops."

———————◆◆◆———————

God already knows the status of your life. You aren't going to start praying and suddenly catch Him off guard: "Hey God, I royally blew it today!" He already knows!

Are you going to try and hide something from God? Just ask David how that turned out when he murdered Uriah (2 Samuel). Nothing is hidden from God. If you believe there is such a thing as a truly secret sin, you are only fooling yourself.

Today, if there is unconfessed sin in your life, make it known and be free. Sin can only weigh you down. You were created to live victoriously, not in bondage to the past. Don't worry about your neighbor's sin; worry about your own. You're not responsible for what he or she does, but you are responsible for you.

So, take a good, long look in the mirror. What do you see? If you see that you need to repent, today is the day. If you see that you need to make some changes, don't be afraid. Ask God to help you and He will make a way for you to find your way back to the Cross. He is just waiting to help you make things right again. Don't put it off for another second!

Isaiah 43:18–19
"Do not remember the former things, Nor consider the things of old.
Behold, I will do a new thing, Now it Shall spring forth...
I will even make a road in the wilderness And rivers in the desert."

Many of you are hurting. Life has left you reeling. The pain dredged up by your past has altered your future. The vivid reminders of failure flash through your mind, haunting you night and day. There seems to be no escape.

In order to move forward, you must let it go—an easy thing to say; a difficult thing to do. The Bible says not to let anyone (or anything) steal your joy. As long as you hold on to what has been, your happiness will be stifled and a healthy tomorrow will remain distant. So just let it go!

Ask God to heal the painful scars. Your future is too bright to be littered with debris from the past. Ask God to touch that part of your life that is broken; to heal your heart, mind, soul, and body. Ask Him to restore what the locusts have eaten and make you whole once again.

Child of God, our days on this earth are short. The older I get, the more I realize this to be true. Make the most of each day, knowing that Christ gave His life to make you His very own. That is how much He loves you. And nothing can separate you from that love.

Ephesians 1:7
"In Him we have redemption through His blood,
the forgiveness of sins, according to the riches of His grace."

———— ◆•◆•◆ ————

There is only one way to heaven: through the blood of Jesus. It is this precious blood that cleanses us from all unrighteousness and writes our names in the Lamb's Book of Life. It is this precious blood that exchanges our rags for riches, giving us the wondrous opportunity to spend an eternity in pristine perfection.

His grace is sufficient. All we have to do is humble ourselves and pray until God shakes the place with His holy presence. There is no mistaking Christ's anointing power—it can heal and restore the most tattered of lives. There is no other way to earn complete forgiveness except through the blood of Jesus that was shed for our sins on Calvary's Cross so that we might be completely redeemed!

What does it mean to redeem something? The dictionary has several definitions. The first one is: "to make an exchange." I love the second one too: "to make something that is bad or unpleasant better."

Jesus Christ certainly took the filthy rags of our sin (something bad or unpleasant) and made us better on Golgotha's hill. He gave His life for ours so that we might live eternally in heaven's paradise. The story of the Cross is the greatest story ever told... a story that gives me and you the opportunity to walk on streets of gold for an eternity. Are you ready?

The Pastor's Blessing

And now may the Lord bless you and keep you. May the Lord make His face to shine upon you and be gracious unto you, giving you His peace. May God give to you the desires of your heart. May you have a hope-explosion in your life that will change you from the inner core of your being until every day you live with a joyful expectancy that God will invade every hour of your day with His divine purpose. In Jesus' name, Amen!

Genesis 17:2
"I will make My covenant between Me and you,
and will multiply you exceedingly."

We serve a God of covenant who always keeps His word. The Bible says there is no shadow of turning in Him. This means that nothing about the Lord changes. What He says, He will do. And what He promises, He will loyally honor and uphold in a covenant relationship, even to His own hurt.

Have you been hurt in the past by others' betrayal? Turn it over to God and know that He will fight for you. Don't rehearse these events until you become old and bitter; today is a new day, and God's fresh mercies are yours.

Focus on being loyal and let God take it up with everyone else. Your life will be rich with contentment and peace when you concentrate on the good things God has in store for you and not the wrongdoings of others. Learn to walk in covenant with the Lord. You will never find a greater Friend.

Jeremiah 33:3
*"Call to Me, and I will answer you, and show you great
and mighty things, which you do not know."*

God doesn't only want to do great and mighty things for you, He wants to do great and mighty things through you.

How can He accomplish this? By answering your prayers. Do you have a dream that God gave you years ago? A dream that seems completely impossible to achieve? He is just waiting for you to call on His name and believe that it shall be done.

When you start getting answers to your prayers, prayer will be the most exciting thing happening at your house. You won't want to go a whole hour without asking God for direction, for a breakthrough, for a friend's need, for a special healing. There is no limit to the things we can ask God to do for us, and there is no limit to His grace.

The Bible says ask and you shall receive. Yes, it is just that simple. Why do we complicate things so much? Just ask according to God's infinite mercy and power. Knock God off His chair, so to speak. Faith like that excites Him! And it will certainly excite you when you see His mighty hand beginning to work in your life.

We serve a big God! Ask for something enormous today, and know that God can and will deliver all that you need according to His riches in glory!

Matthew 5:13
"You are the salt of the earth; but if the salt loses its flavor,
how shall it be seasoned? It is then good for nothing
but to be thrown out and trampled underfoot by men."

*I*t is not what we say we will do as Christians but what we actually make happen. Indeed, actions do speak louder than words. So what are you doing to show your loyalty to the body of Christ? Do you talk about how the church needs a new Sunday School teacher, or do you actually volunteer to teach the class? At some point it is time to step up and do your part for the Kingdom, being salt.

What does the Bible mean by "salt of the earth?" Salt crystals stick together in the bitter cold and the relenting heat. Salt prevents corruption. God's people are not to live by the world's standards but by the commands presented in the Bible. We are to be in the world, not of this world. We are to be set apart for a higher calling.

This doesn't mean that God wants you to be a snob—too heavenly minded to be any earthly good. He simply wants you to be so saturated with the love of the Lord that people want to be like you! They want to know more about Jesus because of what they see in you!

Rise to the challenge of the higher standard set before you and know that God's richest blessings will infiltrate your life in an all-consuming way when you choose to be Kingdom-minded! Reach out to someone next to you and make a difference in their lives for the Kingdom. It will do you both a lot of good!

Matthew 12:25
Jesus knew their thoughts, and said to them: "Every kingdom
divided against itself is brought to desolation, and every city
or house divided against itself will not stand."

The Bible says that a house divided against itself cannot stand. What is the solution? Loyalty is the key to church survival and growth. Christians must stick together, refusing to be intimidated by the world, the flesh, and the devil.

When someone tells you to do or say something that is contrary to the Word of God, don't do it. God's law supersedes man's law. And God sees your predicament. He will guide and protect you, drawing you to the exact place you need to be at an appointed date and time.

Surround yourself with loyal, God-fearing friends and you will live a much more satisfying life. You can lift each other up in times of trouble and bear each other's burdens. Where two or more are gathered in His name, there He is in the midst of you.

If you follow God's mandate to love your neighbor as yourself, you shouldn't have a hard time finding good friends within the Kingdom. This doesn't mean you have to agree on every issue, but at least be unified on the key points covered in the Bible.

Few things in life are sweeter than time spent in the presence of the Lord with God-fearing friends. Just relax and enjoy good Christian fellowship. In God's presence, love abounds.

Deuteronomy 6:10-11
"So it shall be, when the LORD your God brings you into
the land of which He swore to your fathers, to Abraham, Isaac,
and Jacob, to give you large and beautiful cities which you did not
build, houses full of all good things, which you did not fill,
hewn-out wells which you did not dig, vineyards and olive trees
which you did not plant—when you have eaten and are full."

Sometimes God doesn't give you what you want, not because you don't deserve it, but because you deserve something better. God has a great plan in mind for you, and He is just waiting for you to get on board. If you are engaged in behavior that is self-defeating, stop it. Don't set yourself up for failure. This is not the life God wants you to lead. He wants you to be fulfilled and filled to overflowing with joy. He wants your cup to run over!

How can you experience His bounty? Read the Word. Follow His commands. Pray and seek His face. And when God tells you to do something... go out on a limb and JUST DO IT! Don't think about it or take a poll; just do it. You are in for the greatest ride of your life when you follow God's lead!

It is only when we are completely submitted to Jesus that we are truly free. As you invite Christ to take over, He makes all things new. He gives you houses you didn't build and vineyards you didn't plant. His love will begin to restore and refresh you each and every day like never before!

Proverbs 18:10
"The name of the LORD is a strong tower;
the righteous run to it and are safe."

————◆————

*I*f there was ever a time in our modern society when we needed to hear from heaven, it is now. We need God to move on our behalf each and every day, to keep watch over us and protect us, to lead us and to guide us.

We need the favor and blessing of God upon our lives and the lives of our family members. We need an infusion of the Holy Spirit in our households so that we may dwell in peace even when it seems that all hell is breaking loose.

Remember, our God is a strong tower! We can run to Him in the day of adversity and be saved. He is all-knowing and all-powerful. You have never faced an enemy that could not be defeated by Almighty God. When things appear grim and you are surrounded by adversity, look to the One who holds the world in the palm of His hand—who knows your every thought and counts your every tear—and rest assured that everything is going to be alright.

You may feel like the only one on the planet who is trying to live a righteous life, but stand firm, persuaded that the fight belongs to the Lord; He will protect and sustain you when you put your life in His capable hands. Our God is an awesome God!

Genesis 50:20
"You meant evil against me; but God meant it for good,
in order to bring it about as it is this day,
to save many people alive."

Since God already knows what's happening in your life, there is no place you can go where His arm cannot reach—no valley too deep, no forest too dark, no desert too remote, no prison too strong. All you have to do is call on Him. And the Bible promises that He will show you great and mighty things which you have not seen.

As you may recall, Joseph in the Bible had a few bad days. Did your brothers throw you in a pit this morning? If not, you're having a better day than that shepherd boy. Yet the Bible tells us over and over again that Joseph found favor in the eyes of the Lord. For years he endured difficult circumstances and others' betrayals with faith and integrity, and God saw him through.

Cast your cares upon the Lord and He will direct your path. Sometimes you have to fall into the pit before God will carry you to the palace. Use wherever you are as a place to build your faith and trust in the Lord. Good things are on the way!

The Pastor's Blessing

And now may the Lord bless you and keep you. May the Lord make His face to shine upon you and be gracious unto you, giving you His peace. May God grant you the peace that surpasses all understanding; the peace to know that you are favored of the Lord God Most High. May you prosper by His mighty hand and come to understand that He is for you and not against you. Let this year be a year where God's hands full of divine favor reach into every area of your life... physically, spiritually, and emotionally. And may you walk in His divine abundance. In Jesus' mighty name, Amen.

Matthew 6:34

"Do not worry about tomorrow, for tomorrow will worry about its own things. Sufficient for the day is its own trouble."

What is on the top of your "to do" list? Is there something that keeps you awake at night? Something that you waste your time worrying about? Guess what? God says to be anxious for nothing. When you worry, you are essentially telling God you don't trust Him to handle things on your behalf. Is that really the message you want to send?

Today, start living the joy-filled life that comes with the knowledge that God is in control. Concentrate on making this the very best day it can be. The God who created this world and everything in it says that He wants you to have the absolute best every single day of your life! You are so incredibly important to Him that He sent His only Son to die just for you. So lift your head high and believe that God has great blessings on order for you! Live each moment as if it were your last, for you never really know when it will be. No one does. Not even the über rich and incredibly powerful can guarantee their next breath.

God has this day completely under His care, so go ahead and give up your job as general manager of the universe. The world will not stop rotating, and you might just find that you enjoy your life on a whole new level!

2 Chronicles 7:14
"If My people who are called by My name will humble
themselves, and pray and seek My face, and turn
from their wicked ways, then I will hear from heaven,
and will forgive their sin and heal their land."

———————————

What did our forefathers do when America was in crisis? Did they sing a quick song and then jump back into political chaos? No! When America looked like she was about to come crashing down like a house of cards, Benjamin Franklin urged the Continental Congress to fall on their knees and ask Almighty God for guidance. They understood the very simple and yet profound principle that prayer is the key that unlocks the door to wisdom and deliverance.

For everything that America needed during the early days of struggle for survival, prayer was the key. What does America and the world need today? More prayer! Even greater prayer!

Why should we pray? Because God not only hears us but answers when we pray.

God does not need America and the nations of the world, but we desperately need Him. We need to be healed of division and hatred. We need to remember what it means to be united once again. We need to set our trivial "causes" aside and become one body under our loving and gracious God. And this unity begins at home.

It is always better to be reconciled than to be right. Love those who persecute you, and know that when you are doing what God has called you to do, He will take care of those who are coming against you. Nobody can take care of your enemies like God can. "Vengeance is Mine," says the Lord. You do your part, and let God do His.

Psalm 25:2
"O my God, I trust in You; Let me not be ashamed;
Let not my enemies triumph over me."

Today, I'm asking you to turn loose of the things that have held you back. Stop drowning in desperation and despair. Rise up! This year is going to be God's year in your life. It is the year where doors will be opened in your favor, while others will be closed that would cause you harm. Trust Him to handle things without trying to micromanage the details of your life. Turn loose of the reins and allow God to have His way in you!

This year, with the help of Almighty God, you can get over your heartaches, the rejection you've faced, and any controlling relationships! Get over what Satan has done to you too! Turn loose of the resentment and bitterness... those who have abused you and lied about you—turn it all over to the Lord and watch as your life becomes filled with joy once again.

Let the misery melt away and let the Son shine in!

Matthew 28:18
"All authority has been given to Me
in heaven and on earth."

———————

While reading the Good Book is a wonderful thing, it's not what you read or believe that brings the blessings of God on your house, but what you obey. Everything God has created functions by spiritual authority.

Do you feel like God doesn't hear you when you pray? Spiritual authority produces power! The reason many Christians pray without results is not because they aren't saved but because they aren't submitted to God's authority. When God asks you to do something, do you follow His lead or run in the opposite direction? Do you try to make deals with God–"If You'll do this, then I will do that"? Well, guess what? That's not how the system works!

Just be still for a moment and think about the earth-shattering power that God has made available to you. Do you want to tap into that or continue doing your own thing? How has doing your own thing worked out for you in the past? Maybe it's time to allow God to have His way in your life.

God wants to share His amazing power with you. Unlimited power is not just for when the church is raptured and we all go to heaven. Unlimited power is for today!

Luke 15:20
"[The son] arose and came to his father. But when he was still
a great way off, his father saw him and had compassion,
and ran and fell on his neck and kissed him."

The story of the prodigal son is one of my favorites! It is the quintessential story of every person who ever set out in search of something more wonderful than what they already have, only to find it to be an enormous disappointment.

It is the grass-is-greener syndrome. You think you want something you don't have. You believe you need it so desperately that you lose sight of what really matters. So you search the world over, only to find that what you yearned for was right in your own backyard all along. In the mirror you see the reflection of your own worst enemy.

The prodigal son is such a fantastic story because he represents each and every one of us. Anytime we tell God we have a better idea for our lives, or that we want to follow our own path instead of the one He has painstakingly designed just for us, we are the prodigal.

Today is the day to return home and receive the gifts your Father has reserved just for you. He is patiently waiting for you to stop wandering through the far country and come to Him so He can bless you with abundance you cannot contain.

Make no mistake. God will allow you to wander as long as your heart desires. But aren't you tired of doing things your way? Son of God, daughter of God, come home.

John 14:27
"Peace I leave with you, My peace I give to you;
not as the world gives do I give to you.
Let not your heart be troubled, neither let it be afraid."

Everything on the planet is either the truth or a lie, light or dark. Satan presents himself as the angel of light, when in fact he is the prince of darkness. He presents himself as the answer, when in fact he is the source of great lies.

Since time began, Satan has been telling people there is something better waiting for them that God doesn't want them to have. He lured Adam with an apple. What is he dangling in front of you? A better job? A bigger house? A newer car?

What lies have you believed that have caused destruction in your life and robbed you of God's peace? The Bible says that God wants to give you His peace. Meanwhile, you've settled for a counterfeit kind that the world gives and the world can take away.

With God's peace, you can put your head on your pillow at night and sleep like a baby, even when walking through the darkest of days. With this peace you can sing your triumph song from jail, as Paul and Silas did. The peace of God is all-encompassing and all-consuming. Wouldn't you like to have more of it in your life?

Dare to live the life that God has designed for you, not one of your own making. When you follow Him, He will give you the victorious life you were intended to have!

1 Corinthians 10:13
"No temptation has overtaken you except such as is common to man; but God is faithful, who will not allow you to be tempted beyond what you are able, but with the temptation will also make the way of escape, that you may be able to bear it."

---

*D*o you have a habit that is so addicting it has become detrimental to your well-being? Today you can be set free in Jesus' name. I'm asking you to abandon your addiction. Ask God to direct your escape and begin taking away that desire. He can heal you and give you instant relief. Are you willing to let Him work in your life? Are you willing to accept the change?

Once you are set free and given back the life you were called to enjoy, slam the door shut and don't look behind you. Remember what happened to Lot's wife when she looked back at Sodom and Gomorrah? She turned into a block of salt! I'm telling you today, don't look back.

Walk away from relationships and temptations that will bring you into a deeper captivity. Then walk straight into a land flowing with milk and honey as God delivers you from the slavery of the past.

If you will set aside your controlling habits, this can be your most triumphant year—the year you begin to discover anew the goodness of the Lord in the land of the living.

The Pastor's Blessing

And now may the Lord bless you and keep you. May the Lord make His face to shine upon you and be gracious unto you, giving you His peace. May you walk in the knowledge that you are a child of God, that the blood of Jesus has redeemed you. Do not allow the prince of darkness to condemn you, for you have been justified by Jesus' blood, sanctified and set apart, made holy, and honored as a part of the bride of Christ. Rejoice that your redemption is here and that Jesus is the Lord of your life!

Psalm 91:15
"He shall call upon Me, and I will answer him;
I will be with him in trouble;
I will deliver him and honor him."

What did George Washington do when it looked like the American Revolution was lost? At the time, he was leading a ragtag bunch of farmers with pitchforks against the British Army, the finest in the world at that time.

Washington's fan club was calling for him to be fired. Even worse, he knew that a large number of his volunteers would return home at the first of the year and that he (along with his officers) would be hung by King George if they could not prevail. A quick glance at his upcoming calendar looked bleak.

What did Washington do when his life, his reputation, and his sacred honor were all on the line? He knelt in the snow and prayed. I'm sure you have seen the paintings of this magnificent scene. It is a brilliant, patriotic moment.

Washington knew then what America needs to realize today: When we are at our weakest, God is at the top of His game. We can never have a stronger army than when God is on our side. For if God be for us, who can be against us?

Ephesians 4:32
"Be kind to one another, tenderhearted, forgiving one another,
even as God in Christ forgave you."

———◆◆◆———

*D*o you resent someone who has hurt you? Are you harboring bitterness over an event that scarred you so deeply you feel as if life will never be the same? Do you want relief from the raging sea of emotions that are threatening to drown you? Forgive the person who hurt you.

I'm not saying this will be easy, but it is vital for your own mental, spiritual, and physical growth. Why is it so important for you to forgive those who have crushed you in their wake? Because if you hold onto the bitterness and resentment, you are only building a prison around yourself and giving your enemy the key. The one who hurt you becomes your jailer, controlling your life on the deepest level.

The moment you forgive that person, you walk right out of that dark, self-imposed jail cell and into the daylight of freedom. You regain control over your thoughts and emotions. You are no longer bombarded by vengeance and hatred.

Forgiveness will liberate you! It will set you free to focus on the things in your life that truly matter, the relationships that are wholesome and good. You are called according to the purposes of God. Start taking the road less traveled and unload your baggage. Life is so much sweeter when you are unburdened by the past. Be set free today in Jesus' name!

Matthew 18:18

"Assuredly, I say to you, whatever you bind on earth
will be bound in heaven, and whatever
you loose on earth will be loosed in heaven."

---

*H*ave you seen the gladiator movies? When a gladiator gets knocked down in a fight, he loses. And when the standing warrior places his foot on the fallen man's neck, he is the absolute victor.

God wants you to have complete victory in every area of your life! You have absolute authority by the power of Almighty God to put your foot on the neck of your enemies. You are the triumphant one. He has given you the power to bind things on earth so that your enemies will scatter!

Start writing down the things God gives you to accomplish and get to it! Don't let the naysayers hold you back. You and God can determine your future without consulting anyone else. Act as if you can accomplish anything you set your mind to, because with God on your side—you will!

1 Samuel 3:10
"Now the LORD came and stood and called as at other times,
'Samuel! Samuel!' And Samuel answered,
'Speak, for Your servant hears.'"

Are you making any progress on your path? Or are you just going around in circles? It's easy to confuse activity with progress. After all, even a clock that doesn't work is right twice a day. Still, hitting the mark once in a while doesn't mean you're on the right trail.

If you're unsure, stop and wait on the Lord. Get a clear idea of where God wants you to go, then start moving in that direction. It might sound crazy and new to you, but God saw this day coming. He knows your start from your conclusion. Don't be afraid. Like Samuel, you can say, "Speak, for Your servant hears."

Trust in the Lord with all your heart, listen for His guidance—and then go. Just because you don't understand how it will turn out doesn't mean you don't need to head in the direction God is leading. Faith is starting out before you know how it's going to turn out.

God has brought you this far. He will not fail you now.

Matthew 13:45–46
"The kingdom of heaven is like a merchant... who, when he
had found one pearl of great price, went and sold
all that he had and bought it."

———— ◆◆◆ ————

*O*nce there was a Texas man who went to a rock show and purchased a blue rock for ten dollars. He recognized it as a deep blue sapphire. He went home, cleaned the rock, and sold it for five million dollars. The original owner didn't recognize the value of what he had in his hand. His wildest dreams were right in front of him, and he sold them for a mere sawbuck.

You might be continually searching for what you perceive to be the best in your own life... and it's staring you in the face. Start asking the Holy Spirit to open your eyes so that you can see what you already have. God has given you great provision—the perfect answer to the problem He knew would come before you even knew it existed. And He has given you hundreds of promises in His Word to guide you through the problem toward the provision.

Are you giving away your most valuable assets because you don't recognize their worth? Heaven's highway is paved with gold, so God knows a little something about great wealth. He says that all the riches in the world are His, and He promises to meet each and every one of your needs.

Stop scrambling to make ends meet and start seeking His face. He can find a way to provide for you in the most dire of circumstances. If you are only willing to hand Him your sack of rocks, He will lead you toward the greatest treasures you have ever seen.

Psalm 119:162
"I rejoice at Your word As one who finds great treasure."

What is hope? Hope is not wishful thinking. It sees the invisible, feels the intangible, achieves the impossible. Neither is it necessarily getting what you want. If God gave you everything you ever asked for, you would have completely destroyed yourself by now.

Do you want to learn more about the true riches of God that can meet your every need? Do you want to be established in the hope of God? Read the Word and discover the fountain that never shall run dry!

The Bible is not a wish book. The Bible is a book filled with truths. What it says, God will do. The promises found within are not just for ancient Believers but for the church of today.

You have absolute authority to shape the destiny of your life through Jesus Christ. The devil is not afraid of the Believer with a dusty Bible. But the person with a Bible that is falling apart has a life that is not. Strive to be a force the devil has to reckon with—a person who, when you get up in the morning, makes the enemy say, "I wonder what he/she is going to do for the Kingdom today." Be someone who makes a difference!

When you learn how to apply the Bible to your life, it will become the most exciting thing in the world for you to read. Other books are given for information; the Bible is given for transformation.

Mark 4:21
"He said to them, "Is a lamp brought to be put under a basket or under a bed? Is it not to be set on a lampstand?""

---

*T*here was once a schoolteacher who loved art. He was a very talented man who painted majestic nature scenes on canvas at night, after class was over for the day. At one point, he realized he had a choice: he could continue teaching, which he loved... or start painting full-time, which he loved more. He and his wife decided that he would paint for one year and they would live on their savings.

After a year had passed, he held an art show in Dallas and made more than one million dollars by the end of the first week. Today, he is one of the most successful artists in the world because he dared to try a new vision. He turned his talent loose and reached a dimension that no one could have possibly foreseen.

God wants the same thing for you. He has brought you great blessing, and He wants you to display it for His glory. What hidden talent do you have? Don't be afraid to let your light—His light—shine!

The Pastor's Blessing

And now may the Lord bless you and keep you. May the Lord make His face to shine upon you and be gracious unto you, giving you His peace. Let the joy of the Lord inhabit our hearts and lives as we release every weight that has so easily set us back. We declare with all our heart, soul, mind, and body not to look to the right or the left but to focus on You and You alone. We will run with endurance this race that is set before us, that we might indeed receive the crown of conquerors as we hear the words, "Well done, thou good and faithful servant." In Jesus' name, Amen!

Psalm 146:5
"Happy is he who has the God of Jacob for his help,
Whose hope is in the LORD his God."

The world is searching for happiness, traveling near and far in the quest for some unattainable Shangri-La. But true happiness can only be found in Jesus Christ. It's found in Whose you are, not in what you have.

Even when you are surrounded on all sides by calamity and chaos, He holds you in the palm of His hand.

What happened when Peter stopped looking at Jesus as he walked on the waters of the Sea of Galilee? Peter was doing great until he took his eyes off of Jesus and started focusing on the swirling sea around him. Peter's fear got the better of him and he began to drown. Like most of us, he cried out in his panic: "Help me!" But the reality of the situation was that Jesus had His eye on Peter from the very beginning. There was no reason to fear!

Don't let the raging sea of life engulf you, sucking you into a relentless riptide of sorrow and despair. Keep your eyes on Jesus and you will never go wrong!

Psalm 91:11
"He shall give His angels charge over you,
To keep you in all your ways."

---

*H*as life become exhausting? Have you forgotten who you are? Let me remind you: You are a child of the living God! Your sins have been forgiven and buried in the deepest sea, never again to be remembered against you.

You are justified... just as if you'd never sinned. You are royalty! You are an ambassador for Christ. A divine masterpiece that God created as an original. That makes you priceless!

You are so important to the King that He sends His angels to personally guard your every move. You can call on Him in the day of trouble and He will answer. You have out-of-this-world influence that is spectacular! You have significance beyond anything of this earth!

The President might have the Secret Service, but God sends His angels to guard and protect you wherever you are! And my friend, nobody on earth offers service like the King!

Acts 17:28

"In Him we live and move and have our being."

On the road to remembering who you are in Christ, you must recognize that you cannot be all things to all people. So do yourself a favor and stop trying!

Stop allowing the foolish opinions of others to control your own opinions. Don't let someone sabotage your dreams, your destiny, your peace. Don't allow an unkind spirit to creep in and make you feel insignificant or unworthy.

Take control of your life or someone else will. Don't be afraid to be who you are! God designed you as an original. Live your life with gusto, just as the King intended.

The only thing you can truly change is yourself. Today, confront who and what you are so you can become the man or woman God created you to be.

Each of us has a divine destiny that no one else can fulfill. Quit trying to make everyone around you happy; quit struggling to be everything to everyone. Instead, take the bull by the horns and begin living the life that God intends for you. You will never be happier than when you are right where He wants you to be!

Isaiah 32:17
"The work of righteousness will be peace,
And the effect of righteousness, quietness and assurance forever."

———————— ◆ ◆ ————————

*A*re you constantly tired and stressed out? Do you feel excessively worried or depressed? Does your life consist of things you profess to hate and yet you continue to do them anyway? This is self-betrayal.

Don't complain about what you permit. Even a gerbil realizes when it's time to get off the wheel.

If you know you're sinning, don't keep spiraling farther... step away from what tempts you. If you feel you're overweight, don't complain... go on a diet. Don't grumble about your lack of education... go back to school. Stop betraying yourself by sitting back and watching the world pass you by... stand up and do something about it! Even if you do it wrong, God will train you!

If your emotions are marked by worry, cynicism, and hopelessness, take action. If righteousness seems to escape you, reverse course. Stop circling the track and start seeking God's plan for your life. You will never realize your full potential until you ask Him to step in and take over.

Now is not the time to get buried in an avalanche of apathy or the chaos of condemnation. Turn to Almighty God, the Author and Finisher of our faith. He will give you a fresh vision and a brand-new start!

Genesis 1:27
"So God created man in His own image; in the image of God
He created him; male and female He created them."

Stop seeing yourself as other people see you. In your past, some authority figure may have planted seeds of doubt that took root in your life. You have grown to believe that the things this person said about you are true. But today is a new day, and you are called to start seeing yourself as God sees you—as a man or woman created in His image, a person of rare and priceless beauty.

You have absolutely no limitations with the Lord because nothing is impossible to those who believe. If the dearest on earth have left you tattered and torn, look up. Your Redeemer lives! He has the answer for you: more of Himself! He will never leave you nor forsake you. Right this minute, He is arranging things to work in your favor if you will only trust Him.

The moment you cut yourself loose from all the emotional garbage of the past, that is the exact moment you will become free. And oh, how the angels will rejoice!

Your life will exemplify true beauty when you finally see yourself through the eyes of God. Don't let someone else destroy your self-confidence for one more day. Accept the emotional healing of heaven and move forward in Jesus' name!

Nehemiah 8:10
"Do not sorrow, for the joy of the LORD is your strength."

———◆———

*A*re you waiting for some magical event to take place before you can be happy? A graduation, a job promotion, or marriage to the perfect mate? Stop waiting for a future date to be happy, and start enjoying happiness right here and now.

The best-kept secret about happiness is that you must have it inside before you can give it to anybody else. And pasting a fake smile on your face is not happiness. Joy comes from God the Father. Tap into the Source and let Him open the floodgates into your life. There's no need to live in a state of anxiety, fearing what might happen next. As one older woman put it, "Most of the problems I worried about throughout my life never happened."

That's true for most of us. We worry and worry... and then worry some more. Maybe you have a PhD in worry. Stop it! The joy of the Lord is your strength!

Enjoy the journey! Don't keep rushing around in search of happiness, convincing yourself that when you cross some imaginary finish line... ahhhh, there you will find happiness. Today is the day to live life to the fullest. Today is the day to start dancing in the rain.

Habakkuk 2:2
"Write the vision And make it plain on tablets,
that he may run who reads it."

———— ❖ ————

$\mathcal{D}$o you have a vision of where you would like your life to go, the path you would like to travel? Has God inspired a dream deep within that cannot possibly happen without divine intervention? If God gave you the idea, He will give you the ability to obtain all that you need for its fulfillment.

Take out a piece of paper and write down the things you would like to accomplish this month, this year, even next year. Take the time to write out your life goals too. In life you will either live out your own dream or work to help someone else realize theirs. You might as well live your dream. So start making your list.

I'm not talking about a grocery list or a log of bills to be paid. Think big! We serve a great God who has no limits. Write down the things you can only do with God on your side, the things that are hidden behind a mountain of impossibility.

Write today's date and start thinking of what you need God to help you accomplish. And when these things come to fruition, write the date God brought you out to rich fulfillment. He can and will give you the desires of your heart. Begin writing your vision for your future and ask God to take over. He can make a way where there is no way.

The Pastor's Blessing

And now may the Lord bless you and keep you. May the Lord make His face to shine upon you and be gracious unto you, giving you His peace. May you learn to walk in righteous paths of obedience so that you receive the inheritance that God has made possible through the blood of Jesus Christ at the Cross, when He took your poverty and gave you the riches of Abraham. May you walk in that dimension of great faith and receive God's richest blessing. Amen!

Psalm 37:4
"Delight yourself also in the LORD,
And He shall give you the desires of your heart."

When you invite God to come in and take over the desires of your heart, you are releasing your faith and telling God that He is in control. You are making a faith proclamation: "God, these are the things that I need from You. Without Your intervention, they cannot happen."

Once you let God know your specific need, keep praying until the answer comes. Don't give in to fear or doubt, which will surely come your way. You are worthy of God's very best, and He wants you to have the lion's share. Just keep praying... and believing.

Much of what I know about prayer today I saw in action as a child. My mother was a mighty prayer warrior. When she opened her mouth, she made very plain what she was requesting from God. Lives were changed; people were healed; souls were saved; divine revelations were delivered. There were many years that my mother would pray and fast for months on end. And ultimately, heaven reached down and met each and every need. Why? Because my mother never stopped bringing her requests before the Lord. She prayed fervently until the answer came.

When the answer comes, you will know it is from God because it will be what you prayed for, delivered at the time in your life when you are most ready to receive it. Inviting God into your situation is always the right move. Together, the two of you can make big things happen!

Joshua 10:12-13
*"In the day when the LORD delivered up the Amorites before
the children of Israel,... [Joshua] said in the sight of Israel:
'Sun, stand still over Gibeon; And Moon, in the Valley of
Aijalon.' So the sun stood still, And the moon stopped,
till the people had revenge Upon their enemies."*

What would you do with your life if you knew that failure
was impossible? Let me remind you that the Bible says
ALL things are possible to them that believe. So, what are
you waiting for? We serve a mighty God who can help you
overcome any obstacle.

There is a difference between believing and receiving.
You probably believe that God can do something great and
wonderful, but you might not believe that He wants to do it
for you. The reality is that the same God who helped Joshua
can certainly help you!

When Israel needed to defeat its enemies, Joshua spoke
to the Lord and asked for deliverance. And what did God do?
He made the sun stand still over Gibeon, and the moon in the
valley of Aijalon... until the Israelites had their revenge.

Friends, that is powerful! When God takes over, your life
is instantly is filled with limitless opportunities. Your enemies
are defeated in Jesus' name.

God is looking for the person who has enough faith to
move mountains. You might not know what tomorrow holds,
but God does. If you believe in Him, He has promised to take
care of each of your tomorrows. Trust thou in God. When you
trust in Him, you will never go wrong.

Isaiah 61:7
"Instead of your shame you shall have double honor,
And instead of confusion they shall rejoice in their portion.
Therefore in their land they shall possess double;
Everlasting joy shall be theirs."

What do you see in your future? I don't want you to look through the eyes of fear or the eyes of the flesh. Look through the eyes of faith and see health in the place of sickness. See long life in the place of sudden death, and prosperity in the place of "never enough to make ends meet." We serve a God of more than enough!

I want you to see God restoring to you sevenfold what Satan has taken, and your enemies scattering in seven directions as God clears your path of absolute triumph. I want you to see depression being crushed and replaced by a tsunami of joy sweeping over every corner of your life. I want you to be filled with joy unspeakable and full of glory that can only come from God the Father.

Receive it today in Jesus' name, and get excited about what's coming your way! Call upon His holy name and believe that good things can happen for YOU! Look through God's eyes into your future and know this: the best is yet to come!

John 10:28
"I give them eternal life, and they shall never perish;
neither shall anyone snatch them out of My hand."

When God gives you a goal, enjoy the journey but focus on the destination. Keep your eye on the prize! When adversity strikes, batten down the hatches and turn your sights toward heaven. Keep advancing toward your divine destiny. Don't stop, even though at times it is difficult to reconcile fact and faith—the way things are versus the way you want things to be.

You may be inclined to wonder what's going on: "If God is in heaven looking down on me, why is this happening?" Asking why is a genuine response, not a sign of weakness. As human beings we are always seeking answers. And God's Word is filled from cover to cover with the truth that will set you free. When you seek His face, He can guide you through any impasse.

The God of the mountaintop is the God of the valley. Do you trust Him when things go haywire? God sees you, and He holds you close in the palm of His hand. There is no need for you to worry! He's got it all under control.

Though life will not always be smooth sailing, watch for every sign that God is on the horizon, working on your behalf. Anyone can be overcome by fear, but it takes a person of great faith and courage to focus on the destination. Trust Christ to lead you home!

Psalm 5:8
"Lead me, O LORD, in Your righteousness...;
Make Your way straight before my face."

———————

This is the year of your harvest! God is going to lead you to answers you have been seeking for years. Trust that He has your best interest at heart and the answer is on the way. Do not give in! Keep pressing on! This is the year that you and God will sing on the mountaintop, celebrating your greatest victory to date. God can make that happen. Do you have faith enough to move the mountain?

What you thought was impossible is right around the corner. But God wants you to take the initiative. Every miracle in the Bible has two parts—your part and God's part. God's part doesn't start until you start.

The Bible says to ask and you will receive; seek and you will find; knock and the door will be opened. Are you knocking? Are you seeking? Or are you sitting on your couch waiting for a miracle to drop in your lap?

God is ready to lead you down a path of total victory, but the choice is yours. Will you take the initiative and seek His face? Or will you settle for second best? Ask God to lead you in the way everlasting. The taste of victory is never so sweet as when He gives you the most complete answer you never saw coming—that "aha" moment when you are embraced by His presence, knowing that every prayer you sent up has been completely fulfilled.

Romans 5:8
"God demonstrates His own love toward us,
in that while we were still sinners, Christ died for us."

The highest form of courage in life is daring to be yourself in the face of adversity. It takes a brave heart to choose right over wrong, conviction over convenience, and truth over popularity. But these choices measure your life. These choices tell others who you really are and what you're willing to stand up for.

Remember, it is never wrong to do the right thing! Dare to be filled with confidence and move forward like the mighty warrior that you are, fully assured that God loves you!

God sent His only Son to die for you and for me on Golgotha's tree. It is the greatest picture of love that man will ever know. Jesus could have called 10,000 angels to rescue Him from His agonizing pain, but because of His great love, He stayed so that we might be redeemed.

Learn to love yourself like God loves you, and then share His great love with those around you. Recognizing His love inside ourselves is what enables us to give it away.

Philippians 4:7
"The peace of God, which surpasses all understanding,
will guard your hearts and minds through Christ Jesus."

---

*I*f we have peace, no matter what else we may lack, life is beautiful. Without peace, a palace of gold is a penitentiary.

But what is peace? Sometimes God's peace means putting on the whole armor of God and fighting the good fight. Remember David and Goliath? There was no peace in the valley until Goliath was a defeated foe. David confronted him in the name of the Lord and won the battle.

Being in the combat zone with God is better than being alone in your own comfort zone. You can be happier with Daniel in the lion's den than in the palace with the king, because true peace is often found by taking up your cross and following Christ down whatever path He may lead. And you won't know true peace until you make the Prince of Peace your priority.

God's ways are higher than our ways, and His thoughts are far above ours. When He leads you down something that looks different from the primrose path... just keep going. You can be sure, peace is just ahead.

The Pastor's Blessing

And now may the Lord bless you and keep you. May the Lord make His face to shine upon you and be gracious unto you, giving you His peace. Give us the peace that surpasses all understanding, even when the world around us is falling apart. Give us grace without limit that enables us to walk in paths of righteousness. Let us rejoice in the joy of our salvation each and every day, knowing that because Your Son lives, we have our very existence. Because He is a Conqueror, we are more than conquerors. Because He is victorious, we are crowned in victory. In Jesus' name, Amen!

Romans 5:1
*"Having been justified by faith, we have peace with
God through our Lord Jesus Christ."*

What are some of the ways you can have peace through Jesus Christ? There is comfort in death because Jesus is the Resurrection and the Life. You can find rest in the storm because He commanded the wind and waves, "Peace, be still." There is warmth in the darkest valley because "Yea, though I walk through the valley of the shadow of death I will fear no evil for Thou art with me."

Peace is the gift of God, the result of total surrender to Jesus Christ. No matter what is happening in the world around you or what you are facing, you can have peace if you will simply trust the Lord to carry you through. Leave the heavy lifting to Him and just strengthen your faith for the journey. No matter where it takes you, peace will surround in a very real way when you are walking hand-in-hand with the Savior.

Proverbs 28:1
"The righteous are bold as a lion."

---

*T*he difference between being a prince with God and a common drifter is bold persistence.

God is not looking for dash and flash. Duty, discipline, and determination are necessary to finish the race. Are you always starting things and never finishing them? If so, you will never have great success.

Are you struggling to make your dreams come true? Cheer up and stand up! Struggle is proof that you have not yet been conquered. Keep up the good fight! Champions train longer and harder in order to win. The word "no" does not faze them, it only inspires.

When building Cornerstone Church, I heard "no" a lot. There were many reasons not to build where we did: The highway that connects our church to the city, 1604, is called the Death Loop. "It's too dangerous," people said. I was told that no one would drive that far out to attend. But when God tells you to do something, you just get busy. By His grace, our services are filled each and every week, and we are able to reach the nations of the world on a daily basis. And the best is yet to come!

Has God asked you to do something in your own life? Are you weary in well doing? Stay focused! Only the persistent produce fruit. If you're tired and "quit" looks good, don't do it. It's always too soon to give in! Press on. Endure. Fight back. Look in the mirror and say, "There's the winner!" Be as bold as a lion, in Jesus' name!

Psalm 119:165
"Great peace have those who love Your law,
And nothing causes them to stumble."

———◆———

*I*t is unlikely for us all to amass great fortunes, to all become household names, but we can all do something far better than this: we can make peace. It requires a conscious, persistent, sacrificial effort, dedication to the Ten Commandments, and a return to righteousness. But peace is within our grasp.

Are you searching for peace? Be a peacemaker! Start with your own life, then move on to the members of your family and then your community. Flood your home and neighborhood with the love of the Lord. Love one another as Christ loved you. (Remember when you were most unlovable?) Get everything in divine order, and then do more than dream of peace. Make it! Only then will you know the true meaning of God's peace.

Psalm 90:17
"Let the beauty of the LORD our God be upon us,
And establish the work of our hands for us;
Yes, establish the work of our hands."

The favor of God is better than ice cream on a hot summer day! There are few things better than that!

Favor brings the wealth of the wicked into the hands of the righteous. Favor will make you the head rather than the tail.

It is God's desire to pour out His favor on you. He wants to give you houses you didn't build, wells you didn't dig, and vineyards you didn't plant! When you have the favor of God, you can do what others cannot do and go where others cannot go. You can achieve God's destiny in your life. You can believe in things other people cannot see—all through the eyes of faith. When you are favored of God, there is no limitation for you!

If yesterday was your darkest day, you are primed for a joy explosion! Get ready! The Bible says, "Let the redeemed of the Lord say so!"

Proclaim the victory in your life. Child of God, you are redeemed! There is no other life for you than the one that is found at the feet of Jesus.

Isaiah 55:11
"So shall My word be that goes forth from My mouth;
It shall not return to Me void,
But it shall accomplish what I please,
And it shall prosper in the thing for which I sent it."

———————

I often tell my congregation that B-I-B-L-E stands for "Basic Instructions Before Leaving Earth." How ready are you?

Are you preparing yourself and telling those around you about eternal salvation through Jesus Christ? No man knows the hour or the day, and we could be gone before dinner tonight. Don't wait another moment to give your life to Christ!

Are you looking for answers? The Bible can answer every problem you ever thought you might have. Want to get married? The Bible has verses about how to choose the perfect spouse. Are you looking to invest money? Because God owns everything that is, the Bible contains a wealth of wisdom about how we handle what He hands us.

Most books inform; the Bible transforms. It is one of the simplest books to read, and yet it has the power to completely change every part of your life and being. If you aren't taking time each day to unearth the knowledge in this vast treasure, you need to start a daily routine.

Make reading the Word of God a priority, and you will be amazed at the power you unleash over your life as the Lord makes old things new and restores your soul. The Word of God does not return void!

Matthew 5:16
"Let your light so shine before men, that they may see
your good works and glorify your Father in heaven."

---

*O*ne secret of success is to do what you know how to do! God gave everyone a talent. If you use your talent and become your best at that one thing, you'll find success! And it is His desire that you experience success in every area of your life.

But while enjoying your success, remember this one thing: God doesn't just look at what you do; He looks at why you do it. Everything you say and do should be for His glory, not for your own. When we glorify God, we shine the light on the Kingdom, not on ourselves. Then people are drawn to God, wanting to know more about Him.

We are blessed to be a blessing! Great success can be yours during this lifetime if you will focus on doing one thing and doing it to the very best of your ability. Aim high and never give in to self-doubt. God wants you to be a shining beacon of His love to those around you, representing Him by doing all things with excellence.

He created you to bring Him glory. What are you doing with your time and talents that glorifies the King?

Psalm 46:1
"GOD is our refuge and strength,
A very present help in trouble."

Don't depend on God to give you strength; depend on God to be your strength! Call on His name and He will walk beside you as you face the chaos of your day.

Sometimes life can hand us cruel and uncertain circumstances, but one thing is for sure: the Lord is the same yesterday, today, and forever, and is fully willing and able to help you in the day of trouble.

Are you in a situation right now that has you stressed to the max, where you can't see any kind of resolution coming from something so awful? The Word says not to fear but instead to call on God's mighty Name and He will be our refuge. He is our strong tower that the righteous run into and are saved. Start crying out to God and He will send His angels to guard you in all your ways.

When you are down to nothing, God is up to something!

The Pastor's Blessing

And now may the Lord bless you and keep you. May the Lord make His face to shine upon you and be gracious unto you, giving you His peace. May you walk in the confidence that Christ is your Redeemer; that your past has been forgiven and forgotten, buried in the deepest sea, remembered against you no more. May Jesus Christ be the Lord and Master of your life. Amen!

John 19:30
"When Jesus had received the sour wine, He said, 'It is finished!'
And bowing His head, He gave up His spirit."

The Prince of Glory cried out, "It is finished!" The moment those words left His lips, you became royalty, kings and priests unto God. The royal blood of heaven is flowing in your veins. You have the favor of God!

Angels go before you and behind you. The Word of God is in your mouth. The blood of God is on your brow. Nothing is impossible for you! You are heirs and joint-heirs to the throne of God!

You are His and He is yours because of the power of the Cross!

Now that you know the power of heaven is behind you, waiting to answer when you cry out for help, what will you do with your day? Will you use it to give praise and honor to the King? Make the most of every moment. Today is God's gift to you. What you do with it is your gift to Him.

Psalm 55:22
"Cast your burden on the LORD, And He shall sustain you;
He shall never permit the righteous to be moved."

God is greater than the burdens you are carrying. Take your burden to the foot of the Cross and leave it there. You do not have to carry around yesterday's garbage anymore! Today you can be set free in Jesus' name. Free from the fear of tomorrow. Free from the sin of the past. Absolutely, 100 percent free!

Are you a child of the living God? Do you think He wants you to live in a state of defeat or unwavering depression? Absolutely not! He wants you to live in a spirit of worship and service to the King! He wants you to live in abundance and blessing.

How can you fully worship Him if you are constantly worried and afraid? Today, take whatever is bothering you and leave it at Jesus' feet. Tell Him your need and then release the burden; whatever is holding you back... just let it go. There is no need to worry or be filled with anxiety about the future. God is in complete control. When you ask for His help, you can rest assured He has already won the victory.

The Word says the righteous are not forsaken! Count yourself among those who God knows by name and walk in confidence, recognizing that God has destined you for greatness!

Romans 8:1
"There is therefore now no condemnation to those who are
in Christ Jesus, who do not walk according to the flesh,
but according to the Spirit."

⸻

What is the difference between condemnation and conviction? Condemnation is when someone says disapproving things about you, describing your inability to be a certain way or to accomplish certain things.

There are religious people (not godly, but "religious") who go around constantly condemning other people, declaring how unfit they are to be used by God or the church. They do so to hide their own inferiorities and weaknesses.

Don't let these people throw their condemnation on you. Don't let them leave you in a false state of shame or guilt. It is the Holy Spirit's job to condemn, not your nosy neighbor.

When you are truly guilty of wrongdoing, the Holy Spirit will let you know. The moment you are convicted, you need simply ask for forgiveness and you can instantaneously be filled with joy.

Reject foolish condemnation but listen for the leading of the Spirit. Know the difference, so that when the day comes, you can heed the voice of the Father and refuse the voice of a fool.

Colossians 3:15
"Let the peace of God rule in your hearts, to which also you
were called in one body; and be thankful."

$\mathcal{P}$eace in your life is the product of submission to Jesus Christ. We have peace because of the Cross. To the carnal mind, the Cross represents sorrow, suffering, and shame. But that's not so. To the Believer, it *is* the day the Lamb of God forever destroyed the strongholds that Satan had over all of mankind. His head was crushed. He no longer had dominion.

The day Jesus died looked like a day of utter defeat, when it was actually a day of total victory! It was a day of liberation and celebration. It was a day of emancipation. A day of unity for God's people, and the blessed day we were offered eternal life.

If you are seeking peace today, give your burden to the Lord and leave it at the Cross. Then thank Him! You no longer have to carry your sin and shame. You no longer have to suffer in silence. You are more than a conqueror through Jesus Christ!

Matthew 26:39
"O My Father, if it is possible, let this cup pass from Me;
nevertheless, not as I will, but as You will."

———◆———

*J*esus knew exactly what God the Father was asking of Him in the Garden of Gethsemane. And Christ's response was, "Not as I will, but as You will."

What is your spiritual authority asking of you today? Have you heard the voice of the Lord in your life and ignored it because you don't want to give up a habit that consumes you? Are you taking pleasure in something that is contrary to the Word of God?

If God is telling you that His will is different than yours, it's time to adjust your plan. You will never enjoy life more or feel more freedom than when you are a complete slave to Christ. It may be that God is trying to rid you of something that could be potentially fatal to you, or lead you down a path of destruction.

Of this you can be sure: God is intent on sparing you the pain of your own foolish choices. Are you following His lead? He gave His life so that yours could be filled with your heavenly Father's great riches. He is already completely invested in you. What are you doing in return?

Luke 6:31
"Just as you want men to do to you,
you also do to them likewise."

———◆———

Warm someone's heart today with a random act of love. Your love can be the hands of God, reshaping the self-esteem of someone crushed by cruel circumstances beyond his or her control. Put yourself in their shoes. Put your loved ones in their shoes. Wouldn't you want someone to show you the love of Christ if life had just dealt you a cruel blow?

Acts of love and kindness can build faith faster than words ever will. It is the old saying, "Actions speak louder than words." Showing someone the love of Christ can make the difference not only in their day but also in how they view Christianity. When people see you, do they want to have more of what you have? Or do you send them running for the hills?

Think about it. If someone cuts you off in rush-hour traffic, and you see their church bumper sticker as you're pounding the brakes to narrowly miss hitting their car... that's not the best advertisement. No one wants to join that church!

Today, take the opportunity to reach out and do something kind for someone. You will never know the impact of your actions, but God knows your heart and can use you as a catalyst to change someone's life.

Matthew 24:13
"He who endures to the end shall be saved."

Those who persevere are the ones left standing when everyone else quits! And everyone has that day when "quit" looks good. Everyone. Even the friend who seems to effortlessly glide through life as if he hasn't a care in the world.

No one goes through life unscathed. The Word tells us that trials will come. And then what? What do you do when you are facing a challenge in your life? Do you simply throw in the towel? Or do you put on the full armor of God and get ready to fight the good fight?

This year, dive into the great riches of the Holy Bible. God's Word is a lamp unto your feet and a light unto your path. Don't know where to turn? Consult the Word. It is sharper than a two-edged sword when you need to fend off an enemy.

Arm yourself with the Word of God. If you start preparing today, you will be ready when the battle comes. Don't wait until the fight is raging to finally crack open the Bible. Saturate your life and your home in the Word today and get equipped to persevere to the end. God's Word is the absolute truth and your spiritual sword. Keep it with you at all times!

The Pastor's Blessing

And now may the Lord bless you and keep you. May the Lord make His face to shine upon you and be gracious unto you, giving you His peace. May you recognize that He is our Source, the great Jehovah Jireh, the supplier of our every need. It is He who opens the heavens and blesses you with blessings you cannot contain. When God opens the door, no man can close it. Your enemies shall fall before you as Jericho fell before Israel. You shall know the blessings and the abundance that only the Lord can give. In Jesus' name, Amen!

Psalm 144:1
"Blessed be the LORD my Rock,
Who trains my hands for war,
And my fingers for battle."

———◆——◆—◆——◆———

There is no dawn without a night. And there is certainly no victory without a fight! So we should not fear—or be surprised by—the night or the fight.

Warfare is a way of life for the Believer. Get on your knees and take your petition to the Savior. He wants the very best for you and can set angels to flight at the mention of His name. Seek and you will find. Ask and it shall be given unto you. And keep your eyes on the prize as a soldier of the Lord. You are battling for Kingdom territory, not some meaningless clod of dirt. So don't get caught up in worries about which way the wind is blowing or how much stronger the soldier next to you looks.

If you are in the fight of your life, prepare well, battle with all your might in service to your Commander, and expect to celebrate complete victory by the power of Almighty God!

Hebrews 12:2
"Looking unto Jesus, the author and finisher of our faith,
who for the joy that was set before Him
endured the cross, despising the shame, and has sat down
at the right hand of the throne of God."

Do you like to shop? I don't like to shop... ever. But my wife loves it. For her it is a religious experience. If she gets home and doesn't like an item, she will return to the store the next day and exchange it for something else.

I want to remind you today of the greatest exchange ever made. This exchange was made on Calvary's Cross, and gave each and every one of us the opportunity to spend eternity in heaven. We were purchased with the shed blood of Jesus Christ.

We brought our sickness and disease, our sin and shame, a future without hope or promise. In exchange, Christ gave us health and healing... and complete redemption. If you have not given your life to Christ 100 percent, stop what you're doing right now and ask Him to come into your heart. Rededicate your life to Him! It will be the greatest gift you ever give yourself... and the reward program is out of this world!

The exchange of a lifetime. Little is much when God is in it.

Ephesians 6:16
"Above all, taking the shield of faith
with which you will be able to quench
all the fiery darts of the wicked one."

———————

If what you're doing doesn't produce resistance, it isn't worth doing. If you are doing what God has called you to do and you're neck-deep in hot water, shout Hallelujah! You're in the perfect place for God's richest blessing!

Consider this: Kites rise against the wind, not with the wind. Ships sail against the tide. So when something happens in your life, what do you do? Sing or complain? Square your shoulders and start working with God to resolve the situation, or sink back into your couch and moan another verse of "Nobody Knows the Trouble I've Seen"?

Trials will always be a part of life. What will you do when that day comes for you? In the life of a Believer, the only answer is to cry out to God and put on your spiritual armor so that when the enemy shoots in your direction, his darts will not penetrate your protective shield.

What are you waiting for? Take a stand today for righteousness' sake. Insulate yourself with the Word of God and then fight! Greater is He who is within you than he that is in the world!

Isaiah 52:12
"You shall not go out with haste, Nor go by flight;
For the LORD will go before you,
And the God of Israel will be your rear guard."

---

*J*ehovah Shammah means "the God who is there." He is there when you need Him, and He is good all the time—yesterday, today, and forever.

His angels go before you to prepare your way, and behind you to be your rear guard. He guides and provides. He leads in paths of righteousness for His namesake. He restores your soul and makes your path straight. He is as close as the mention of His name.

We serve a God who cannot fail. He makes streams in the desert and turns your darkest night into a golden day. When you are feeling alone or afraid, He is right beside you.

Have confidence in Christ and you will not be challenged by the opposition. With God on your side, all you have to do is sling the rock and the giant is going to fall!

Matthew 17:20
"Jesus said to them, 'Because of your unbelief; for assuredly,
I say to you, if you have faith as a mustard seed, you will say
to this mountain, "Move from here to there," and it will move;
and nothing will be impossible for you.'"

———————

Stop hiding from success because you're afraid to fail. Failure is a necessary part of life that can motivate you to be a better person than you ever dreamed possible. Stop fearing risk. Have faith in God. With Him all things are possible.

Yesterday's failure does not determine your future. Stop taking ownership of one day that was less than stellar, and move on. Let your scars be a reminder of things you have overcome, not things that have conquered you. The choice is yours. Have faith that God wants something better for you than what your mistakes might dictate.

If you continue to dwell on your past failures, you will never achieve tomorrow's success. It doesn't take much to believe that a great big God who has never failed you can actually take you to the place you need to be; can help you accomplish your ultimate goals, no matter how lofty.

Reach for the stars, and don't be surprised when you grab them on the way back down! God has things destined for you that are far greater than you have ever dreamed possible. Believe in God and watch the mountain of impossibility that has held you hostage begin to melt in the presence of the Lord.

Psalm 139:24
"Lead me in the way everlasting."

———————

Need direction in your life? Pray that God will open the doors you can't open and close the doors that need closing. He has a divine plan carved out just for you, a specific purpose that no one else on earth can fill.

Maybe you are in the middle of a life-altering decision and you don't know which way to turn. Seek His face, and wait. Tell Him to make the way so plain that there won't be any doubt about what you should do. And then listen when He sends the answer.

When God begins to lead you in a certain direction, don't be afraid to leave people and places behind and walk toward the brilliant future that He has crafted just for you! Sometimes He must remove certain people from your life who would keep you from your divine destiny and distract you from what He has in store.

What you walk away from can often determine what God can lead you to. Trust that He knows what is best for you, and keep marching up the path as He guides you in the way everlasting.

Psalm 1:1-2
*"BLESSED is the man Who walks not in the counsel of
the ungodly, Nor stands in the path of sinners, Nor sits in the seat
of the scornful; But his delight is in the law of the LORD,
And in His law he meditates day and night."*

When you love the world and its attractions, it will completely control you. It will affect your thought life, the words that come out of your mouth, and your actions. The world will prevent the joy of the Lord from saturating your soul because you will always be searching for a pot of gold at the end of some non-existent rainbow, chasing a fairy tale. That "grass is always greener" syndrome didn't work out so well for the Prodigal Son, and it won't work out for you; I can assure you of that.

God wants to inject your family with joy, with peace, and with love. He does not want the enemy to destroy your children, to manipulate your marriage, or to corrupt your home. If you long to know the true love of God, learn His commandments and then live by them.

The Word of God is filled with the good news of Jesus Christ. It may have been written more than 2,000 years ago, but the promises still ring true today. He is a covenant God and He changes not. If you're looking for mighty things to happen in your life—things that only God can do—begin to saturate your mind and spirit with the Word. It will refresh you in ways you never imagined possible.

The Pastor's Blessing

And now may the Lord bless you and keep you. May the Lord make His face to shine upon you and be gracious unto you, giving you His peace. May you walk in the knowledge that Jesus Christ is your Lord and Savior, that heaven is your future home, and that you have been sanctified and justified by the blood of Jesus Christ. You are wearing the robes of righteousness, the signet ring of a child of the living God, and the shoes of a son, not the bare feet of a servant. You are precious in the sight of the Lord. In Jesus' name, Amen!

John 10:10
"The thief does not come except to steal, and to kill, and to destroy.
I have come that they may have life,
and that they may have it more abundantly."

Do you have people in your life who are constantly dragging you down? Maybe they don't have anything positive to say, or they are constantly pointing out your faults. Refuse to accept an inferior role just because someone tries to assign it to you. Don't allow anyone to continually dredge up your past mistakes. These people are joy killers who only want to rob you of happiness... which they clearly don't possess.

You are a child of the King! God has designed you for greatness, not to be trampled under someone else's dream. Don't get lost beneath any poor opinions of you. That's not God's opinion. God loved you so much that He sent His only Son to die for you. He loves you!

If someone is a constant flow of negativity, distance yourself from them. Nobody needs a Negative Ned or Nellie in their life. They may be telling you how your life should be, but you don't have to listen. Rise to the destiny God has for you and enjoy being filled with the abundance of the Lord!

The joy of the Lord is your strength. Make up your mind today that no matter what comes your way, nothing is going to steal your joy.

Matthew 19:26
"Jesus looked at them and said to them,
'With men this is impossible,
but with God all things are possible.'"

———————————

God doesn't need a lot to accomplish a lot. All David had was five stones; all he needed was one.

If you feel like you are down to nothing, God is up to something. In our weakness, He shows His greatest strength, carrying us to safety when we merely call on His name.

Does it seem the only light you can see in the tunnel is on the front end of a freight train? Know that Jesus Christ, the Light of the World, can shine His radiance on the darkest situation and turn your mourning into dancing. His arms are open wide; run to Him and be safe!

If you are facing overwhelming obstacles, know that you are next in line for a promotion in the Kingdom. God is doing a good work in you, and He will not stop until He has crafted you into the perfect servant for His kingdom. He wants you to fulfill your divine destiny and to be a giant slayer. So claim your victory and start down the road of His choosing. Nothing is impossible with God!

Psalm 107:29
"He calms the storm, So that its waves are still."

Sometimes, what looks like a disappointment is simply God getting us into a position to see His greatness!

Have you recently been through something that felt like a setback? You thought things were going along just fine and all of a sudden a black thundercloud just unloaded on your day. Lightning seemed to strike out of nowhere. The bad news pelted you like hail at every possible angle.

Have faith in God! Today's storm is going to bring tomorrow's rainbow. Do not fear! The SON who shines brightest after the darkest storm has overcome the world.

How can you enjoy walking in divine health until you have understood what it means to be sick? How can you understand how great freedom is until you have been bound? How can you appreciate true joy without knowing the aching pain of tragedy?

Today, God can free you from the heavy weight on your heart. Maybe this is something you have been dealing with for years. Just ask God to set you free—to calm the waters of your stirred-up soul—and have faith that the answer is already on the way! Our God can—and will!

Psalm 35:27
"Let them say continually, 'Let the LORD be magnified,
Who has pleasure in the prosperity of His servant.'"

———◆•◆•◆———

*Y*our circumstances may not look favorable, but don't let your conditions disrupt your acceptance of God's gifts. He has made His best available to you. I challenge you to say to yourself each and every day: "By the grace of God, I am blessed and highly favored!"

When you start talking like that, demons will scatter, sickness and disease will begin to leave your body, fear and doubt will run out the back door of your house. When you proclaim that you are favored, your low self-esteem is transformed into the boldness of a lion; your timidity and insecurity vanish! You will have streams of Living Water coursing through your veins.

Favor isn't "every day is filled with sunshine and roses." Favor means you can have the peace of God as the storm rages on. It means you can walk through the fire and not get burned.

Start proclaiming His favor and watch how the peace of God begins to saturate every corner of your life. "I am blessed and highly favored!"

Isaiah 64:6
"We are all like an unclean thing, and all our
righteousnesses are like filthy rags."

"We all fade as a leaf, and our iniquities, like the wind, have taken us away."

One drop of Jesus' precious blood can remove the sins of the world. One prayer in His holy name can grant eternal salvation. That, my friend, is power.

The Kingdom of God functions on that divine power. Do you know how to tap into it? Have you ever seen it in action? It has the capability of shaking the earth to its very core! This is what you gained at Calvary.

At the Cross you traded your poverty for untold riches. You gave up hopelessness for the blessings of Abraham. You gave up your filthy rags in exchange for a robe that is whiter than snow and gained divine favor for life.

Celebrate the power and majesty of Christ Jesus, and share the wonder of His great love with those around you, especially the least deserving. Truly, none of us deserves the gifts afforded us at the Cross, but God's grace still made it possible.

Psalm 16:11
"You will show me the path of life;
In Your presence is fullness of joy;
At Your right hand are pleasures forevermore."

Make up your mind today that no matter what comes your way, nothing will steal your joy. Your attitude can dictate whether you have a good or bad day, so decide that it's going to be wonderful! Of course, difficult times come, but in His presence is fullness of joy, even if the day is a complete disaster.

No one makes it through life without a few bruises and scrapes. Falling down is never the problem... staying down is. The enemy comes to rob, to kill, and to destroy. Don't give him what he wants! When he starts telling you how horrible your life is compared to your friends and relatives, remind him that he is in charge of exactly NOTHING.

Concentrating on what you don't have or can't do is simply self-defeating behavior. Instead, focus on what you can do and what you have already accomplished by the grace of God. Life is too short to focus on the negative! So when bad news punches you in the gut and sends you reeling, come back with your boxing gloves on, ready to fight. When God is in the ring with you, no enemy can defeat you!

Isaiah 53:4-5
"Surely He has borne our griefs And carried our sorrows;
Yet we esteemed Him stricken, Smitten by God, and afflicted.
But He was wounded for our transgressions, He was bruised for
our iniquities; The chastisement for our peace was upon Him,
And by His stripes we are healed."

---

*I*f you feel rejected and betrayed, realize that Jesus has already borne your pain. Rejected by those around Him, Jesus bled and died in your place after being mocked. He was herded through streets crowded with people chanting, "Crucify Him!" and betrayed by Judas for 30 pieces of silver... then left to die by those closest to Him. From a human perspective, He knows how you feel. From a heavenly perspective, He has already conquered whatever you are facing.

When you are feeling rejected by the dearest on earth, cry out to God. He can give you peace when the burden is beyond human comprehension, and He will begin to heal that place in your heart that seems irreparably broken. He knows the pain you are suffering and has already paved the way for your complete emotional healing.

Jesus paid the full price for your pardon. He is your Savior and Redeemer. This means that regardless of your tragedy and pain, He has already paid the ultimate price. The remedy for every human problem is found at the Cross.

The Pastor's Blessing

And now may the Lord bless you and keep you. May the Lord make His face to shine upon you and be gracious unto you, giving you His peace. Lord God of heaven, mend every broken heart that has been destroyed or wounded by selfish behavior. Give us the heart of God—willing to love our sister or brother in Christ even as God loved us—and the strength each day to constantly demonstrate that love so that when the world sees our relationships, they long to be in them rather than avoid them. Heavenly Father, build up our marriages and strengthen our homes. Help us to teach another generation God's picture, the perfect vision of love. We come before Your throne and ask You to put a hedge of protection around our homes, around our marriages, around our children. In Jesus' name, Amen.

1 Samuel 17:47
"The battle is the LORD's."

———◆◆◆———

$\mathcal{R}$emember this verse the next time you feel as if you're fighting an uphill battle all alone. The battle is the Lord's and the victory is already on the way.

Without God, you can do nothing. With God, there is nothing you can't do. When you give the battle to God, supernatural things begin to happen both in the heavens above and in the earth below. As we release our problems to God, He will release angels to surround us, to protect us, and to guide us down the path of total resolution.

Are you sick in your body? He can heal you from the top of your head to the soles of your feet. Are you broken and bitter from yesterday's pain? He can restore to you what the enemy has taken, giving you finished houses and planted vineyards.

Do not be afraid of what tomorrow holds, for we know Who holds tomorrow. Take your burdens and leave them at the foot of the Cross, knowing that the very best is yet to come. We were not designed to be independent. We were designed to be dependent upon our Creator, to seek Him first. He knows your need. Now turn it over to Him and smell the sweet scent of utter victory as the Rose of Sharon completely destroys your enemies. For what Satan means for evil, God can use for His good.

Psalm 119:73
"Your hands have made me and fashioned me;
Give me understanding,
that I may learn Your commandments."

———————◆———————

You are unique. When you were born, the creativity of heaven fashioned a person the world has never seen before and will never see again. So why do you allow others to paint the picture of your identity? No one else should determine who you will be or what you can accomplish in this lifetime. Only God. He has big plans for you. Don't let anyone deter you from your true purpose.

Get up and give God the glory! Since you were created in His likeness, then truly great things are ahead. Don't let a bad day slow you down, and don't get absorbed in what's going wrong with your life. Stay focused instead on helping others, sharing the love of Christ, and winning the lost. The days of building a life around your troubles are gone. Don't whine but shine!

Ephesians 6:11
"Put on the whole armor of God, that you
may be able to stand against the wiles of the devil."

In the life of every Believer, fighting for what is good, pure, and right is a way of life. We are not called to simply take a seat and watch as the movie of our life rolls tape. We are to stand up and speak up! We are called to be the salt and light of the earth! We are told to focus on Christ! When we are intent on Him, nothing and no one can derail us from the important work He has for us to do!

What are you doing today to make a difference for the Kingdom in your heart? In your home? In your community? Start sharing the love of Jesus with those closest to you and you will be surprised at how infectious it can be!

And the Bible tells us when we have done all that we know to do, what next? Having done all... STAND!

Mark 11:22

"Jesus answered and said to them, 'Have faith in God.'"

———————

God will not allow a storm unless He has a divine purpose for it. Trust in God's faithfulness. He did not save you from last year's marriage crisis, complete financial devastation, your home foreclosure, your business implosion, a doctor's diagnosis... just to let you drown in a puddle this year. So don't make a mountain out of a molehill.

What God has done for you in the past, expect for your future. He never changes, and He has your very best in mind, wanting you and your soul to prosper.

Faith means stepping out before you know how it turns out. It means following God's will for your life, not carving out your own plan and asking God to squeeze into it. It means you are quiet, listening, attentive... and God is doing the talking, the leading, the guiding.

Delight yourself in the Lord and tell Him the desires of your heart. He is available to not only meet but greatly exceed your wildest expectations if you will simply give Him the chance to intervene on your behalf.

Colossians 3:9–10
"[You] have put off the old man with his deeds, and have
put on the new man who is renewed in knowledge
according to the image of Him who created him."

———◆———

Shake off anything or anyone that is holding you back. Make room for God to do something new in your life! Don't be afraid of change. How can you have something better unless you get rid of what you have?

Good is the enemy of better, and better is the enemy of best. Let go of what's in your hand and let God give you what's in His. It will be His firstfruits, not the rubbish you have grown accustomed to.

Insanity is doing the same thing over and over again and expecting different results. So I'm telling you, stop the insanity! If you are looking for a fresh start, let God take you in a new direction that fits the new person you are!

Clear the way for Him, and brace yourself; abundance is about to rain into every realm of your life!

John 15:11
"These things I have spoken to you, that My joy may remain in you, and that your joy may be full."

———————◆◆◆———————

*H*appiness is not dependent on the type of house one resides in; it depends on the type of person who resides there.

I have known many people living in enormous mansions that are immaculately decorated with exquisite furnishings gathered from the far corners of the world—and they are completely miserable. The joy of the Lord does not reside in their homes or their hearts.

This is a choice! You set the tone for your home by deciding who and what your priorities are. If you don't make a conscious decision to fill the rooms of your home with the love and joy of the Lord, something else will seep in... and it will not be uplifting.

Turn the TV set off and read the Word. Make God a priority in your home. Pray together as a family. Don't tuck your children into bed with video games. Joy is a choice.

Choose to serve the Lord both in and out of season and things will begin to pick up at your house. You will experience joy like never before as your cup runs over with the goodness of the Lord.

1 Thessalonians 5:24
"He who calls you is faithful, who also will do it."

Our feelings are real and they are powerful, but they are not more powerful than God and His truth.

If God has told you something is going to happen in your life, don't doubt it for one second. Noah built the ark before anyone had ever seen a drop of rain. If God is telling you to start a new season, close the door behind you and get ready for blessings to fall all around you. Great things are ahead as long as you follow His lead!

At God's word to get moving, don't look for a second opinion... If you second-guess Him, you can miss out on your blessing entirely. Seek His face and do as He says. Whether or not you "feel" like something good is going to happen, know that God will never leave you nor forsake you.

Don't base your actions on your emotions; this can lead you down a toxic path. Just stay the course that has been laid before you by the Architect of the ages.

Trust that great things are on their way to you, and enjoy the journey! God is faithful, and He will do as He says!

The Pastor's Blessing

And now may the Lord bless you and keep you. May the Lord make His face to shine upon you and be gracious unto you, giving you His peace. May God restore your confidence, so that you might walk with a supernatural strength and courage you have never known before. May God remove the barriers that are before you and open the doors that have been closed. May God send His angels before you to prepare the way so that when you arrive, everything is in divine order for your complete success. May God give to you, to your business, to your family a successor so that success can be sustained for several generations from the fruit of your labor. May the God of heaven anoint you now to be successful in all you do because the Lord delights in the prosperity of the righteous. In Jesus' name, Amen!

Ecclesiastes 3:1
"To everything there is a season,
A time for every purpose under heaven."

———— ⋅•⋅ ————

God has a perfect time for everything. Learn to wait on Him instead of constantly rushing through life. Waiting on the Lord brings Him honor and gives you divine peace. It also means that you will arrive at the perfect destination in your life, right on time. Nothing God does is by mistake or on accident; it is all by design. Trust that God has it all under control.

If you choose to complain about your life, you are essentially saying you don't trust God to take care of you. You are saying you don't trust His ability to send you what you need. Do you really think that your ideas are better than His?

Today, stop trying to knock down doors that are closed for a reason. When the timing is right, God will open the doors that are good for you, and close those you don't need to walk through. Waiting is never fun, but it is an essential skill that must be mastered in the life of every Believer who desires a deep and meaningful walk with Christ. In the end, it is our walk with Christ that will benefit us in both this life and the life to come.

Matthew 5:44
"I say to you, love your enemies, bless those who curse you,
do good to those who hate you, and pray for those
who spitefully use you and persecute you."

Keep honoring God and do what you know is good, pure, and right. Keep treating people according to the Word of God that commands us to love our neighbor as ourselves. When you do, you are making it possible for heaven to bless you and take you right where you need to be.

Don't pay attention to those around you who seem to skate through life veiled in deception and manipulation. There is no honor in that! These liars will all have their day; their ease will be over when the trumpet sounds. Instead, focus on YOU! What does God want you to do, regardless of how others are treating you or what they say behind your back? You're a child of the King! Don't worry about these people.

When someone treats you poorly, remember to leave them to the Lord. If they are doing something they shouldn't, pray about it and let God take care of it. Trust me, when God takes care of something, He takes care of it so completely that no stone is left unturned.

Rather than wasting your time on what others are up to, think on the things that are of good report and stay tuned on the Lord. When you choose to attend to what is pure, evil will have to flee. Your time will not be consumed with anger and bitterness but with the peace that passes all understanding.

1 Peter 5:6–7
"Humble yourselves under the mighty hand of God,
that He may exalt you in due time, casting all your care
upon Him, for He cares for you."

God has heard your prayers and He has a plan for you. You may not realize how close you are to your breakthrough, but hold on! Help is on the way! Just stay the course.

Don't you dare give up! When it looks like all you can do is throw your hands in the air and wave the flag of defeat, know that God is busy fighting your battle. Humbly surrender to the King of kings and you will never experience a greater victory!

The key to a rich and successful life is to cast your cares on Him. Ask Him to lead you down paths of righteousness for His name's sake, toward your very own land of promise. He will bring you to streams in the desert and quench your parched soul. Have you lost your way? No matter... you can pick up and get back on track, right where you left off. Simply ask God to point the way and make your path straight.

When you remove wickedness from your life, you are making room for God to flood your soul like never before. You are sweeping out the anxiety left behind by the enemy. The hurtful words of unworthiness that once seared your soul are washed away. Turn to the healing balm of Gilead; His touch can make you whole.

John 13:34
"A new commandment I give to you, that you love one another;
as I have loved you, that you also love one another."

No matter how many times you fail, God will always love you because God's love is not based on you... but on Him. His love is as limitless as the ocean's drops of water or the beach's grains of sand. There is no way to contain His love as it splashes over you, drenching your soul.

Do you love yourself? Do you love others? You cannot reach out and share the love of God with others until you first learn how to love yourself. Why should you share this great gift of God's love? Because we are most like Him when we love our neighbors as ourselves.

Often we judge others on their actions, while we only judge ourselves on our intentions. Give people the benefit of the doubt and apply forgiveness liberally. It is easy to condemn... but that's not our job. We don't know what anyone is going through or their particular battles. Leave those things to God.

We are called to love one another as Christ loved the church. We all fall down. We all fail and come short of the glory of God. Instead of pointing out someone else's faults, worry about your own—that should give you plenty to do.

When life knocks you down, dust yourself off, get back up, and get in the game. God's love for you is immeasurable. Get ready to dive right in and soak up every drop!

Luke 12:32
"Do not fear, little flock, for it is your Father's good pleasure
to give you the kingdom."

———————

Why are you worrying? God has already solved your problems and knows exactly where your life is headed. If you will trust Him, He will steer you in the right direction, so there is no real reason to worry!

You cannot add length to your life by worrying. If that were true, we would all be alive for centuries! The Bible tells us not to worry for good cause—God is our Provider, Defender, our Rock and Fortress, a strong tower to run into in the day of trouble.

When you made the decision to believe on the Lord Jesus Christ, you were saved. In that moment, you were granted God's entire kingdom and an eternity in heaven. Today, begin believing that all things are yours through Jesus Christ. Cast aside your cares and anxieties and follow Him to a place of secure refuge.

Psalm 27:14
"Wait on the LORD; Be of good courage,
And He shall strengthen your heart."

———◆———

Wait, I say, on the "LORD!"

Quit being discouraged over what didn't work out. It's not over until God says it's over. He may well be working behind the scenes on your behalf, beyond where your eyes can see.

Have you ever been drowning in a problem? I mean a problem so big that you just couldn't possibly swim your way out of it?

You pray and get pretty enthusiastic about it, maybe fast a few meals. Still, you feel like nothing is happening. So you call in the big guns and get your prayer partners to join you. And when nothing happens 30 minutes later, you're asking, "God, where are You?"

Waiting on the Lord is a lifelong lesson. The sooner you learn it, the better off you will be. When the time is right, God's plan will completely unfold and you will be left saying, "Aha! This is what God had intended for me all along!"

Be encouraged today. God is the Master of the "Aha" moment and He will complete the good work He has started in you.

Job 23:10
"He knows the way that I take;
When He has tested me,
I shall come forth as gold."

You may be going through a fire, but God will bring you out on the other side, better than you were before.

One year as I was traveling, I came across a goldsmith who was taking his tool filled with gold in and out of the fire. Each time he pulled the melted gold out of the flames, he would gently brush the impurities off the top layer—and back into the fire the gold would go!

I asked him how he would know when the impurities were all flushed out and the gold was ready. His reply was thought-provoking: "I place the gold in the fire until I can see my reflection in the metal."

This is what God does with us. He will continue to allow fires to come our way until we are a reflection of Him. Fires are not to resign us but to refine us.

The Pastor's Blessing

And now may the Lord bless you and keep you. May the Lord make His face to shine upon you and be gracious unto you, giving you His peace. May you walk today with divine confidence that nothing can be greater than the power of God within you, which will heal you and restore you in this day of new beginnings. The best is yet to be because the Lord is with you and no one and nothing can defeat you! In Jesus' name, Amen!

2 Chronicles 20:15
"Thus says the LORD to you: 'Do not be afraid nor
dismayed because of this great multitude,
for the battle is not yours, but God's.'"

———◦·•·◦———

*A*re people attacking you—telling you what you are incapable of doing or demeaning your value? Shake off the negative comments and hold your head high! God will promote you in spite of what anyone else says or thinks.

Many times people compensate for their own insufficiencies by attacking others, thus deflecting their own shortcomings. If they can shine the spotlight on your mistakes, then no one will look at theirs. But be sure of this: God did not design you to be a doormat! Enjoy being who you are; there is no one else on planet earth just like you. Celebrate what makes you unique... God does.

Rather than fretting, focus. Get busy on the task at hand, fully expecting the blessings of heaven to rain down on your life, today and every day.

Philippians 2:14
"Do all things without complaining and disputing."

$\mathcal{D}$on't complain about what's wrong. Be grateful for the opportunity to experience each day.

When you complain, you allow the enemy to invade your life; you make room for him to intrude and change your attitude to stinking thinking. Once you crack that door, the floodgates of negativity can burst open, allowing all forms of it to enter your home and heart.

Physicians love to treat patients with a "can do" attitude. They always fare better than those who spend their waking hours complaining.

It is the same with the Great Physician. He doesn't want to hear complaints; He wants to hear praises. He wants your life to resound with joy from one day to the next, until each year becomes a testimony of your walk with Him.

Today is a rich gift to you from God. Spend it wisely!

Luke 21:28
"Now when these things begin to happen,
look up and lift up your heads,
because your redemption draws near."

God has seen every hurt you've been through, counted every tear you've shed, recorded every injustice. And He will pay you back, restoring what has been taken so that you will dance instead of mourn.

What have you lost that has broken your heart? What battle wounds have left you reeling? Do you feel all alone?

When nobody believes in you, believe in God. He sees what others can't, and He is able to heal that place in your heart that seems irreparably broken.

When things look their worst, look up; your redemption is near. Don't listen to harsh words spoken in anger. Don't seek approval from others. Listen for the promises found in God's holy Word. He can fill the void left by others with His enormous love and never-ending mercy. His grace is sufficient for you!

2 Corinthians 13:4
"Though He was crucified in weakness, yet He lives
by the power of God. For we also are weak in Him,
but we shall live with Him by the power of God toward you."

———————

Your day of trouble will show exactly what you are made of. When you come face-to-face with opposition, do you run and hide? Or do you turn and face it head-on, bold in the greatness and might of God?

No one enjoys trouble. No one wants to face difficult circumstances. But these are just the places where God shows up and shows off. These are the places where our faith is deepened and our spirits renewed.

Our weakness puts His power on full display. Trouble strengthens you and gives you a spine of steel. It's a reminder that your strength is not enough; you need Almighty God on your side.

God sees what you are facing, and He is telling you today that He is sufficient for your every need!

Isaiah 64:8
"Now, O LORD, You are our Father;
We are the clay, and You our potter;
And all we are the work of Your hand."

Sometimes while we're waiting for our circumstances to change, God is waiting for the circumstances to change us.

If you are faced with challenges you don't understand, embrace them. Seek God's face and ask Him how to tackle the problem, knowing that if you don't do it God's way the first time, He will give you many more laps around the same mountain. It is so much easier when we listen to the still, small voice of the Holy Spirit that is guiding us toward our divine destiny.

No one enjoys trials or tribulation. No one. But each life is a culmination of good and bad, sweet and sour, heartbreak and elation. Praise the Lord in and out of season, because He is molding you to be the outstanding individual He created before time began. Challenges are not a punishment; they are a potential source of great improvement!

Numbers 23:19
"God is not a man, that He should lie...
Has He said, and will He not do?
Or has He spoken, and will He not make it good?"

———————

*R*elease your faith. God is shifting things in your favor right this very minute. Believe it and receive it in Jesus' name. This is not a gimmick but a fact.

The Bible is filled with great truths. Are you ready for favor to cover your life? It can happen right in the middle of your greatest crisis! The sun doesn't have to be shining for you to receive what God has to give!

Right now, as your day is being peppered with bad news, you might not be able to see that something wonderful is headed your way. But the Lord is already working behind the scenes to not only meet but exceed your every need.

Don't be afraid to make necessary changes! He is moving the wrong people out and the right people in. He is taking you to a higher place that will elevate you far above what any of us deserves. Release the very little that you have in your hand toward God, and He will release the entire universe in His hand toward you.

Isaiah 46:9–10
"Remember the former things of old, For I am God,
and there is no other; I am God, and there is none like Me,
Declaring the end from the beginning."

When life hits you square in the jaw, don't just lay there. Rise up! The only failure in being knocked down is staying there.

Champions get back in the game and give it their very best shot. Abraham Lincoln was defeated in multiple political races before becoming the sixteenth President of the United States. Born into poverty, he faced defeat throughout his life but remained persistent in his pursuit of excellence. He failed in multiple business ventures and even suffered a nervous breakdown; but because he never gave up, America was changed and the captives were set free by the Emancipation Proclamation.

So, what's holding you back today? Don't give up; get up! This is the day the Lord has made, and you have much to rejoice about!

If you quit now, emancipation in your own life might never be proclaimed. Get busy with God's plans for you. He has promised a bright future filled with great hope.

The Pastor's Blessing

And now may the Lord bless you and keep you. May the Lord make His face to shine upon you and be gracious unto you, giving you His peace. May you know in the depth of your soul that God sees your need and He is meeting it right now. The answer is being provided even as you read this. You will discover the answer with exceeding joy, and be blessed beyond imagination because the provisions of God are greater than what we can ask or think. In Jesus' name, Amen!

2 Corinthians 12:10
"I take pleasure in infirmities, in reproaches, in needs,
in persecutions, in distresses, for Christ's sake.
For when I am weak, then I am strong."

———————

God knows all your flaws, mistakes, and weaknesses. He also knows that you're amazing.

We were not designed to handle all of life's hardships on our own. We were created to serve. We were created to seek. We were created to be dependent on our Creator.

When we are serving God, we seek Him out first. We ask for Him to guide us in the way everlasting and to help us when life becomes difficult. And though God does chasten us at times, He always does so with our very best in mind.

We are disciplined so that we can be true disciples of the one true God, so that we can shed His light and love even though we are flawed.

Today, let your light so shine before men that all around you can see the glory of God. Give your flaws, your weaknesses, the parts of you that are broken and in need of repair, to Almighty God. Then watch as He weaves them together in a pattern that reflects His image.

Matthew 11:28
"Come to Me, all you who labor and are heavy laden,
and I will give you rest."

---

*A*re you exhausted? Is life dragging you down and you don't know where to turn? God says, "Come to Me! If you're tired, come to Me!"

Life has seasons just as the earth does. Sometimes we're in a season of great joy where all is right with our world, and sometimes everything seems to come crashing down around us as we enter a season of heart-wrenching sorrow. But we can learn as much from the sorrow as we can from the joy.

Today, if you are in the middle of a great storm, turn to the One who, with only a word, even the winds and waves obey! Find your way to the throne of grace, and He will give you rest so sweet that nothing can penetrate the protective shield of peace around you.

Give God the opportunity to invade your life with a time of great refreshing! You will be so glad you did!

Luke 9:62
"Jesus said to him, "No one, having put his hand to the plow,
and looking back, is fit for the kingdom of God."

Jesus taught the persistence principle during His time on earth. Look toward a bright future in Him, not at yesterday's mistakes. Yesterday is over! Every page of the Bible says to press on, to win, to fight back against the enemy. That day is over, and great things are just around the bend for you, child of the Most High God. Don't let anyone make you think otherwise, for greater is He that is in you than he that is in the world.

Do you think something in your past is so terrible that God can't forgive you; that you can't move forward into a life of service to the King? Put on His whole armor and act like a soldier of the living God! Rejoice in this day that you've been given and go forward to a bright tomorrow!

Give yourself the gift of forgiveness and be set free from the chains that bind you to the past. Satan would like to remind you of the times you have royally screwed up, but Jesus would like to remind you of what you have already overcome. Find freedom today in Jesus' name. No other name has such power!

2 Corinthians 5:17
"If anyone is in Christ, he is a new creation;
old things have passed away;
behold, all things have become new."

When you become a new creature in Christ, you get a new attitude. You get rid of your stinking thinking! You get new friends and a brand-new vocabulary. You start going to places you used to shy away from... like the church house. (And you will love going!)

It's okay to leave your comfort zone, to walk away from your creature habits. God is standing before you with arms open wide, ready to give you an out-of-this-world, head-to-toe makeover. Are you ready for it? Can you handle a cup full of blessings that is filled to running over?

When you fall deeply in love with Christ, you start obeying the law of God because His law is truth! If you are tired of your old life and desperately searching for hope and peace, may I present Jesus Christ of Nazareth! He is the Prince of Peace and our greatest source of hope. He is the Way, the Truth, and the Life. No one comes to the Father except through Him.

Today is the day to rededicate your life to Christ and put the past behind you. Let God arise and let His enemies be scattered. There is nothing more important than God. Get rid of the old you and move forward with the new you... fully restored and ready to grab life with gusto!

1 Peter 1:7
"That the genuineness of your faith, being much
more precious than gold that perishes,
though it is tested by fire, may be found to praise,
honor, and glory at the revelation of Jesus Christ."

God allows trials in our lives to show us His awesome power. These are not merely demonstrations to punish you but to reveal to you the unmitigated power that can be unleashed in heaven and on earth in your hour of need. Such power He has promised to share with us: what we bind on earth, He will bind in heaven. Do you have that kind of faith?

The Lord is faithful to deliver us in our day of trouble. When we are faced with complete catastrophe, He doesn't send someone else to lend a hand. He shows up Himself— God is with us!

No matter what trial you are facing, God can bring you out and give you complete victory! He does not promise us gentle winds, but He does promise a safe landing for those who call upon His name.

When you are in the minority position, if you are doing God's will, you are in the perfect spot! When everything around you is telling you to bend and bow before something (or someone) you know does not honor the Lord, God will honor you for standing up and speaking up. Faith under fire can be difficult, but the taste of victory is never sweeter than after a hard-fought battle!

Matthew 4:1
"Jesus was led up by the Spirit into the wilderness
to be tempted by the devil."

Jesus was led into the wilderness by the power of the Holy Spirit. This means that God took Him on purpose to the place where He was tempted by the prince of darkness himself. Coming out of this trial, Jesus immediately began His miracle ministry. He had been tested, and now the power and anointing of God the Father was upon Him. With this anointing He turned the world upside down.

What trial have you faced? How have you used it for the Kingdom? Have you used your testimony to change the lives of others for Christ, to win lost souls? Or do you tuck your story in your pocket and save it for yourself? The Bible says we will be known by our testimony. What are you doing with yours?

God gives us these opportunities to grow, and to lead others to Him. Let this be the day you begin sharing your own story of triumph over evil, of victory over the grave, of complete healing. Whatever your story, start telling it. Whatever your song, start singing it.

The days are short and the time of Christ's returning grows closer with each passing moment. Don't wait another day to share the good news of what He has done in your life— someone needs to hear of His amazing grace! You never know how many lives you will change by sharing your testimony. God will do the rest!

Psalm 84:11
"The LORD God is a sun and shield;
The LORD will give grace and glory;
No good thing will He withhold
From those who walk uprightly."

---

*E*veryone at some point makes wrong choices. Sometimes these choices can lead us down a path that is very painful. But His grace is greater still.

Forgive yourself. God has forgiven you, so give yourself some grace and move on. Quit talking about your past and rehashing old mistakes! God has moved on, and so should you.

Grace is God's power to forgive you, and His grace is greater than all your sin. Today is a new day! When Satan reminds you of your past, remind him of his future. God doesn't consider your past when determining your future. Your past is dead and buried in the deepest sea. Leave it there! Satan will try to use guilt as a weapon to crush your spirit, to keep you from achieving the will of God in your life. But Satan is a liar and a defeated foe. So why are you listening to him when he reminds you of your mistakes?

Forget those things that are past and move toward a bright tomorrow. It is yours in Jesus' name!

The Pastor's Blessing

And now may the Lord bless you and keep you. May the Lord make His face to shine upon you and be gracious unto you, giving you His peace. O Lord, Your grace is sufficient! Thank You that the best is yet to come in our lives! Though we can identify a barren place today, You—through the promises in Your Word—will erase it and move us to a place of great abundance in our lives. We yield our spirits to You and say, "Whatever You ask or require of us, we are honored to serve You." You will not fail us! You have not left us! You have not forsaken us! You have supplied all our needs. We are not going backward; we are claiming Your promises for a bright tomorrow in Jesus' mighty name. Amen!

Isaiah 41:13
"I, the LORD your God, will hold your right hand,
Saying to you, 'Fear not, I will help you.'"

— • —

I have often said from my pulpit, "Child of God, the Lord is on your side and everything is going to be alright." But who is God?

In Genesis, He is the Seed of the woman. In Exodus, He is the Passover Lamb. In Leviticus, He is the High Priest. In Numbers, He is the Cloud by Day and the Fire by Night.

In the Psalms, God is our Rock, our Fortress, our High Tower, our Shield and our Buckler. In the New Testament, He is the Lion of the Tribe of Judah, the Lamb of God, the Prince of Peace and the King of all kings. He is the Alpha and the Omega, the First and the Last, the One who Was and Is and ever more Shall Be.

He is the fourth Man in the fire, Immanuel—God with us, and the Hope of Glory. He is the Champion of Calvary who took away the sins of the world. I could go on for pages describing the many attributes of God the Father and His Son, Jesus Christ. But I want you to clearly understand: this is the Team standing squarely in your corner, cheering you on to victory. Face today with full confidence, knowing that victory has been secured!

Daniel 3:17–18
*"Our God whom we serve is able to deliver us from the burning
fiery furnace.... But if not, let it be known to you, O king,
that we do not serve your gods, nor will we worship
the gold image which you have set up."*

Don't think for one second that God's delays are God's denials. When the three Hebrew lads were facing a most certain death for disobeying the king, they knew that only God could save them. But this verse says that even if God did not save them, they would still honor Him and refuse to bow to the idol.

Their loyalty to God did not depend on God doing what they wanted Him to do; their commitment was unconditional. Disappointment would not lead them to disbelief.

The three Hebrew boys knew that God had the power to deliver them. If He chose not to, they wouldn't become bitter. They would die as living monuments to Him, refusing to bow to the gods of this world.

We all know how the story ends: God showed up in the fiery furnace and the Hebrew boys were saved. The king was so shocked that he ordered the entire nation to once again worship the God of Abraham, Isaac, and Jacob.

When the flames of disaster are licking at your heels, God will show up right on time. Refuse to worship worldly gods that offer riches, fame, or other fleeting forms of happiness. Feelings last but a moment. Faith is forever.

Psalm 34:17
"The righteous cry out, and the LORD hears,
And delivers them out of all their troubles."

———————

*I*f just for today... take a break from your full-time job of worrying! The world will still revolve on its axis and you might just be surprised at what else you can accomplish when you aren't fretting over things you can't control in the first place! Take off your "General Manager of the Universe" badge and relax. God has it all under control!

If God is for you, who can be against you? If your best friend is walking out the door, God is still closer than any brother. In the middle of the raging tide, He can walk on water. In your greatest day of trouble, He is still the Prince of Peace. So what are you in need of in this moment? Are your finances failing? Is your heart shattered seemingly beyond repair? Cry out to Him, and let His sweet fragrance fill your life.

When you leave your problems in God's hands, His peace will surround you like air. Let your heart rejoice in Christ your Savior, for your Deliverer has come.

Matthew 6:25-27

"I say to you, do not worry about your life, what you will eat or what you will drink; nor about your body, what you will put on. Is not life more than food and the body more than clothing? Look at the birds of the air, for they neither sow nor reap nor gather into barns; yet your heavenly Father feeds them. Are you not of more value than they? Which of you by worrying can add one cubit to his stature?"

———————

The Bible says that worrying is a sin. Worry actually means there is something you can't control, some happening over which you cannot have your way. In reality, it is a personal distrust and irritation with God.

In Matthew 6, God tells us five separate times not to worry! The Bible is the owner's manual to the soul, the complete blueprint by which to live your life. It says that we were created for worry-free living. We were designed for a life without tension, turmoil, and Tylenol.

So what is weighing you down today? Why have you shifted your focus to something completely out of your control? Give it to God! Jesus has already defeated every enemy we will ever face. The total victory is ours over the world, the flesh, and the devil. They are powerless against us!

Today, I encourage you to begin a new, carefree lifestyle. Allow Jesus to lead the way, and you'll learn what unadulterated joy is all about.

Isaiah 40:31
"Those who wait on the LORD
Shall renew their strength;
They shall mount up with wings like eagles,
They shall run and not be weary,
They shall walk and not faint."

---

*A*dversity comes to all men and women alike; it is not a respecter of persons. If you have a pulse, then you've seen your own personal snapshot of adversity. Perhaps your encounter with adversity is like a sequence of novels: you wonder if it will ever end! Guess what? There's more coming your way!

Gold is tried in fire; the righteous are tried in the furnace of adversity. The brightest crowns being worn in heaven today have been tried and polished, glorified through the furnace of tribulation.

So, are you in the middle of the fire? Congratulations! God has a blessing coming your way. Stand firm!

Adversity doesn't make you weak or strong; it reveals who you really are deep down inside when nobody's looking. Wait upon the Lord and He will sustain you. He will renew you. His strength will be with you until your last breath on this earth!

Psalm 144:15
"Happy are the people whose God is the LORD!"

———————

*W*orry is trust in the unpleasant assurance that disaster is looming. Worry is belief in defeat and despair.

It is a polluted stream that surges through your mind, drowning out all sources of optimism. It is interest paid on trouble before it happens. Have you ever noticed that when you anticipate how horrible something is going to be... it turns out to not be as awful as you thought?

Most of the trouble we expect in our lives never comes. So why do we waste so much time fearfully awaiting the proverbial drop of the other shoe? If we spent that much energy being joyful in the Lord, our lives would be contagious.

Today, I encourage you to be happy with who you are and where you are in life. If you don't like something, change it. Don't waste your time worrying about it.

You are a unique individual. You are God's masterpiece! Live like the heir to the throne that you are, and enjoy each day for the true gift that it is! You are an ambassador for Christ!

1 Corinthians 4:20
"The kingdom of God is not in word but in power."

———— ◆◆◆ ————

*P*ower is exciting, and it changes things! Jesus turned water into wine, made the lame to walk, walked on the water, and made the blind to see. He raised the dead and fed the multitudes with one boy's sack lunch.

The Bible says that the Kingdom of God comes with great power, and that all power is given unto God in both heaven and on earth. We can tap into this unlimited power for our own lives. What are you in need of today?

Jesus has power over sickness and disease, power over demon spirits. He has power over the circumstances in your life, power to save you from drowning in your own personal brand of misery and despair.

He can conquer the fear that controls you and crush the enemies that torment you. He can break the chains of addiction that bind you. Today, you can be set free from anything that is keeping you from fulfilling the will of God in your life if you will only ask in faith believing. Then watch the mighty hand of God take over and clean house!

The Pastor's Blessing

And now may the Lord bless you and keep you. May the Lord make His face to shine upon you and be gracious unto you, giving you His peace. That which You have done for us in the past, heavenly Father, we claim in faith, believing that You will do it again! We receive a new dawn and a new direction, knowing that You are making a way where there seems to be no way. Your lovingkindness shines down on us. Today, You will go before us and lead us down paths of righteousness for Your namesake. Amen.

Psalm 40:2
"He also brought me up out of a horrible pit,
Out of the miry clay, And set my feet upon a rock,
And established my steps."

———————

God can open the doors of opportunity that have been closed. He can bring you the perfect companion to spend the rest of your life with. He can lift you from the black hole of defeat and plant your feet on the Solid Rock. He can reverse your finances and put a song in your heart when the burden seems too great to bear.

You are not a second-class citizen in the Kingdom of heaven! You are riding with a first-class ticket paid for in advance at Calvary's Cross. Lift your hands and rejoice! You're not going to just get through this by the skin of your teeth; you will be more than a conqueror through Jesus Christ when the dust settles!

God wants your heart to be filled with joy unspeakable, not to be troubled! Ask your heavenly Father to fill that void in your life, to meet your need... then you get ready for the heavens to open up and rain blessings on your parade! God delights in giving heaven's very best to His children!

Psalm 100:5
"The LORD is good; His mercy is everlasting,
And His truth endures to all generations."

---

*Y*ou have to believe that no matter what has come against you, no matter how unfair it was, things are shifting in your favor.

Do you feel like you are facing giants? Are you completely alone? Blinded by a depression so deep that you can't see your way through? Hold on! Help is on the way! When you are down to nothing, God is up to something with mercy that never quits and truth that never fails!

Remember the old donkey that was tossed into the well? Everyone heaped garbage on top of him... until one day he walked on top of the garbage and was freed from the well. When God's favor is on you, nothing and no one can take it from you. Be strong and courageous! God is on your side and great things are headed your way!

If you have just run into a brick wall, this is only a temporary setback. Ask God to help you over it and rejoice by choice! Once you've ascended that wall, you'll see: a new day has dawned.

Acts 10:38
"God anointed Jesus of Nazareth with the Holy Spirit
and with power, who went about doing good
and healing all who were oppressed
by the devil, for God was with Him."

Jesus' entire ministry can be described in one sentence: He went about doing good. Can the same be said of you?

What you do for someone else, God will bring back to you pressed down, shaken together, and running over. If you really want to be blessed of God, find someone who needs help and then help them! The blessings that will be returned to you will be exponential, and will come your way when you need them most.

Don't be afraid to get your hands dirty—we are most like God when we serve. We serve God when we help others.

You don't have to like someone to meet their need. Reaching out to show God's love in action is the best way to "tell" someone about God. They will know we are Christians by our love.

This year, offer the love of God to others like never before. Our world is hurting and in need of a revival. If you share this greatest of gifts with just one person, and they share it with one more, think of the number of lives you can affect by the love of God, which knows no bounds.

Ezekiel 34:26
"I will make them and the places all around My hill a blessing;
and I will cause showers to come down in their season;
there shall be showers of blessing."

If God has a job for you to do, get busy doing it! He will give you whatever you need to complete the task, with room enough to spare!

He has a specific purpose for you that no one else can fulfill. The place of God's power is released in the place of God's purpose. When you find where God wants you to be, He will turn His almighty power on right there.

It may be a place that is completely out of your norm, completely out of your comfort zone. Guess what? Make yourself comfortable! There is no better place to be than right where God wants you. He will use you for His glory right where He plants you. His grace will carry you through and you will be blessed because you followed His lead.

Are you tired of running around in circles while accomplishing absolutely nothing? Live the dream God has given you. Therein is the true meaning of fulfillment.

Proverbs 23:7
"As he thinks in his heart, so is he."

———◆◈◆———

*B*e like King Solomon: he recognized that spiritual strength is far greater than physical strength. With spiritual strength you can conquer your greatest enemy without lifting a finger! God will do your heavy lifting.

What are your thoughts? Are they focused on bitterness and resentment, or on goodness and lovingkindness? Do you reach out to help others or strive to make a difference for the Kingdom?

Your thoughts are heard in heaven. When no one else knows what's going on in your pretty little head, God does. The greatest battlefield upon which you will ever fight is your mind. It's a fight you can't afford to lose.

What are you feeding your mind? Do you watch endless hours of television and read one or two Bible verses each week while you grace the church house with your presence?

You probably know that whatever you put into your body will determine your physical fitness, your overall strength. Do you take care of your physical self? In like measure, you need to care for your spiritual self. The Bible commands us to control our thoughts and tells us that we are responsible for what we think. What you put into your system is exactly what you will get out. Are you storing up Bible verses to replay in your mind the next time you come face-to-face with the enemy? Or are you too busy looking at pornographic images?

Today and every day, fill your mind with thoughts that are good and pure. If you want to live a joy-filled life of service to the King, open the Word and absorb the truths found inside. It will revolutionize your life!

Psalm 62:8
"Trust in Him at all times, you people;
Pour out your heart before Him;
God is a refuge for us."

———◆◆———

Start believing the verse that says that ALL things are possible to those who believe. Why? Because it's true! If you think you can, you will. On the other hand, if you think you can't, you won't. If you think you're beaten, you are. If you think you'll fail, you will.

If you're in a storm, keep rowing. If you're in a fight, fight to win. If you've been knocked down, you're not defeated until you stay down.

Trust in the Lord at all times and fight the good fight of faith. Wipe the mud off your face and get up! Everyone faces difficulties. Behind closed doors everyone has problems. So stop thinking how easy your neighbor's life looks and start focusing on your own victory that is just around the bend.

God sees what you're going through. He knows your need and your heart. His deepest desire is for you to become a runaway success story. He even sent His Son to redeem you from your past so that your future could be ridiculously bright! So why do you remain in a rut, focused only on the negative? Move forward in faith! Open the Bible and invite the God of all hope to invade your life today. Victory awaits in Jesus' name!

Colossians 3:2
"Set your mind on things above,
not on things on the earth."

---

*H*aving our minds set on eternal things gives us a sure source of confidence that will endure no matter what life throws our way. Your attitude embraces faith or wallows in doubt; it celebrates victory or settles for self-pity. Have you ever noticed how long your bad day lasts when you begin to feel sorry for yourself? Self-pity, anger, bitterness, anxiety, fear, doubt, and other toxic emotions can take on a life of their own if you allow the enemy to steal your joy and set the tone for your day.

Satan always attacks anyone God is getting ready to promote. If you are under fire, it means your promotion is on the way! Don't get so discouraged that you miss out on the great things God has in store for you. Don't let the enemy steal your blessing! Remember, a tiny acorn must push through the hardened ground before it can become a mighty oak tree.

Struggle is living proof that you haven't given up and the enemy hasn't won. Today's tragedies will become tomorrow's triumphs. And tomorrow's triumphs can turn into testimonies that will change the most unsuspecting person's life for the better. Allow God to have His way in you, and your trials will mold you into someone who can be used to shine His light in an otherwise dark world.

The Pastor's Blessing

And now may the Lord bless you and keep you. May the Lord make His face to shine upon you and be gracious unto you, giving you His peace. May you walk in the confidence that You and God are a majority in any crisis in which you find yourself. The victory is already yours in Jesus' name! Stand upon the Word of God, for it is eternal and unchanging, Holy Spirit-inspired, the inerrant truth that will never fail you! Hallelujah to the Lamb of God!

Philippians 4:4
"Rejoice in the Lord always.
Again I will say, rejoice!"

———————

*H*ave you ever noticed how worry comes at a bad time—generally at a time of crisis? Just when you need a clear mind and steady nerves to make a great decision... here comes your old pal Worry!

Like a dark cloud to hide the sun, worry drains you of all creative ability. Worry robs you of rest and sends your heart rate soaring. It's not what you're eating; it's what's eating you!

Today, God is reminding you, "I am from everlasting to everlasting. I have defeated your greatest enemies in the past and will continue to fight your battles in the future. Your problems have already been solved. Rejoice and be exceedingly glad! For greater am I, the One who is in you, than he that is in the world!"

Do you feel alone and lost, walking through the deepest crevice you have ever traveled? He is already there. Rejoice! Are you on the mountaintop? Rejoice! The Bible says a merry heart doeth good like a medicine. When you rejoice, you are allowing the Great Physician to apply the balm of Gilead on whatever ailments you have.

Decide today to REJOICE by choice!

Romans 5:3-4
"Not only that, but we also glory in tribulations,
knowing that tribulation produces perseverance;
and perseverance, character; and character, hope."

Persistence, strength, and endurance... they're what the Bible is about. Winners never quit, and quitters never win!

Is what you're doing meeting resistance? If not, it isn't worth doing. Without the resistance of water, a ship cannot float. Without the resistance of air, a plane cannot fly. Without the resistance of gravity, you cannot walk.

If you're up against a wall, climb over it. Dig under it. Go around it. Get a truckload of TNT and blow it up! But don't ever think about quitting. Persistence is why the turtle won the race.

You may not look like the most equipped person for the job, but in spite of all the odds stacked against you, being persistent means you are willing to go the distance and do what God asks you to do. If God gives you a task, just get started. He will equip you along the way. And remember, if you are willing, He is able. Press on, and as the struggle continues, you'll be surprised at how the depths of your character get revealed.

The God of all hope can mold you and make you into someone who can withstand the test. You will go from mama's little biscuit eater to a fighting machine, ready to tackle anything the devil throws your way with a smile on your face and a song in your heart.

Matthew 10:22
"He who endures to the end will be saved."

———◈———

*Y*our strength in heaven is not measured by what you can do. Your strength is measured by how you endure the weaknesses of others. Think about that for a second. Adversity is an opportunity for those who have the mind of Christ. Why? Because adversity shows what you are really made of; it reveals your true character.

A rubber band is effective only when it's stretched. A kite flies against the wind. God will not use you until He puts you through the furnace and sees how you react. With the mind of Christ, however, you are victorious, so refuse to be intimidated!

Endure the road that has been set before you. His Word promises you will be greatly rewarded if you faint not. The race may look long and difficult from your vantage point today, but I encourage you to stay in it. The splendor of heaven will be so worth it for those who endure to the end.

Isaiah 61:3
"To console those who mourn in Zion,
To give them beauty for ashes, The oil of joy for mourning,
The garment of praise for the spirit of heaviness...
that He may be glorified."

The test of your attitude is seeing what it takes to stop you. Do you give up easily? Or when tragedy strikes, do you grab your boxing gloves and fearlessly run to face your opponent, knowing that if God be for you, no one dare be against you?

At some point in life, people are going to throw trash your way. They will try to dump their garbage on you. But you are a child of the Most High God! Use the garbage they are throwing at you as a stepping-stone toward your own spiritual destiny.

Don't hang onto the negativity they pelt you with. Find the promises God has given you in His Word and hold them tight until you cross the finish line. Even if you feel like you aren't reaching the level of success you're striving for, do everything as unto the Lord, giving it your all. He will take your simple actions, and turn them into a beautiful symphony.

Colossians 3:17
"Whatever you do in word or deed,
do all in the name of the Lord Jesus,
giving thanks to God the Father through Him."

God will not judge you in eternity for what others do wrong, but He will reward you for what you do right. People are unreasonable. They're illogical. They're self-centered. Love them anyway.

If you do good, people will accuse you of being selfish and having ulterior motives. But do good anyway. Honesty and frankness make you vulnerable. Be honest and frank anyway. Your kindnesses today will be forgotten tomorrow. Still, get up each day and give it your best! The biggest people with the best ideas can be shot down by the smallest people with the tiniest minds. Think big anyway. What you spend years building may be destroyed in a minute. Go ahead and build.

Give the world the best you have and someone is going to criticize you. It's okay—give your best anyway. With the help of Jesus Christ, none of this is impossible for you!

James 1:2–4
"My brethren, count it all joy when you fall into various trials,
knowing that the testing of your faith produces patience.
But let patience have its perfect work, that you may be
perfect and complete, lacking nothing."

One year when I was visiting Hebron, Israel, I came across a potter who was diligently working with a lump of red clay on his wheel. When he started, the clay certainly didn't look like much. The potter continued to manipulate the clay, doing his very best to morph it into the desired shape. Then the clay was placed on a tray and shoved into the fire. After a few moments, he brought the hot clay out of the kiln and thipped the end of it with his finger. This process of placing the clay pot into the fire was repeated several times, so I had to ask: "How many times will you thip the edges? When will the pot be complete?" The potter said, "I keep testing the clay until the time comes when I thip the edges and it sings."

This is a lesson we can all stand to learn. When God hands us a trial, it is our turn to sing. Not whine, just shine.

The trial you are facing is taking you to the perfect testimony. When the Master Potter starts thipping you along your rough edges, just do your best Pavarotti imitation and give God the glory. He is doing great things with your life.

1 Chronicles 16:34
"Oh, give thanks to the LORD, for He is good!
For His mercy endures forever."

———————

Sometimes people have trouble remembering the goodness of God. They have one bad day and think the buzzards are circling.

I encourage you today to remember God's amazing grace. Remember when you were lost in sin, and the loving hand of God reached down into the gutter where you were and snatched you out. He washed you in His precious blood, redeemed you, and set you free. Angels wrote your name in the Lamb's Book of Life and you received the certificate that guaranteed eternal life. Do you remember that day of joy?

Remember the day the doctor came into your hospital room and told you there was no medical hope. Then the Great Physician walked in and His healing power surged from the crown of your head to the soles of your feet. Remember when your marriage was falling apart at the seams and the God of all hope reached down and mended your hearts.

Choose today to give God thanks for the good things He has done instead of reminding Him of what still needs to be taken care of. While there is air in your lungs, use it to glorify His holy name!

The Pastor's Blessing

And now may the Lord bless you and keep you. May the Lord make His face to shine upon you and be gracious unto you, giving you His peace. May you have the peace that the world can't give. May you live with joy that is unspeakable and full of glory, knowing that you are sons and daughters of the Most High God. May you come to know that where your foot falls, God goes with you. The power of God's Word lives in you because Christ your Savior lives in you. Let this week's battles turn to triumph as every enemy is defeated! In Jesus' mighty name, Amen!

Psalm 145:18
"The LORD is near to all who call upon Him,
To all who call upon Him in truth."

———————

We serve the God who gave us the awesome power of prayer as a means of direct communication with Him. All we need to do is ask. That's it.

There are people who would give a fortune to be able to talk to the President for just a few minutes, but you have the opportunity to talk directly to the King of kings and Lord of lords for as long as you please. And best of all, He hears your every word.

Today is the day and right now is the time. Whatever you are needing, call upon His mighty name and know that it shall be done in Jesus' name! Your human mind cannot begin to grasp the great things He can do, if you will only free Him to have His way in your life.

Proverbs 8:35
"Whoever finds me finds life,
and obtains favor from the LORD."

———————

*Y*our wisdom can become intellectual idolatry.

The Bible says that God's Word is truth. If you believe anything beyond the Word of God, you are investing in a lie, plain and simple. If you are a Believer, every answer you need for your life is found in the Bible. Don't lean on your own understanding; lean on what God tells you is true.

Fear and doubt can sway you in the wrong direction and blow you off course. Hold tight to the truth found in God's Word. Cling to it like a life vest on a sinking ship when the storm is raging, and know that the promises found within the Sacred Text are always true. The Bible's truths will not only set you free but can navigate a course that will make you a success story that shines light on the Savior... on your Source.

Right now, what you see in front of you is not the whole picture. Only God knows what is coming your way. Trust that He knows what is best, and continue seeking His will. He will never lead you in the wrong direction!

Jeremiah 9:24
"Let him who glories glory in this, That he understands and knows Me, That I am the LORD, exercising lovingkindness, judgment, and righteousness in the earth. For in these I delight,' says the LORD."

————◆◉◆————

There is a divine spark in you that can only be satisfied by the presence of God.

A bird is satisfied with last year's nest. A dog is satisfied to chew on an old, dry bone. A cow is satisfied to chew on its cud. But the only thing that will satisfy you is to be in the presence of the living God. If you don't know Him, please call our prayer line today at 800-854-9899 and we will be happy to lead you in a prayer that can grant you eternal salvation. It is never too late. No matter who you are or where you've been... it is never too late.

You will never be satisfied until you surrender to Christ. He's the only one who can bring you true joy in the midnight hour and the peace that surpasses all understanding. He knows every thought, every word, every deed. And He loves you beyond comprehension.

He can touch the area of your life that needs it most and bring you utter peace of mind. If you are scrambling for an answer to anything, stop your scrambling and look up. Jesus Christ IS the answer. He is the Source of your greatest success, and His lovingkindness is greater than life!

John 15:5
"I am the vine, you are the branches.
He who abides in Me, and I in him, bears much fruit;
for without Me you can do nothing."

⸺⸺⸺◆⸺⸺⸺

When God created plants, He spoke to the ground and plants came forth. As long as plants stay in contact with the dirt, they live. If you remove the plants from the soil, they immediately begin to wither.

When God created you, He breathed His Spirit inside you. As long as you stay connected to Him, you will thrive—you can grow to become anything God wants you to be. But the moment you decide you no longer need God, you will begin to shrivel like a plant plucked from the rich soil. And when the branch is separated from the vine, the life begins to slowly leak out of it until one day there is no life left.

If you have a dream in your heart, today is the day to tap into the Source and start making that dream a reality. Sing your song. Beat your drum loudly for all to hear. Make today the very best day you can and blossom with all you have.

We are not promised tomorrow. Stay rooted in Jesus and He will send you rain in the drought when all those around you are in need. As long as you're connected to the living Vine, your future will shine!

Matthew 6:9–13

"In this manner, therefore, pray: Our Father in heaven, Hallowed be Your name. Your kingdom come. Your will be done On earth as it is in heaven. Give us this day our daily bread. And forgive us our debts, As we forgive our debtors. And do not lead us into temptation, But deliver us from the evil one. For Yours is the kingdom and the power and the glory forever. Amen."

Until the day she passed from this life to the next, my mother would recite the Lord's Prayer every night. She taught this prayer to us at home at a very young age. She then taught my children this prayer, along with many fully animated Bible stories, in her kitchen when they would visit. In her final days on this earth she would ask her great-grandchildren, "Do you know the Lord's Prayer?" When they would nod, she would say in her not-so-shy manner, "Well, let's hear it!" She knew there is power in prayer, and my mother was a Grade-A prayer warrior!

Do you know where to start today in your conversation with God? Start with the Lord's Prayer. Get to know God like He's your best friend. Call upon His mighty name; He tore the temple veil in two to make sure we knew: we have an all-access pass to the throne room of God Himself.

When Jesus walked this earth, He didn't teach His disciples to preach, but He did teach them how to pray. When you pray, you unleash the power of heaven on this earth. Demons quake and angels are put to flight.

If you aren't utilizing prayer in your daily life, you are missing out on one of God's greatest gifts to His children. Prayer is communion with God. It is unleashing heaven's best on your life. It is keeping your enemies at bay. It is fighting your battles in the heavenlies. It is a tool like no other. If you don't know how to pray, start here: "Our Father in heaven, Hallowed be Your name..."

John 10:14
"I am the good shepherd; and I know My sheep,
and am known by My own."

God Almighty, the Creator of heaven and earth, wrote the Bible to give you an inside peek at who He is and what He's all about. His detailed love-letter invites you to know Him on an intimate level and be His ambassador to the world. The more you know about Him, the deeper your relationship with Him and the more you can share His love with others.

God calls you to be His own. Whatever you ask in His name, He will do it. When your enemies come against you, He will scatter them to the four corners of the earth.

When I was traveling through Israel on one occasion, a large number of sheep were blocking the road. How we were ever going to maneuver a car through the mud and around the sheep without running them over, we didn't know. Thankfully, their shepherds saw us approaching, and each began to call their herds. In that moment, three different flocks of sheep immediately began walking toward their individual shepherds. Why? Because they knew their master's sound.

Not a moment slips by that you aren't at the forefront of God's mind. But do you know the sound of His voice? Do you listen when He leads you down paths of righteousness? Learn to listen! He might just be leading you out of harm's way.

Luke 10:19
"Behold, I give you the authority to trample on serpents
and scorpions, and over all the power of the enemy,
and nothing shall by any means hurt you."

———— ◆·◆·◆ ————

What do you want to accomplish this week, this month, this year... over the course of your lifetime? Write it down, then get ready! Because the moment you write down what you want God to do in your future, fear will be the first guest to come knocking on the door of your soul. Fear will say, "Hey! You're thinking way too big here! Be reasonable!" Another voice will tell you, "You're not worthy of that! Who do you think you are?"

What's the answer? When fear knocks at the door, send faith to answer. Faith will respond by saying that you are a child of the living God, royalty sanctified and purified by the blood of Jesus Christ, with all authority in His name to have whatever the Bible says you can have and be whatever the Bible says you can be!

If you don't already have one in place, start constructing a clear plan for what you and God are going to accomplish together, knowing that all things are possible to them that believe.

The Pastor's Blessing

And now may the Lord bless you and keep you. May the Lord make His face to shine upon you and be gracious unto you, giving you His peace. Let the Word of truth be the seed that God uses to bring a barn-bursting harvest into our lives as we walk in paths of righteousness for His name's sake. Because He has redeemed us, we are more than conquerors! We have overcome the world, the flesh, and the devil. So let us live in victory, knowing that beyond a shadow of any doubt, we are triumphant because of what the Lord has done. In Jesus' name, Amen!

Matthew 21:22
"Whatever things you ask in prayer,
believing, you will receive."

I'm sure you believe that God can do anything. But do you believe that God will do it for you?

God is looking for a time and a people who will give Him the opportunity to demonstrate His majestic power. Right now I want you to see the Lord coming into your life and telling you to not only write out your vision for the future but to start working toward the goals you have set forth. This vision should include you and God walking in harmony according to His laws and precepts.

There is no obstacle you are facing that God's promises cannot conquer. There is no valley so deep that God cannot guide you through. So, get started! Don't look through the eyes of fear or the flesh. Look through the eyes of faith: See health where there was sickness. Gain where there was lack. Life where there was death.

I want you to see a new dawn replacing the darkness that has overshadowed your hopes for so long. I want you to see God restoring to you what Satan has stolen. I want you to see depression being crushed in your life and joy sweeping over you like the sunshine after a storm.

Get excited about what God has in store for you! Make your plan and watch as He helps you unfold greatness in your life on the grandest scale!

1 Corinthians 13:13
"And now abide faith, hope, love, these three;
but the greatest of these is love."

---

*G*od has given us three great treasures: faith, hope, and love. These treasures will give you self-confidence to try again when you have failed miserably. These treasures will give you the ability to win when the odds are stacked against you. These treasures will give you the capacity to not only dream the impossible dream but to achieve it.

Hope is God's gift to every Believer. Whatever you place your hope in (whether a person or things) will determine the validity of your hope. Is your hope in God? Or in the things of this world? God has tailor-made plans for you, plans that expose His unsearchable riches.

Does that sound like something you might be interested in? Then have faith in God, our greatest Source of hope when the going gets rough. Above all, share the love of Christ with those around you. Love your neighbor as yourself.

God loved you so much that He sent His only Son to die in your place. Don't keep it to yourself—give it away! There is no greater love!

Psalm 28:7
"The LORD is my strength and my shield;
My heart trusted in Him, and I am helped;
Therefore my heart greatly rejoices,
And with my song I will praise Him."

When you really know Jesus, the joy of the Lord is your strength and song. You will have faith that is infectious, that generates enthusiasm, when others would lose heart. Do you have this joy in the battle today?

Are you facing trials in your life? Have they caught you by surprise? Maybe you feel like you were run over by a truck that then backed over you to finish the job. What does the Word say about that? Be patient and continue praying. Your answer will come.

With the Lord as your Shield and Defender, taking things in your own hands is the worst mistake you could make. God sees your position in the battle, He has His eye on the enemy, and He knows exactly what you need. Hold your ground and don't shrink from the battle. His help will come at the appointed time.

Psalm 3:3
"You, O LORD, are a shield for me,
My glory and the One who lifts up my head."

———❖———

*P*raise God, the Glory and the Lifter of your head. Praise Him for the good things in your life and for the trials. He alone is worthy! When you begin to praise God, the rest of the world just melts away. The evil of the day moves into the background as God takes center stage.

You have been placed on this earth with a divine purpose. You have a destiny that no one else can fulfill. You are unique! You are blessed and highly favored of God! You can accomplish more in one hour with God's favor than most people can in a lifetime.

It's not how long you live but how strong you live. Joseph went from the jailhouse to the penthouse in one day. He found great favor with both God and man. Are you looking for God's favor in your own life? Take advantage of the Holy Spirit's anointing and tap into the Source of all life, knowing that every good and perfect thing comes from above.

You are called with a holy calling. The vision you have for your life is inspired by the fire of hope, which comes from God's anointing. This hope should impassion you to work with God to reach your divine destiny. Go after it with your eye on the prize, for nothing is impossible with God!

Joshua 1:8

"This Book of the Law shall not depart from your mouth, but you shall meditate in it day and night, that you may observe to do according to all that is written in it. For then you will make your way prosperous, and then you will have good success."

———◆◆———

$\mathcal{K}$ing Solomon said whoever is in love with money never has enough. Surely, the person who loves wealth is never satisfied with his income or his possessions.

So what is success according to God? Success is not money. It's not power, because absolute power corrupts absolutely. Adolf Hitler had great power, but he was not successful.

Success is not reaching a goal. Most people have what I call "Destination Disease." They believe that if they can arrive at a certain place in their lives (such as being named the president of their company or living the life of a millionaire), then they will be successful. Nothing could be further from the truth. Success is not a destination; it's a journey. Achieving a goal doesn't guarantee contentment.

Make it your goal to seek God's will for your life. In His presence your soul will be satisfied. Walking hand-in-hand with the Savior, even during times of unspeakable sorrow, is our only guarantee of knowing true joy.

Meditate on His Word, and God will direct you down paths of righteousness. You will never regret a single day spent in His presence.

Psalm 32:7
"You are my hiding place; You shall preserve me from trouble;
You shall surround me with songs of deliverance."

———— ◆ ————

*H*ave you ever had a really bad day? A day where you wish you could just run and hide somewhere? Well, you're in good company! Most of us have been there. And if we haven't been there recently, we are surely on the way to our next crisis.

Just before the Christmas of 1776, George Washington had an entire week that was going poorly, to put it mildly: the Continental Army had to win the war, or England's king would hang him and his officers when spring rolled around.

So what did he do? He rode his horse out into the woods of Valley Forge and knelt down in the bitter cold snow. He then prayed to God that this great nation would long endure and that his volunteer squadrons would win the battle.

By the end of that prayer, Washington felt renewed enough to head back and meet with his leaders, giving them a token that said, "Victory or death!" He didn't worry about the criticism surrounding him, or the impending threat of death. Washington trusted in Almighty God to see him through overwhelming odds and became one of the greatest leaders this country has ever known.

When your day of trouble arrives, get down on your knees. The same God who watched Washington kneel in the snow sees you kneeling beside your bed. He is not a respecter of persons and He will preserve you just as he did the Continental Army. Nothing can shorten His arm—He can reach you just where you are, delivering you from even the greatest foe.

1 John 3:18
"My little children, let us not love in word or in tongue,
but in deed and in truth."

———◆•◆•◆———

The message of God's love is urgent for your personal survival and for your family. If you want to thrive as a unit and be salt and light to the world (as we are called to do), you need a joy infusion.

What are you doing to show the love of the Lord to those around you? Love is not what you say, love is what you do. Talk is cheap. Don't tell someone you love them; show them!

God's love is a Divine flood that soaks into every fiber of your being! The Bible describes it as a love that overflows.

God loved you enough to send His Son to be born in a cave with stinking animals, to endure years of hatred and scorn, and to finally end up on Golgotha's Cross. He did this, not because He had to but because that's how much He loves you!

Don't be afraid to show those around you the love of the Lord. Go out of your way for people. Help others in their hour of need. It won't tarnish your image if you actually lend a hand once in a while, for this is when you are most like Christ.

The Pastor's Blessing

And now may the Lord bless you and keep you. May the Lord make His face to shine upon you and be gracious unto you, giving you His peace. Walk in this divine assurance: that the victory is already yours, your enemies have been defeated, the answers are already on their way. The Lord of heaven is the God of all gods and there is none like unto Him, not in the heavens above or on the earth below. From everlasting to everlasting, He is God and He will demonstrate Himself to be a miracle-working God in your life. In Jesus' name, Amen!

Philippians 4:13
"I can do all things through Christ who strengthens me."

———— ·•·•· ————

$\mathcal{I}$ want you to transform your attitude from "I can't" to "I will by the grace of God." Your Father in heaven is all-powerful and He deeply desires to give you the very best. In order to receive it, you need to anticipate that you will receive His best. If you think you are going to succeed, you will. If you think you are going to fail, you will. So, focus on achieving excellence in all that you do, and get ready to loose the floodgates of rich success!

Our majestic God has promised to each and every one of us a life without limits. How can we, as mere humans, even begin to mentally grasp the greatness of God? Right now I want you to remove from your mind anything that would limit Him, anything that would limit His power in any way. And then you are only just beginning to understand how truly awesome He really is.

Understanding that He can help you achieve any goal you set your mind to, what would you do if you knew you couldn't possibly fail? God is on your team! What will you do? You have absolutely no limitations, so don't adopt a defeatist mentality. The minute those thoughts flood your mind, your success goes right down the drain.

What happens when someone harms one of your children? When someone says or does something unkind to them? You unleash heaven and earth to make it right, to get them what they need, to come face-to-face with their enemy. God does the same thing for His own children, only His resources are limitless.

Exodus 2:5
"Then the daughter of Pharaoh
came down to bathe at the river."

———————

Let me give you the secret to success in one sentence: Find out what God wants done, and do that. Because if God tells you to do it, He will bless it. It's guaranteed to work! The word "impossible" is simply not in His vocabulary.

When Pharaoh's daughter went to bathe in the river, she saw a basket containing baby Moses in the reeds. She walked into the water as far as she could go and stretched her arm out, but she could not reach the basket. Hebrew scholars say that God supernaturally extended her arm so that she could pull the basket from the reeds.

The point is, when you are doing the will of God, you go just as far as you can go. Wade into the water until you're as deep as you can get on your own. Stretch your arm as far as you can stretch it, and if it needs to go farther, God will extend your arm for you, reaching that blessing and dragging it back to you.

Why? Because there is no limitation with God.

James 2:17
"Thus also faith by itself,
if it does not have works, is dead."

---

*Y*ou will never possess what you do not pursue. You can't launch into the deep and stay on the beach. You cannot accomplish a great dream without taking action.

In the Bible there are two kinds of people: dreamers and doers. Do you just dream, or actually "do"?

Maybe you've dreamed for years but have never taken the first step toward accomplishing your dream. I challenge you today to get off the beach and get into the water. Start swimming toward your objective. Go as far as you can go, and God will do the rest.

God is waiting to bless you with blessings you can't begin to comprehend. Turn Him loose and your life will soar on the wings of eagles. The only thing stopping you from achieving absolute, off-the-charts success... is you. Let go of your fear and start moving today toward the goal that Christ has set before you.

Psalm 139:7
"Where can I go from Your Spirit?
Or where can I flee from Your presence?"

―――――・◆・―――――

"If I ascend into heaven, You are there; if I make my bed in hell, behold, You are there."

God's presence has no limit. You can cut yourself off from people, but you cannot hide from God. You can go home today and unplug your TV, disconnect your phone, lock the cat outside... but you cannot hide from God.

I went swimming in the pool one time with my cell phone in my bathing suit. It killed my phone in a hurry! And I really didn't mind too much. I've always said that after I die, if I hear a telephone ringing on the other side, I'll know that I have gone to the wrong place.

You can disconnect from the world in a hurry, but you can never disconnect from God. When you are in the dark and feeling totally alone, God is still there. He can see you. He knows your movements before you make them. He knows your thoughts before you think them. He knows your words before you speak them. His ways are higher than your ways.

You can pretend to be someone fake and phony to those around you, but God sees. He sees your secret sin. He also sees your good deeds that no one else sees. His point of view is out of this world, and His Word promises that He will repay evil for evil and good for good.

I challenge you today, if you have unconfessed sin in your life, bring it before the Lord and start a new chapter in your life. Get things right and get plugged into God. It is the only way to live a successful life!

Jeremiah 32:17
"Ah, Lord God! Behold, You have made the heavens
and the earth by Your great power and outstretched arm.
There is nothing too hard for You."

Listen to what I'm about to say: "God's greatness is measured by what he CAN'T do." No, that's not a typo. And it might sound like an oxymoron, but it's not. What is an oxymoron? A phrase that sounds like it has contradictory elements... like "family vacation." You can either take your family, or you can take a vacation.

There are several things God cannot do, including: He cannot be given a problem that He can't solve. He can never leave you nor forsake you. He cannot break His promises. Isn't that great news?

In your darkest moment, when you receive the worst of news and your heart nearly stops beating from the burning anguish in your soul, I want you to know that God is standing right beside you. He never left you for a second, even as the dearest on earth passed you by.

As your heart is breaking and your pillow becomes soaked with tears in the deep recesses of the night, He is there. And He wants you to know that He will restore to you what was taken. He does not want you to be ashamed of your past. Place your hand in His and get ready for the journey of a lifetime. It's going to be epic!

Psalm 71:16
"I will go in the strength of the Lord GOD;
I will make mention of Your righteousness, of Yours only."

———◆———

*A*re you facing a Red Sea moment in your life? Do you have an impossible trial looming, and you can already feel your anxiety rising? Are you surrounded on every side? Unsure where to turn? Is fear choking the life out of you? Are your enemies powerful? Do you feel as if you have lost the battle before the first shot has been fired?

I have great news for you today: you serve a majestic God, and you can go forward with His strength, not yours!

He will scatter your enemies like straw on the summer threshing floor. He is your Fortress, a high tower you can run into for safety. He is Jehovah Shammah, the God who is there when you need Him. No need to feel like you are fighting this battle alone; He is the Friend who is closer than kin.

He says to call on Him and He will show you great and mighty things. He has promised that you can walk through the fire and not get burned. If God could part the Red Sea to allow Moses and company the several days they needed to get their families and livestock to the other side... He can certainly do the same for you. Ask whatever you will and it shall be done in Jesus' name!

Deuteronomy 8:10
"When you have eaten and are full, then you shall bless the LORD your God for the good land which He has given you."

Today, I challenge you to break the shame barrier in your life. Does a past tragedy haunt you? Something you never speak about?

Maybe a member of your own family did something horrible to you and you feel like somehow it was your fault. Perhaps your mother or father never affirmed you, and you grew up steeped in self-doubt, insecurity, and shame. Maybe you often wonder, "What's wrong with me?"

If there is a stain in your past, a flaw you can't scrub out, a scar that won't go away, know that Jesus paid the ultimate price for your sin and shame at Calvary's Cross. He has cleansed you and made you whiter than snow. You no longer have to wear your shame as a cloak; Calvary exchanged your filthy rags for robes of splendor.

Your past is forgiven. Your sin is buried in the deepest sea. You are royalty, sons and daughters of the Most High God. You are loved and precious in His sight! Are you getting the picture here?

You are blessed beyond measure and justified by faith... just as if you had never sinned. Today, be set free in Jesus' name. Break the chains of bondage over your life and give God the glory—both for the great things He has done in your past, and the ones He will continue to do in your future!

The Pastor's Blessing

And now may the Lord bless you and keep you. May the Lord make His face to shine upon you and be gracious unto you, giving you His peace. Give us such a hunger and thirst for the things of God that we would desire nothing more than to continually feast upon the truth of Your Word. May our faith be built so that our enemies are defeated in the mighty name of the Lord Jesus. Help us to pull down the stronghold of sickness. May the church be a house of healing for wounded lives, broken bodies, and souls in need of Your special touch. May Your favor explode in our lives today as You continually demonstrate Your lovingkindness! Amen!

Isaiah 42:8
"I am the LORD, that is My name;
And My glory I will not give to another,
Nor My praise to carved images."

God shares His glory with no one.

The Lord's Prayer tells us, "For Yours is the kingdom and the power and the glory forever. Amen." When we get to heaven, we will receive crowns to cast at His feet. Why? Because He is the one who made it possible for us to get there in the first place.

Jesus didn't come to earth because He needed us. He came because we needed Him. The way of the Cross leads us to our eternal home.

If you try to take God's glory, He will take His anointing from you, and He might even take your life! So be warned that the glory belongs to the LORD. When you share His message, do not add to it or take away from it. The Word needs no further interpretation. It was inspired by Almighty God, and its message is life-changing and true.

What are you in need of today? Start by giving God the glory, then look up—showers of blessing are headed your way!

Luke 2:11–12
"There is born to you this day in the city of David a Savior,
who is Christ the Lord. And this will be the sign to you:
You will find a Babe wrapped in swaddling cloths,
lying in a manger."

*T*oday, you have reason to rejoice... for Christ the Savior was born.

As you celebrate this day, keep CHRIST in Christmas! And keep in mind: it's not about the gifts under the tree but about the One who died ON the tree to redeem us from our sins. He is the greatest Gift of all.

This Gift grants you eternal life. This Gift sets the captive free and heals all of our diseases. Born in a humble stable next to stinking cattle, Baby Jesus came into this world in the most lowly of ways. But He is coming back to rule and to reign at the right hand of God the Father.

As your family gathers from near and far this Christmas, remember the true reason for the season. Amid the chaos of tinsel and toys, dinner parties and late nights spent wrapping the perfect present for Uncle Joe, remember the Child who was born to die in your place.

Thank You, God, for the Babe in Bethlehem's manger who has granted each and every one of us the gift of eternal life!

Philippians 3:13-14
"Forgetting those things which are behind and reaching forward
to those things which are ahead, I press toward the goal for
the prize of the upward call of God in Christ Jesus."

What you are able to walk away from will determine what God can bring you to.

God wants to set you free from the addiction that has been ruling your life for years. Are you willing to walk away from it? God wants to heal your marriage, but are you willing to walk away from the things (and people) that have become more important than your spouse?

God wants to reunite your family, but are you willing to walk away from your ungodly behavior that drove them away? God wants to restore your finances, but are you willing to give up a few vacations or luxury items in order to tithe?

God longs to bless you far above your ability to take it in. But are you willing to follow Him? Are you willing to walk away from what keeps you from fulfilling your divine destiny?

If you know you're so far off track that you have no clue how to restore the closeness you once shared with the King, you are in the perfect place for the most remarkable comeback of your life. God sees you right where you are. Reach out to Him, and get ready to walk away from the things that have built a wall between you and God.

There is no high like the Most High! And He can elevate you to a place of total communion with Him. Walk away from the chains that bind and into the loving arms of your Savior. He's waiting!

Ezekiel 36:26
"I will give you a new heart and put a new spirit within you;
I will take the heart of stone out of your flesh
and give you a heart of flesh."

---

*B*e willing to change your plans when God changes your heart.

You might be at a place in your life where you think you have it all figured out. Everything seems to be moving along just fine; it's all smooth sailing. But guess what? If you're not where God wants you to be, it's time to head in a new direction.

God's plans are not always our plans. His ways are not always our ways. But I can tell you from experience, if you will follow His lead, the path will take you somewhere far greater than you could have ever anticipated. The path may not be strewn with rose petals and rainbows, but it will make you into a servant—someone God can use to further His kingdom.

As we get ready to close out the year, many of you will start making resolutions and big plans for the coming year. It's a clean slate, so why not start the year out right?

The Bible says to write your plan and make it plain. Then you can easily see how far the Lord has brought you, through good times and bad. Pray about your plans. God will give you the desires of your heart, but He will never take you down a path that will endanger your eternal soul. Remember, He sees your end from the beginning.

So I say again, if God changes your heart, be willing to adjust the sail on your ship. God might be directing you toward deeper waters that will bring you into closer communion with Him.

Psalm 37:25
"I have been young, and now am old;
Yet I have not seen the righteous forsaken,
Nor his descendants begging bread."

———◆◆◆———

*M*y grandmother Swick used to say, "If you always save everything you have for a rainy day, God will make sure to give you a rainy day."

The point is this… enjoy today! If someone has a need you can meet, help them out. Give what is due to God (your tithe) and then enjoy the rest. God gives us a harvest of abundance, not so we can hoard it but so that we can share it. He gives us the provision so that we can live a rich and full life in Him.

Live in the here and now without the fear of tomorrow. Be anxious for nothing! Don't base your happiness on some future event that may or may not ever take place. No one is promised tomorrow. Make the most of today; God has already taken care of all of your tomorrows.

You can store up your treasures in heaven by tithing, sharing the love of the Lord, and following His commands. Do you own your possessions, or do your possessions own you? If you're storing up your earthly possessions to the point of misery, then you need to rethink your plan. God has something better to offer you. Seek first the Kingdom, and all these things will be added unto you!

Hebrews 12:2
"Looking unto Jesus, the author and finisher of our faith,
who for the joy that was set before Him
endured the cross, despising the shame, and has sat down
at the right hand of the throne of God."

———————

It was the priceless value of your eternal soul that drove Jesus to endure the Cross.

You have heard it said that you can't be everything to everyone, but to Jesus Christ you are a priceless treasure. He is the Pearl of great price that willingly gave His life for you. If you were the only one on planet earth, He would have bled and died just for you.

Don't sell yourself short. God created you a little lower than the angels. His love for you is so deep that He remained on the Cross to become your Redeemer, even though He could have called down 10,000 angels to deliver Him to heaven.

No one will ever love you like God does.

When life becomes difficult and the pain of your soul is choking out every positive reminder of the blessings in your life, meditate on this one thing: God loved you enough to send His only Son to die in your place.

The story of Calvary is the only one we need.

Romans 1:7
"Grace to you and peace from God our Father
and the Lord Jesus Christ."

———◆———

*Y*ou are not living until you discover God's amazing grace!

No message in the Word of God can heal you, inspire you, encourage you, and bring you joy unspeakable like the message of God's amazing grace.

Grace can move mountains of guilt and shame! It can calm the troubled sea of your soul. Grace can bring you through the fire without the smell of smoke upon you. It is the unmerited favor of God upon your life, even when you are least deserving.

Grace is an ocean without a shoreline, its depths unknown. Its healing, life-changing waters have never been charted because they have no boundary.

Grace will set you free from the tyranny of the past and wash away the stain of mistakes scattered across the fabric of your life. If you are a prisoner to someone else's foolish opinions or unreasonable demands, grace can set you free. Your future is not controlled by your past—your past ended last night. Your future is unlimited by the grace of Almighty God!

The Pastor's Blessing

And now may the Lord bless you and keep you. May the Lord make His face to shine upon you and be gracious unto you, giving you His peace. May you walk with self-confidence, with joy and divine knowledge that your destiny was written in the chronicles of glory from the creation of time. God saw you today and knew exactly where you were going to be. You are on the highway to heaven. Celebrate with joy unspeakable—great things are on the way for you, blessed child of the living King! Hallelujah to the Lamb of God who sits upon the throne, who rules and reigns forever and ever. Amen!

Galatians 5:22-23
"The fruit of the Spirit is love, joy, peace, longsuffering,
kindness, goodness, faithfulness, gentleness, self-control."

As we come to the close of another year, I encourage you to meditate on the positive aspects of your life. Focus on a loving Savior who died to grant you eternal life walking streets of pure gold and on His Spirit, who empowers you to display the character of Christ.

Open the Word of God and let it come alive in your life. Let it take root in your soul! The peace that comes from above is like no other. It is a peace that suffers long and offers calm where chaos has been.

Guard your joy. Happiness is fleeting, but the love of the Lord and the favor of God last a lifetime.

Cherish each day for the priceless gift that it is. Time is running short. Gabriel's trumpet could sound at any moment, and we who are alive in Christ could be called up to meet Him in the sky. Nothing else needs to take place in Biblical prophecy to prepare this earth for the second coming of Jesus Christ.

Are you ready to meet your Savior face-to-face? If not, close out this year by asking God to forgive your sins and make your path straight. And when you have set things right with your Savior, live, love, and be happy, doing good to others. There is no better way until you are basking in the presence of the Most High God!